What Happened to the Children
Who Fled Nazi Persecution

WHAT HAPPENED TO THE CHILDREN WHO FLED NAZI PERSECUTION

GERHARD SONNERT
GERALD HOLTON

palgrave
macmillan

WHAT HAPPENED TO THE CHILDREN WHO FLED NAZI PERSECUTION
© Gerhard Sonnert, Gerald Holton, 2006.

First published in 2006 by
PALGRAVE MACMILLAN™
175 Fifth Avenue, New York, N.Y. 10010 and
Houndmills, Basingstoke, Hampshire, England RG21 6XS
Companies and representatives throughout the world.

PALGRAVE MACMILLAN is the global academic imprint of the Palgrave Macmillan division of St. Martin's Press, LLC and of Palgrave Macmillan Ltd. Macmillan® is a registered trademark in the United States, United Kingdom and other countries. Palgrave is a registered trademark in the European Union and other countries.

ISBN-13: 978–1–4039–7625–3
ISBN-10: 1–4039–7625–2

Library of Congress Cataloging-in-Publication Data is available from the Library of Congress.

A catalogue record for this book is available from the British Library.

Design by Newgen Imaging Systems (P) Ltd., Chennai, India.

First edition: December 2006

10 9 8 7 6 5 4 3 2 1

Printed in the United States of America.

Transferred to digital printing in 2007.

To all those who persevered despite great odds.

Contents

List of Tables

List of Figures

Preface

Statistics can be strange. I would not have thought of statistical analysis as an art form, but in this group portrait of some 28,000 children who were forced to flee from Nazi-dominated Central Europe with or without their parents and to resettle in the alien language culture of the United States, it is precisely that. The authors sketch broad outlines drawn from large comparative databases, then add the major features and details of various subtle colorations, then fill in the contextual background, and finally draw with great skill a multitude of individual faces in verbatim quotations from questionnaires returned by the former refugees, now mature men and women reflecting on their childhoods and careers. The group portrait, vivid in the end, does not appear all at once. It emerges gradually as the authors first sweep across the canvas, then work back and forth, touching up details that are not quite precise, noting certain vaguenesses and clearing them up, and returning to adjust patches that were altered by shifts in the developing background. Only then is the finely depicted group portrait complete—and what a picture it turns out to be!

It was obvious that these émigrés children—a small percentage of the German and Austrian children whose lives were convulsed if not destroyed by the Hitler regime—faced large obstacles in adjusting to a strange new world, a world where the anchors of parental guidance and support were weakened or distorted, where linguistic expression and all that it involves had to be relearned and pathways found into the mainstream of the life around them. It was obvious too that the United States in general was not welcoming to this largely Jewish immigrant group and that they would have to face, if not anti-Semitism, then at least public indifference to the difficulties of their lives. Yet one also knew in some vague and impressionistic way that some, at least, of these disadvantaged children succeeded in overcoming the obstacles they faced and coped successfully with the problems of life in the United States. But not until now has the full measure of the group's success been recorded.

Of their parents, the adult refugees from Hitler's Europe, much has been recorded and much has been discussed. Especially well known is the extraordinary galaxy of intellectuals among them who contributed so much to American life in almost every field of endeavor: science, social science, humanistic scholarship, literature, music, finance, art, and architecture. By the early 1960s their accomplishments were so clear that historians began compiling memoirs and studies of their professional experiences and wrote essays interpreting the impact of their work; archives were created that documented aspects of the lives of all the adult refugees who could be traced. Not all of these adult refugees were creative intellectuals, or creative in any sense. Some professions—law and medicine particularly—were difficult to transfer from European to Anglo-American culture, and often careers in such fields were never reconstructed, with disastrous effects on family security and self-esteem.

Such turmoils of adult lives disrupted by emigration and the difficulties of reestablishment are familiar themes in American history, though seldom has there been such a cohort of well-educated middle-class exiles as those who fled Nazi Germany. But what of their children? While the lives of immigrant children have occasionally been imagined in novels and documented randomly in reports of social workers, there is no tradition of historical study of what the "second waves" have experienced. Torn from the culture of their origins before maturity and forced often to witness their parents' insecurity and desperation as they coped with the problems of resettlement, the children bore extra burdens and, one would have thought, could have survived only with disabilities. But the picture that emerges from the details in this book is just the opposite. It is so unexpected, so surprising, that at times it defeats explanation.

Despite all the disruption in their lives, despite the anguish and traumas these uprooted children suffered, in relation to any comparable group— native Americans of their age group, Jewish Americans of their age group, Jewish American children of American parents, of immigrant parents, of one immigrant parent, of immigrant grandparents (all permutations are explored)—they were immensely successful. They were—and still are— successful in terms of financial security, fulfillment in their careers, domestic stability, physical and psychological well-being (with documented exceptions), and the capacity and willingness to contribute to the life of their communities.

Why? How did this happen? How can this be explained? One of the most arresting parts of this book is the authors' efforts to answer these ultimate questions. Having established in detail and with subtlety the facts of these remarkably successful careers, they reach beyond the numbers, the tables, and the mathematical models, into the less certain spheres of cultural studies, sociology, and social psychology. They write of cultural capital, of "distinctiveness advantage," the power of transmitted values and statuses, psychological toughness, the consequences of alienation and guilt, instant adulthood, and success as revenge. There are no numbers here, only sensitive probing, empathy, imagination, and the recognition of silent, latent aspirations.

This work of sophisticated social science is indeed a work of artistry. For all its quantitative formalism it tells a moving tale of children who flourished in a time of great adversity, and explores the sources of their strength.

At the end, the authors suggest that their work may have broader implications, that their findings may in some way apply to the children of other ethnic groups now and in the future of our increasingly diverse society. One hopes the authors will turn to these broader questions, "tease out," as they say, "the circumstances that facilitate integration," and extract "positive lessons for current young refugees/immigrants" so that they too may turn the challenges they face to their advantage and contribute similarly to the nation's welfare.

Bernard Bailyn
Department of History
Harvard University

Introduction

The plight of refugees is one indicator that, throughout recorded history, our species has exhibited a stubborn tendency of turning on itself, clan against clan, tribe against tribe, nation against nation, class against class, and religion against religion. Here, on the dark side of the human condition, we find large-scale oppression, expropriation, enslavement, persecution, expulsion, even genocide and, as a result, a never-ending stream of refugees. For most people, the sheer numbers are too painful to contemplate. In the case of the United States, the proverbial land of immigrants since its beginnings, the refugee issue is now not just an abstraction, but still very much with us. Between 1996 and 2000, for example, an annual average of about 70,000 new refugees arrived. Even though that number drastically dropped in the wake of the 2001 terrorist attacks, more than 25,000 entered the country in 2002 and again in 2003.[1] At the same time, worldwide numbers are even more sobering. In 2005, the Office of the United Nations High Commissioner for Refugees reported on its website that, at that time, it was helping 17 million people in 116 countries.

Publications about refugees have clustered around two opposite poles: either statistical reports and analyses of large, often undifferentiated numbers, or specific accounts of the fate of an individual or family, autobiographical or journalistic in style.[2] Our study that resulted in this book was located at an intermediate level, aiming to combine the strengths of these two opposite approaches. Our task was to create a collective biography of a specific, especially vulnerable refugee cohort, based on detailed research that covered both representative statistics and personal experiences.

We undertook a five-year-long in-depth study, using social science methodology, of one particular group of refugees—those who came as children or youths from Central Europe to the United States, during the 1930s and 1940s, fleeing persecution from the National Socialist regime. These young refugees belong to the few lucky ones, for out of roughly 1.6 million children in Europe targeted by the National Socialists, it was estimated that only 100,000 survived.[3] Some 28,000 in number, the surviving children we studied are, to define the parameters of our project more precisely, chiefly those who were born in Germany or Austria between 1918 and 1935 and came to the United States in their youth. We decided to concentrate on those coming from Central Europe—and not on their fellow refugees from Eastern Europe or other parts—so as to study a cohort with a relatively homogeneous origin in terms of a common native language, culture, and schooling. We wanted to examine their fates in their new country, their successes and tribulations. In short, we wanted to know what happened to the children, when they arrived and as they matured.

Having survived a tremendous amount of adverse circumstances in Europe (e.g., usually physical and psychological abuse, persecution, often the destruction of their families, the loss of family property, of their friends, and indeed of their identity as future citizens), their start in the United States was typically also inauspicious. America certainly did not roll out the welcome mat for these young refugees. On the contrary, the country's attitude was, on the whole, cold, if not hostile. As we will discuss below in more detail, the guiding principle of the United States immigration policy in those days was to keep the number of immigrants as low as possible. Those who made it into the country encountered a largely unsympathetic indigenous population who in general liked neither immigrants nor Jews, and still suffered from the economic malaise of the Great Depression. One needs to remember that, during the Depression, at least 25 percent of the workforce in the United States was unemployed, the Gross Domestic Product fell by half, and poverty was widespread.

In light of these handicaps, it might not have been unreasonable for an observer in the 1930s and 1940s to expect that this cohort of young refugees, on the whole, would spiral into despair, deviance, and social anomie, constituting a long-term social problem, and adding a net burden to their new country. And to be sure, there was a share of individual tragedies among this cohort of young refugees, of troubled behavior, and of serious psychological suffering. But we may hint here at a central finding out of the many results of our research: We found that, on average, the young refugees eventually triumphed against long odds and made extraordinary accomplishments, as became evident when measured against the corresponding data we obtained for American-born comparison groups.

The extent to which the young refugees, on the whole, eventually came to achieve relatively high social positions and made positive contributions to the nation is nothing short of astounding. Our cohort of refugees who arrived at a young age included a remarkable number of those who became distinguished persons, such as Alfred Bader, Lotte Bailyn (née Lazarsfeld), Eugene Braunwald, Carl Djerassi, Lukas Foss, Peter Gay, Hanna Gray, Henry Grunwald, Geoffrey Hartman, Henry Kissinger, Herbert Kelman, Eugene Kleiner, Gerda Lerner, Felix Rohatyn, Robert Rosenthal, Henry Rosovsky, Lore Segal, Fritz Stern, and many, many others. And as many as four members of this cohort eventually won a Nobel Prize in science: Eric

Kandel, Walter Kohn, Arno Penzias, and Jack Steinberger. Our book also explores some of the possible explanations of the *prima facie* improbable success, on average, of this refugee cohort. We shall show, for example, the significance of the concept of *"cultural capital"* (Bourdieu) and of the transmission of that capital across generations. Some of our findings about what contributed to the success of the "Second Wave" may be applicable to the current waves of young refuges and immigrants.

To preview here the scope of our study further, we present some highlights of what it does and does not address. First, as indicated, the book does not focus on immigrants who came as adults, but on those who came as children and youths, a cohort that we call the "Second Wave,"[4] to distinguish them from the much studied "First Wave" of adult refugees in the 1930s and 1940s who arrived in the United States having already entered a career. In particular, when one thinks of European refugees who came to the United States in flight from National Socialism, what is likely to come to mind first is not our group of children, but a crop of accomplished adults, indeed of intellectual, artistic, scientific, and creative luminaries—including Albert Einstein, Enrico Fermi, Hannah Arendt, Thomas Mann, Else Frenkel-Brunswik, Kurt Weill, Walter Gropius, and many others of world renown who sought refuge from persecution in the United States. Their seminal achievements and contributions are widely recognized. The fate of this elite has so far also garnered the lion's share of the scholarly interest in the refugees from National Socialism, and it has spawned an extensively researched field called *Exilforschung*.

While the primary focus of immigration studies—both in general and about the Central European refugees from National Socialism—has, with good reasons, been on adults (and, among the refugees from National Socialism, on the famous First Wavers), flight and immigration pose a somewhat different set of opportunities and challenges for children and youths; and their experience, too, deserves attention.[5] For instance, the family unit often was broken up in the course of the flight—in many cases forever: among our survey participants who were separated from both parents when fleeing from Central Europe, 38 percent never saw either parent again. A central point of interest of our study concerns the complexities of the young refugees' identity formation, and how they brought about, in many cases, a sort of alchemical reaction between the European and American styles and modes of thought and action.

Amazingly little scholarly study existed on this younger cohort of refugees from Central Europe—those who had to start their careers in America. Heeding Lewis Coser's (1984:xiii) exhortation that the younger generation's "careers in this country might well be a very important subject of study," our project addressed this lacuna.

While focusing on those who arrived as young refugees,[6] our study provides an additional twist. The refugees of our group typically experienced the by far most dramatic and haunting times of their lives in their youth—marked by National Socialist persecution and a sometimes daring escape. It is little surprising, therefore, that what has received most attention so far is the story of how they escaped and survived. Yet more than half a century has passed since then. Those once young refugees now have lived most of their lives in the United States and are senior citizens. Therefore it was high time to focus on what happened to the former young refugees as they built their lives and careers in their new country.

Another difference between the present study and the increasing number of publications and writings about the "Second Wave" is methodological. Most accounts have been autobiographical and journalistic; our project, by contrast, chose a scientific approach to draw a representative picture of that whole cohort.[7] For instance, we do not dwell on the "big names" among the former young refugees, but examine, for the total refugee group, the spectrum of their eventually achieved socioeconomic status, a concept which we operationalized, in accordance with sociological tradition, as being composed of three core components: the achieved income, education, and occupational prestige (in chapter 4).

In using social science methodology for our study, we considered it advantageous to employ the strategy of methodological triangulation (a strategy we had already tried out successfully in an earlier research project[8])—bringing together various methods that complement one another and conjointly paint a fuller, more complex, and ultimately more accurate picture than any single method could if applied in isolation. To be sure, using several methods instead of just one substantially increased the time and labor put into this research project; but we have found that the added benefits were well worth these added costs.

The three principal methods we used were, first, the analysis of existing large and representative data sets (i.e., "secondary data analysis," in social science jargon); then our own extensive questionnaire survey containing more than 100 questions, carefully designed and tested, of which we received 2,500+ responses that were entered into our database; and third, also 100 semi-structured interviews we conducted with former refugees around the country, each typically lasting between one to two hours. With our questionnaire survey and the interviews, we have created a large and unique database, whose value will even grow in the future, as fewer and fewer members of this group will be available to tell of their experiences by themselves.[9]

In the course of our research, we carried out a large amount of statistical data analysis; but, in this book, we have kept the technical aspects of statistical analysis in the background as much as possible so that the text remains accessible to the general reader. (A more detailed description of the data and methods we used in our study is given in the Appendix.)

The purpose of analyzing large existing datasets, such as the United States Census and the National Jewish Population Survey, was to gain a representative picture of the broad socio-economic achievements of the former refugees as a group. We have already noted a few individuals with stellar achievements, but such lists do not necessarily say much about the accomplishments of the whole cohort. In any group large enough, one will be able to round up a few success stories. But we wanted to know quantitatively how well or badly the immigrants did *as a group*. Using the large datasets had the crucial advantage that they could counteract what is called response bias. This made them an important corrective to our own questionnaire survey, which was necessarily somewhat biased toward high achievement, primarily because high achievers are more visible and could be easily identified from published compilations containing former refugees.

Those previously published and available large datasets were, of course, not designed with our research focus in mind; so we had to glean important additional information from our extensive questionnaire survey. We distributed that survey as widely as we could, using multiple sources for finding recipients—for instance, associations of former refugees, lists of refugees such as that kept by the United States Holocaust Memorial Museum in Washington, DC, a variety of other compilations, and referrals from study participants. We also sent a version of the questionnaire survey to suitable comparison groups of American-born persons.

The statistical analysis of both the large datasets and our own survey, while necessary, could, of course, not fully tell what individual refugees experienced, and how they have lived their lives.[10] To capture the spectrum of complexities and idiosyncrasies of the refugees' life stories, we felt it indispensable to conduct those semi-structured interviews, so that former refugees could tell their stories in their own words. Only through this method were we able to access the former refugees' specific experiences and memories that were often crucial in shaping their life course. The readers will find passages and excerpts of those interviews throughout the book, to illustrate general findings from the other methods and to add insights that could only be gained this way.

Furthermore, our study aims to bring together stories about our refugee groups that are usually being told separately and in different scholarly traditions. The first of these dichotomies is that between achievement and anguish, between socioeconomic success and psychological trauma. Studies in clinical psychology with former refugees have focused on the enduring after-effects of childhood traumatization, on the "post-traumatic stress syndrome." These studies have typically looked at clinical populations, that is, at persons who had sought help for psychological troubles. Not surprisingly, studies of this kind highlight refugee anguish. There are, however, some studies emphasizing resilience and triumph against the odds for the children touched by the Holocaust in some way (e.g., Gilbert 1996, Helmreich 1996, Kahana, Harel, and Kahana 1988). These studies segue into the second, sociological, story, which is a primary result of our project: the revelation of remarkable achievements.

But these two stories are the two sides of the same coin; they belong together, and we have tried to draw them together. It became apparent to us that this interplay is highly complex. For instance, as we shall see, the deprivations and terrors endured during their youth often accelerated the former refugees' maturation process and reinforced their determination to succeed. The popular notion of the "hungry boxer" (who is assumed to fight more ferociously than a well-fed opponent) might well apply here. Furthermore, from our interviews in particular, there appeared to be no overwhelmingly strong relationship between socio-economic success and psychological well-being. One might have expected that those with psycho-logical problems would be unable to be highly functional in their careers—or, conversely, that those who enjoy career success might be better able to come to terms with perhaps initially troubling experiences. Such a correla-tion might hold in extreme cases; but it was not conspicuous in our sample. Here one cannot give answers, but can point out the complexities. The research area thus defined is actually a fascinating one that might well be pursued further in collaboration with psychologists.

The second dichotomy relates to the cultural outlook of the refugee group. It would have been easy to tell the story of our cohort exclusively as an analogy to that of the elite intellectuals of the First Wave, picturing them as radically modern and cosmopolitan, from a major metropolis, such as Berlin or Vienna, high-achieving, committed to the ideals of high culture or *Kultur* as they would call it, and strongly secular.

Many Second Wave refugees were indeed like that, but certainly not all. We became increasingly aware of an alternative story to be also told: of refugees who had come from middle-class or lower middle class homes, and who themselves led comfortable lives but did not obtain positions of particularly high socioeconomic status. These were certainly not as glamorous as the others, and they have tended to be neglected somewhat by scholars in the field; but there do exist a few excellent studies of particular communi-ties of this type. That alternative story emerges from in-depth studies such as Steven Lowenstein's (1989) portrayal of the German-speaking Jewish community in Washington Heights, New York City, and Rhonda Levine's (2001) work on German Jewish refugee cattle dealers in Upstate New York. These social scientists have brought to view young Central European immigrants from small-town or rural backgrounds, who were conservative in their general worldview, and were strongly rooted in Jewish traditions, perhaps more strongly than their average American-born counterparts.

Washington Heights was, of course, a major initial settlement area of the Second Wave refugees; but, by the time of Lowenstein's study, many of those with outward-looking and mobile tendencies had left, so that the remaining community featured a continuation or recreation of a more modest community- and religion-oriented Jewish group, harking back to small-town Germany. And between these two immigrant subgroups—stylized here for maximum contrast—there were multiple hues and transitional variants. Again, in our study of our cohort, we take account of both types, and we present quantitative data indicating the relative sizes of these groups.

Context

In these introductory pages, it is useful broadly to locate our specific group of young refugees within the larger universe of immigration and refugee movements. For example, one needs to keep in mind that the Central European refugees entered the United States at a time, in the 1930s and 1940s, when the immigration stream into this country was exceptionally small. By historical standards, immigration had been reduced to a trickle by the end of the 1920s (see table in Waldinger and Lee 2001:32). The numbers began to pick up again after World War II and reached new heights after 1965 when a new U.S. immigration law relaxed immigration restrictions and thus marked the beginning of what is called the "New Immigration" (now mostly from non-European countries of origin, in contrast to the predominantly European "Old Immigration").

Furthermore, immigrants certainly do not all fit the same pattern. Immigrants can and have been classified in many different ways, but the following basic distinctions should suffice to set the wider stage. Three variables that appear useful here are the motive of migration, the type of migrant (especially in terms of skills and socioeconomic background), and the migrants' definition of their situation.

The first distinction, though in some cases not clear-cut, is that between immigrants who came to better their (often dire) economic situation versus refugees (typically having been targeted for political and/or ethnic reasons) who came to the United States leaving an oppressive regime, who escaped persecution, or were expelled from their homes.

The second distinction pertains to the immigrants' background and skills. The classical story and fabric of the American Dream is that immigrants, typically young adults, would come from humble and uneducated backgrounds and would enter the lowest rungs in the American labor market (which, from their perspective, however, might be perceived as a great step up, compared to what they had been used to); and that they themselves, and especially their children, would work their way up in the American society. There has been, however, a numerically smaller group of highly skilled immigrants (often from elevated socioeconomic backgrounds in their home country) who have come to the United States to enter intermediate or even upper positions in the socioeconomic hierarchy. This last type of immigration—though certainly a minority phenomenon within the larger immigration streams—has become more frequent.

Many adult Central European refugees from National Socialism could be counted among that latter type of highly educated immigrants. In contrast with highly skilled immigrants taking advantage of greater economic and career opportunities, however, the refugees, having migrated essentially to save their lives, in many cases painfully realized that their skills and qualifications had become obsolete in the new country, so that they experienced the threat of social *declassement*. As we found, growing up after arrival in a family caught in such circumstances posed particular challenges to some of the young refugees.

The third distinction pertains to how the migrants perceive their situation. Some may view their sojourn in the United States as a merely temporary phase. The core of their identity and the focus of their interests remains the home country to which they hope to return. If the migration occurs for economic reasons, immigrants of this kind would be some kind of migrant workers. But where the migration was caused by persecution, those immigrants would be considered exiles, fleeing from their country because of its hostile government, but hoping (or even actively working) for an overthrow of that government, and intending to return after the regime change.

There were indeed some exiles, by that definition, in the First Wave of refugees, and they typically returned to their former home countries in Europe in order to participate in rebuilding them. But, by contrast, a large proportion of the members of the (adult) First Wave, and a huge proportion of the (young) Second Wavers could be considered *émigrés*, or refugees having become permanent immigrants. They settled in the United States for good and consider it their home. This does not, however, mean that, on the whole, they have severed all ties to their countries of origin. We examined the Second Wave refugees' relationship to their home countries in detail, and we found this issue particularly fascinating for our group, perhaps more so than for most other immigrant groups.

Furthermore, in studying the effects of our young refugees' early experiences on their later lives and careers, it was important to realize that we were dealing here with the superposition of two different effects, an "immigrant" effect and a "refugee" effect. On the one hand, there is the common experience of immigrants—the change in culture and living environment, and the ensuing challenges of adjustment that all young immigrants go through when they move from one country and one culture to another. On the other hand, there are the particularly harrowing circumstances in the background of the young refugees, including the oppression and persecution in the home country and, in many cases, the hazardous escape.

Finally, as we set out to document the outcomes for our cohort of young refugees from Central Europe and to identify some of the conditions and determinants for these outcomes, we should emphasize that, at the most fundamental level, we see the key for the successes in the "fit" between the displaced youths and the setting to which they tried to adapt. In somewhat more technical terms, we conceptualize the, on the whole, remarkable achievements of this cohort as a result of the advantageous interaction between the socialization, skills, experiences, and cultural values with which the youngsters arrived and the opportunity structure (Merton) they found in the United States. To strengthen this analysis, we paid particular attention to internal differences in cultural capital and socialization within the refugee cohort, and we traced the powerful processes by which socioeconomic status is transmitted across the chasm of persecution and flight. In short, this book tries to tell a sociological story that is coherent and makes theoretical sense, going beyond simple amazement—which certainly is hard to avoid—at this cohort's collective achievements.

To preview just a few of the fundamental characteristics of the refugee group under study. Of the 1,571 former refugees who responded to our questionnaire survey, 7 percent arrived in the United States at age 6 or younger, 31 percent were 7 through 12 years old, 44 percent were 13 through 18 years old, and 19 percent were older. In the broad categories of the United States census, 30 percent of their fathers had been professionals in Europe, 38 percent had been managers, and 32 percent had worked in other occupations. The young refugees thus came from an elevated socioeconomic background, on average—and they themselves, as a group, became highly successful in terms of socioeconomic status. Among our group of refugees, 58 percent were found to have become professionals. An additional 25 percent were managers, and only 17 percent worked in other occupations.

Uses for Today

Our research results concerning the tribulations and eventual success, on average, of this cohort of young refugees are, we believe, not only of historical and sociological interest. The findings of the conditions and the many factors that, in our study, made eventual success more likely can well be instructive for current waves of young refugees arriving in this country. Despite obvious differences between then and now, we believe there are continuities of many sorts, and that our results, therefore, contain positive lessons for many young refugees and immigrants at this time, as well as for policy makers in governmental and nongovernmental organizations active in this area. Moreover, some of these differences themselves may be instructive in helping pinpoint factors that influence how young refugees adjust to life in their new country.

Plan of the Book

The first section of our book sets the stage for our examination of the lives and careers of our cohort of young refugees by addressing a few basic questions: who were the refugees who entered the United States in the 1930s and 1940s, where did they come from, and why did they have to leave? Based on the material gathered from our participants through questionnaires and interviews, we shall depict how these youngsters grew up in Central Europe and what they experienced after the National Socialist regime took power. We will also describe the various routes the refugees, young and old, took to safety. (By concentrating on former refugees who came to the United States, we cover an important, but certainly not the only, destination of the refugees' escape routes.)

The second section portrays the situation in the United States that the arriving refugees had to face. As mentioned, the refugees were not universally welcomed, but there were great humanitarian efforts to help them. We will cover official immigration policies, the mood of the population, as well as the variety of organizations and individuals who played an active role in helping the refugees come to, and establish themselves in, America.

In the third section, we describe the process of settling in, for both the refugees in general and the refugee children in particular. The fourth section then presents our findings on the basic socioeconomic outcomes for the former young refugees. Large and representative databases, such as the U.S. Census, the National Jewish Population Survey, as well as our own questionnaire survey, allowed us to generate a quantitative picture of the achievements of the former young refugees as a group.

The fifth section turns to the complex identities that the refugees developed over their life courses. We will touch on language acquisition, the ethnic options available to the former refugees, and on attitudes and behaviors that preserved remnants of their Central European origins.

The sixth section discusses possible causes for the observed remarkable socioeconomic success of the former refugees as a group. Of particular importance in this discussion will be the concept of cultural capital and the modalities of its transmission across the generations. Other potential determinants under study include the family and community circumstances in which the young refugees grew up, as well as age at arrival, and gender. We also look into the relationship between collective identities and socioeconomic outcomes. Finally, we discuss psychological factors, stemming from the refugee experience, that may have facilitated the refugees' success in many cases.

However, the psychological constitution of many of our participants was highly complex and ambivalent. Often, we found, the socioeconomic successes and societal contributions were motivated by intense emotions of anguish and insecurity. We describe this constellation as *socialized benefits and privatized costs* of the refugee experience. In the seventh section, we glimpse into the private anguish of many former refugees who are still impacted by the aftereffects of a trauma they received during a childhood marked by great upheaval. We investigate how early experiences of this kind are related to later outcomes and emotions, and we present a few illustrative types of reactions vis-à-vis those early experiences.

In conclusion, we express the hope that there will be potential lessons for current waves of child refugees arriving in America that might be learned from the experience of our group of young refugees.

Acknowledgments

In the course of this project, we have been given help and support from many individuals and organizations, and we are sincerely grateful to all of them.

We thank the Andrew W. Mellon Foundation for its generous grant that made this research project possible. We gladly acknowledge some additional grant support from the William F. Milton Fund and the Clark/Cooke Fund, both of Harvard University.

While one of the authors (G.H.) found this project of interest also for autobiographical reasons, the research itself was directed by a scholarly approach and methodology. In this endeavor, we have been very fortunate to receive sage advice and guidance from members of a distinguished Advisory Committee. The committee consisted of Bernard Bailyn, Lotte Bailyn, W. Robert Connor, Lewis Coser, Mary Frank Fox, Howard Gardner, Nathan Glazer, Hanna H. Gray, Inge Hoffmann, Stanley Hoffmann, Jerome Kagan, Stanley Katz, Herbert Kelman, Walter Laqueur, Kenneth Prewitt, David Riesman, Robert Rosenthal, Neil J. Smelser, Michael Sokal, Arnold Thackray, Mary Waters, and Spencer Weart. They all have our deep gratitude. We mourn the deaths of two of our advisers, David Riesman and Lewis Coser, who died during the course of the project.

Other scholars and experts in this area who were not formally part of the Advisory Committee also kindly offered us their help and useful suggestions. Among those, we would particularly like to thank Daniel Bell, Herbert Strauss, and Roger Waldinger, as well as Carol Kahn Strauss and Frank Mecklenburg of the Leo Baeck Institute, New York City, and Col. S. J. Pomrenze of the Hebrew Immigrant Aid Society (HIAS). We also acknowledge gladly that the American Academy of Arts and Sciences' Committee on Studies initially vetted our proposed research project that resulted in this book, and recommended it with respect to its scholarly and intellectual interest.

Our administrator, Joan Laws, not only expertly assured the smooth running of the project, but also participated in the analysis of the interview transcripts. Most of the interviews with former refugees were conducted by our keen interviewer, Alexandra Gross. Rabbi Robert L. Lehman distributed questionnaires and did some interviews for us in New York City and vicinity right up to the sad event of his death in 2003. Our Faculty Aides Lauren Hult, Megan Berry, Tina Wang, and Frederic Clark competently assisted with various aspects of our research. Wesley Cheong helped with the design of the data entry form for our electronic database, and Tripti Thapa and Mark Benson conscientiously entered a multitude of data into it. We thank all of them for their contributions.

To identify participants for this study (in addition to those we found through publicly available sources), we turned to a number of organizations and associations of, or connected with, former refugees from Central Europe, and we are very grateful for their help in facilitating the distribution of our questionnaires. We thank these organizations and acknowledge with gratitude the individuals in them who helped us: Martin Goldman and Megan Lewis of the US Holocaust Memorial Museum, Washington, DC, Iris Posner of One Thousand Children (OTC), Inc., Kurt Goldberger of the Kindertransport Association (KTA), Frank Harris of the Nürnberg-Fürth group of former refugees, Judy Rapaport of the Safe Haven Museum & Education Center, Oswego, NY, and Ruth Einstein and Haven Hawley of the William Breman Jewish Heritage Museum, Atlanta.

Numerous individuals we contacted told us about other family members or friends who also belonged to the population under study. Thanks to them, we were able to reach many more former refugees than we could have otherwise.

A final word of heartfelt thanks is owed to all those who filled out questionnaires and gave us interviews, to the former refugees as well as to the members of the comparison groups. Without their generous willingness to participate in this project, our study would not have been possible.

Gerhard Sonnert
Gerald Holton
Jefferson Laboratory
Harvard University

Chapter 1

Exodus

To understand the young refugees' later lives, it seems important, even necessary, to know something about what happened to them during the 1930s and 1940s. Where did all those refugees come from, one might ask, and why did they have to leave their own countries? This chapter recapitulates and summarizes some pertinent facts and figures, based on the widely dispersed data in the existing literature, so as to set the stage for the presentation of the results of our own research in the next chapters. Most of the chapter describes the refugee movement of that period in general; a later section then focuses more closely on children who became the subjects of our "Second Wave" project.

Who Left and Why

In his grand study of European refugees, Malcolm Proudfoot (1957:21) noted that in connection with World War II, some 60 million European civilians were forced to move.[1] The magnitude of this displacement was unprecedented and much of it was made possible by the advanced bureaucratic and technological means at the disposal of ruthless governments. The tragic chain of events was set in motion on January 30, 1933, when the National Socialists, led by Adolf Hitler, took over the German government. Whereas, at first, the refugees came only from Germany, the expansion of the German sphere of influence later forced many Europeans of other nationalities also to take flight.

The number of German-speaking emigrants, old and young (mainly from Germany, Austria, and parts of Czechoslovakia) would roughly amount to 500,000. Most of them were Jews (as defined by the National Socialists, not necessarily by the targeted individuals themselves); 30,000 were political opponents or dissidents for some other reason. A numerically smaller, but highly influential, segment was composed of members of the cultural, intellectual, scientific, and artistic elite (Handbuch 1998:1, Strauss 1983:xii). These three groups of refugees overlapped to some extent, as substantial proportions of the political and cultural groups were also Jewish (or at least would be qualified as such by the National Socialists).

Targets of Ethnic Persecution

In the late eighteenth century, there began a protracted process of Jewish emancipation and assimilation in Germany (and Central Europe). By the early nineteenth century, large numbers of Jews had availed themselves of the new opportunities opened to them by legal and political emancipation (see Elon 2002, and, for a wider perspective, Slezkine 2004). Many left the traditional Jewish communities in small towns and villages for the cities; left the jobs to which, for centuries, they had been restricted—mainly peddling and small-scale trading—for successful careers in commerce, the professions, and scholarship; and gave up the religion of their ancestors for a highly assimilated, modern belief system that worshipped the universalist ideals of the Enlightenment in the form of a *Bildungsreligion* derived from the classic German thinkers and poets. By 1933, German Jewry, on average, was in a thoroughly assimilated condition, which Gerhart Saenger (1941:10) described as follows: "Apart from certain religious customs, preserved by the more orthodox persons, there was no peculiarly Jewish culture. There were no differences in clothing, attitudes and gestures, or language. 'Yiddish' was merely bad German to the assimilated Jew, considered as slang rather than as a separate language." Saenger emphasized social class as the overriding organizing principle of German society. In contrast, Herbert Strauss (1981:236, orig. in German) argued that despite the thoroughgoing processes of assimilation, the German Jews retained a kind of ethnic culture so that they could be considered "an at least potentially ethnic group" (also see Berghahn 1984). The strength of this ethnic culture correlated inversely with the degree of modernization. Jewish traditions were stronger in the remaining rural pockets of *Landjuden* communities than among the Jews in the big cities,[2] and they were also stronger among the *Ostjuden* who had immigrated to Germany from Eastern Europe.

Cultural assimilation went hand in hand with a rise into the ranks of the Central European bourgeoisie. By the early twentieth century, the socioeconomic composition of German and Central European Jewry, on the whole, differed markedly from that of the non-Jewish populations; Jews were present in substantially larger proportions in the commercial and professional classes. However, the trend of successful integration met with increasingly virulent resistance from segments of the non-Jewish population. The forces of anti-Semitism were gathering strength and finally triumphed when Adolf Hitler and the National Socialist German Workers Party (NSDAP) came to power in Germany in 1933.

From that point on, the German government pursued increasingly draconian policies of oppressing, expelling, and finally annihilating, the German and then the other European Jews (for a summary, see Strauss 1983; also Kaplan 1998). The initial goal was to clear Germany of its Jewish population that according to the 1933 Census numbered about 500,000 (Davie 1947:6). Almost immediately after the National Socialists came to power, they orchestrated boycotts of Jewish stores and professional offices, which culminated on April 1, 1933. Furthermore, they enacted a series of anti-Semitic laws—the most notorious of which were the Nuremberg racial laws of 1935. These laws reduced Jews from the status of regular citizens to that of societal outcasts without rights. The so-called *Kristallnacht* ("crystal night," sometimes loosely translated as "night of broken glass"), a country-wide pogrom of November 1938 signaled the beginning of a brutal expulsion campaign. Tragically for the Jewish population, during the war that soon followed, German policy shifted dramatically from expelling the Jews to exterminating them. Thus, in the course of the Holocaust, an estimated 6 million Jews perished in all Europe.[3]

From Germany alone, more than a quarter million Jews fled or were expelled, as indicated in table 1.1. It shows that Jewish emigration dropped

Table 1.1 Jewish Emigrants From Germany (To All Other Countries)

1933	37,000–38,000
1934	22,000–23,000
1935	20,000–21,000
1936	24,000–25,000
1937	23,000
1938	33,000–40,000
1939	75,000–80,000
1940	15,000
1941	8,000
1942–45	8,500
Total	265,500–281,500

According to Benz 1998:5–6, cf. Davie 1947:8–10, Strauss 1980–1981, 1983:xv.

somewhat after the first year of National Socialist rule, but then reached a dramatic peak in 1938 and 1939, caused by the increase in harsh policies in the aftermath of *Kristallnacht*. Whereas in the years before 1938, Jewish emigration still had some remote semblance of an orderly process, in which some property also could be transferred out of Germany, utter chaos reigned after *Kristallnacht*, as huge numbers of persons, robbed of all their means and threatened with arrest, were either forcibly driven out or frantically tried to escape. In the war years the refugee stream understandably dwindled to a trickle, as the German government embarked on its extermination program.

After Austria was taken over by Germany in March of 1938, the National Socialist government made an accelerated effort at driving the Austrian Jews out. "In Germany the gradual elimination of the Jews from the economic and cultural life of the nation took five years; in Austria five days sufficed" (Saenger 1941:29). Whereas before the so-called *Anschluss* (annexation) an estimated 206,000 Jews lived in Austria, the Census of May 17, 1939 counted only 95,000. Thus, within little more than a year, about 100,000 Jews—constituting roughly half the former Jewish population of Austria—left the country or were imprisoned in concentration camps (Benz 1998:9, Davie 1947:9). By the beginning of World War II in September 1939, only about 75,000 remained in Austria.[4]

A total number of 17,000 Jews emigrated from the ethnically German region of Czechoslovakia, called Sudetenland, after that area was annexed by Germany, and from Bohemia and Moravia after these areas, too fell under German control (Tartakower and Grossmann 1944:32). The German government in October of 1938 deported more than 15,000 Polish Jews who resided in Germany; but they were equally unwanted in Poland, which had earlier stripped them of their citizenship (Tartakower and Grossmann 1944:32). The Polish Jews thus were left languishing in the frontier zone. Outraged by this event, Herschel Grynszpan, whose parents were among the deportees, shot and killed the German diplomat Ernst vom Rath at the German embassy in Paris. It is this incident that provided the pretext for the *Kristallnacht* (Cesarani 2000:8).

Most Jews in Germany and in other Central European areas were secular and assimilated and had developed a deep sense of German or other Central European identity and patriotism. For them, the events that were unfolding were simply surreal. Unlike the political refugees who had quickly grasped the situation, many Central European Jews did not immediately realize the danger they were in. They believed that the government would not actually follow through on its anti-Semitic rhetoric, or that it might even quickly disintegrate. For them, the catastrophe when it did happen was also epistemological: their worldview collapsed. The hardest hit of all were the so-called non-Aryan Christians who were suddenly robbed of their most meaningful collective identity, often the only one they had—that of being a German (or other Central European)—and fell into "a complete spiritual vacuum" (Saenger 1941:39).

In addition to the large group of assimilated and rather apolitical Jews, one might perhaps distinguish three further subgroups among the Jewish migrants: Zionists, strongly religious or orthodox Jews, and political far-leftists. In contrast to the bewildered assimilated Jews, these other groups all had some explanation for what was happening. For the Zionists, it was the ultimate proof that their analysis was correct, and that the grand experiment of assimilation was but a perilous illusion. For the strongly religious Jews, it was the latest in a long series of persecutions visited upon the Jews by hostile Gentiles, or perhaps some kind of divine retribution. "This persecution has been inflicted upon you because you have forgotten the religion of your fathers and relaxed in faith," a rabbi was reported to have put this idea succinctly to his congregation (Saenger 1941:49). This may have been an extreme view, but, in various ways, religion helped many people to cope. One of our interviewees, who had left Germany immediately after Hitler's rise to power and lived with his family in a neighboring country, recalled, "of the many people who visited us in one way or another from Germany, those that had religion and adhered to it to some extent, not necessarily fully, seemed to be able to adjust best to whatever happened to them. Those that were completely away from religion took it the hardest. And that impressed me very much." As Herbert Strauss (1981:238) noted, persecution by the German government caused even many assimilated Jews to return to old Jewish explanatory models.

And as for the political far-leftists, they could fall back on Marxist crisis theories of monopoly capitalism and on their typologies of fascism that explained the events as historically inevitable stations along the way toward the equally inevitable destination of a classless society. For them, National Socialism was a particularly nasty, yet ultimately a futile attempt of capitalism to halt its own demise. Most Jewish far-leftists actually would have preferred to think of themselves not as members of the Jewish group, but as members of the political exile group to which we now turn.

Political Opponents

The new government of Germany on coming to power in 1933 immediately began to dismantle the existing democratic system of the Weimar Republic. It swiftly moved to round up and incarcerate its visible political opponents—mostly activists of the Communist and Social Democratic Parties—yet many of the activists did manage to escape.

In mid-1933 a second and more organized phase of politically motivated flight began. Suppressed in Germany, political parties built up exile organizations abroad with the purpose of supporting and coordinating a German resistance. It has been estimated that, in 1935, the political refugees from Germany numbered about 5,000–6,000 Social Democrats, 6,000–8,000 Communists, and nearly 5,000 other opponents of the National Socialist regime (Röder 1998:21). By the outbreak of war in 1939, the total number of political exiles from Germany, Austria, and the German-speaking parts of Czechoslovakia was estimated at nearly 30,000. The largest group of them (9,000) lived in France, 7,000 went to Spain, where many of them participated in the Spanish civil war siding with the loyalists, 5,000 landed in Britain, and smaller groups dispersed to various other European countries (Röder 1998:23).

After their flight, the political refugees clearly considered themselves exiles rather than permanent emigrants. Their goal was to combat National Socialism, to return to Germany after the Hitler government was overthrown, and to shape the emerging Germany according to their political and social vision. The commitment of political exiles to the overthrow of the National Socialist regime and the support of clandestine operations within Germany impelled many of them to remain close to the German borders. Therefore, as the German sphere of influence expanded, they often had to flee several times, for example, from the Saarland or from Czechoslovakia. France also proved not to be a permanent safe haven, and many exiles who could not leave France in time were interned or even returned by French authorities to Germany.

In sociological jargon, one could distinguish persecution based on ascribed characteristics from that based on achieved characteristics.[5] This distinction illuminates crucial differences between the Jewish and the political refugees. Immediately after coming to power, Hitler's regime set out to imprison its prominent political opponents because these veteran activists of the political struggle were deemed potentially dangerous. The large mass of mostly apolitical Jews constituted no such political danger, and the policies of expulsion and annihilation in their case developed at a slower pace. Their stigma was based not on their political action but on their race, and therefore was indelible. By contrast, even Communists were not beyond redemption in the eyes of the National Socialists (as long as they were of the right racial stock) (Tutas 1975). If those supposedly misguided victims of *jüdisch-bolschewistische* (Jewish-Bolshevik) propaganda saw the error of their ways, they were warmly welcomed into the fold of the National Socialist state and its organizations. This, of course, happened mostly at the rank-and-file level where many former Communists swiftly entered the National Socialist party or allied organizations. Even some of the non-Jewish rank-and-file political refugees were invited to return to by the National Socialist government, though only a small part of them accepted this dubious offer (Röder 1998:18).

Cultural Dissidents

Numerically, the intellectuals, writers, and artists in the First Wave who left Germany because of their opposition to the National Socialist regime formed the smallest of the three refugee groups, but they were the most visible and influential contingent, and they also have received the most scholarly attention.[6] Because these refugees included the most brilliant representatives of German culture, there was a sense that German *Kultur* itself was migrating alongside luminaries such as Thomas Mann, who self-confidently proclaimed, "*Wo ich bin, ist Deutschland*" (Where I am there is Germany). (Stephan 1998:30) Gerhart Saenger (1941:269) likened the exodus of the intellectual elite from National Socialist Germany to the flight of scholars to Italy after the fall of Byzantium in 1453, and to the expulsion of the Huguenots from France. The emigration of world-famous intellectuals, especially those who were neither Jews nor political activists (such as Thomas Mann), was a source of acute embarrassment to the German government.

According to Alexander Stephan's (1998:31) estimate, over 11,000 individuals can be counted among the cultural dissidents, although this group, as already indicated, overlapped considerably with the other two, as many of the intellectuals were also Jewish and/or Leftists. Among the intellectual and artistic refugees, about 2,000 were from academe, 2,500 were writers and journalists, and 600 worked in radio broadcasting. In addition there were artists from the theater (4,000), the movies (2,000), photography (200), dance (120), and other arts.[7] Those who left Germany immediately after Hitler came to power in 1933 typically considered themselves exiles. They directed their efforts toward ridding Germany of Hitler and rebuilding the country. Those who left later tended to be emigrants rather than exiles. They focused on continuing their careers in the countries of their refuge and typically did not want to return.

Through the Eyes of Children

Having surveyed some basic and general features of the refugee movement as well as its approximate magnitude, we now turn to more personal and individual views of these dramatic events as they unfolded. Our study participants, who at that point were children and youths, told us about how they experienced the onset of National Socialism and also about the havoc it wreaked in their lives.[8]

Most young refugees had been raised, as a matter of course, to become regular and fully loyal young Germans or Austrians. (Or, as sociologists might put it, they had been socialized into the mainstream culture of those Central European countries.) From many questionnaires we received shone memories of what once had been a "normal" childhood in Central Europe and in many cases a very comfortable one too. (More than 70 percent of the survey participants reported that, by their own definition, they came from an upper-middle class [or, in a few cases, upper class] background.) Our survey showed that the participants' tastes, activities, and hobbies, when they were still children, were much in line with the general culture that surrounded them in their home country. For instance, the favorite books they mentioned were among those that German or Austrian children would be expected to read, or to be read to—books like *Struwelpeter, Heidi, Doktor Dolittle, Biene Maya, Peterchens Mondfahrt*, or *Max und Moritz*, the most famous of the beloved humorous cartoon-stories by Wilhelm Busch. The Grimms' *Fairy Tales* were also a favorite, along with books by Erich Kästner, especially *Emil und die Detektive*. Among the books older children had liked were those by Dumas, Verne, Hugo, *Tonio Kröger* and *Nathan der Weise*, Ernst Haeckel's *Welträtsel*, and Greek and Roman, as well as German mythology. But one participant simply wrote, "all books by Karl May." That extremely popular author of the "Wild West" genre of books was by far the most frequently cited author among the male participants. Popular reading among the girls was the *Nesthäkchen* book series.

Among other well-liked activities mentioned were hiking, bicycling, and sports. Many girls enjoyed knitting, crocheting, or similar activities. Boys tended to like model trains and football (soccer). Stamp collecting was a popular hobby, but mostly among the boys. An astonishingly large number of participants mentioned that they listened to classical music and opera, even at an early age. Many children liked the lighter fare of waltzes, operettas, *Schlager* (pop songs), and *Wanderlieder* (hiking songs). A few participants said they had enjoyed "martial music," and some mentioned Hebrew or Jewish songs.

For the older children, the demanding school curricula (especially those of the *Gymnasien*, a type of secondary school that prepared the pupils for university studies) imparted large amounts of knowledge as well as a particular ideal of a comprehensive liberal arts education, or *Bildung*, as it was known in German. Numerous participants mentioned that the superior academic training they had received at Central European schools and at

Gymnasien allowed them to thrive in American institutions of education. One participant, for instance, noted that a "relatively stronger educational process gave me 'a leg up' when I entered the American school system."

In those early days was shaped the *cultural baggage* with which the children arrived in America. In a subsequent chapter we shall explore in detail the remnants of the early cultural formation that (contrary to the expectations of some assimilation theorists) persisted through the young refugees' later lives and careers.

Suffering under National Socialism

The rise of the National Socialists to power—in 1933 in Germany and in 1938, by the *Anschluss*, in Austria—changed life completely and irretrievably for Jewish children as well as for their parents.[9] Whereas the onset of the regime was somewhat gradual in Germany, everything changed much more rapidly in Austria after the *Anschluss* In the post–*Anschluss* Austria, between March 11, 1938 and September 1939, over 250 official orders were issued by the government authorities placing various limitations on the life of Jews. The firing of "undesirable" teachers; orders to parents to cease their economic activities; prohibition of using playgrounds, cinemas, theaters, and so on—all these arbitrary orders strongly affected the youngsters and their parents.

In the National Socialist Reich, any so-called non-Aryan was exposed day and night to the possibility of any kind of assault, freely chosen by mobs and uniformed men. But all the early oppressions were just a dress rehearsal compared with the main events to come. On November 9 and 10, 1938, as already mentioned, there occurred the horrid, meticulously planned and executed Pogrom throughout the NS-occupied lands, to which the perpetrators gave the perfumed name *Reichskristallnacht*. Up to that point, some Central European Jews could deceive themselves that the horror would not last. Especially the veterans who had fought for Germany or Austria in the frontlines of World War I thought that their venerable status would give them immunity from persecution. It did so only at first, but eventually most veterans had to realize that their status had lost its currency. At least, people at this time were still permitted to emigrate, after a payment of a large sum to the authorities, called a *Reichsfluchtsteuer*, on top of the huge "fine" assessed to the Jewish community to repair damages done to their own premises by the mob!

The human mind, it appears, does not systematically sample and average large numbers of events to arrive at an understanding of the overall situation. Often it seems more affected by the power of a single poignant episode than by abstract analyses of social structures and processes. Such pivotal experiences—though, in the larger scheme of things, perhaps relatively random or insignificant events—tend to color a person's perception and memory from then on. We questioned our interviewees about such experiences, asking them to recall any memories they held most vividly from their time in Central Europe.

The thoughts of one of our participants, for example, returned to the boat he treasured in his boyhood. It was the loss of this boat that deeply affected him. "I had a kayak on the river . . ., which I loved and used a lot and went out with friends. And it was almost the worst thing for me that the Nazis did when they decided that Jewish kayaks could no longer be on the river, or could no longer be stored in the warehouse. And that was an enormous shock to me. I was quite young at that point; I must have been 13 or something like that and that certainly stuck in my mind."

Fascination of Power

Recalling their boyhood in the very early days of the National Socialist regime, some of our interviewees said that, to their parents' horror, they were fascinated by certain public displays of strength and community and would have loved to join the *Hitlerjugend*[10] or participate in other ways. It may be an enlightening exercise—although, of course, to be taken with a grain of salt—to classify whole political regimes along the typical trajectory of individual psychological development. In such a scheme, one might well align National Socialism with preadolescence or adolescence. Again, granting that it had many other features also, one would be struck by the numerous traits that made it especially attractive to some boys (and those older ones who developmentally remained stuck at that stage)—the marches, flags, drums, uniforms, the glorification of strength and the projection of power, the intense group spirit and camaraderie, aggression, militarism and violence, and the maltreatment of deviants and outsiders.

One interviewee told us that, as a boy of only about five years of age, he was fascinated with the National Socialist parades (of which there was no shortage), although, at one time, his enthusiasm led to a strange incident. "I do remember on the day of the *Anschluss* when the German Army was marching down the [street] and I was watching them from my—it was a second- or third-floor—balcony. And somehow, I was playing with a drum. And the drum fell out of my hand and fell down from the balcony onto the sidewalk and happened to land near a couple of German soldiers, who promptly ran up the stairs and knocked on the door and came into the apartment and wanted to know who was sabotaging their parade. So it was a little frightening when the Germans came into the apartment with their guns drawn and made life a little bit—very miserable for us.'"

School

Nonetheless, the children had to learn quickly and painfully that they did not belong in the new "Reich" that was being constructed and that they were now considered the enemy. One prime arena in which this lesson was taught was the schools, where the Jewish children were increasingly marginalized until they were no longer permitted even to attend public schools and were transferred to special schools run by Jewish teachers. Before this enforced move, mistreatment could come from both teachers and fellow students. Being bullied and beaten up by other boys was rather common and frequent for the "non-Aryans," as many of our participants told us. The teachers' behavior varied. Even though the regime was totalitarian and did not suffer dissent or deviance gladly, there was some leeway for acts of decency, and the children observed this closely and they still remembered. Some interviewees had kind words for teachers who had treated them correctly or even tried somehow to help them. Here is an example from a refugee from Germany.

"And on the whole, I must say the professors, the teachers were quite fair to me. I had very little trouble with the teachers and they gave me decent grades and, you know, you had to get up and say, 'Heil Hitler' when they came into the room. That sort of thing was de rigeur. You just had to do it. But apart from those embarrassing things, they were quite fair, and I can't remember that any of them singled me or the other Jewish children out for prejudice or discrimination. The other students was another story. On the whole, you know, I was good friends with a lot of them and particularly the kids who lived right around us. . . . And I knew the kids of all of those families and we went back and forth to each other's houses for birthday parties, or just to play, or to go on bicycle trips and stuff. We were all on good terms. That sort of cooled very much in, oh, '34, '35 gradually. That cooled, and suddenly they didn't want to be seen with me anymore."

Many participants, of course, did encounter teachers who were National Socialist fanatics and went out of their way to torment the non-Aryan students. Here is a story told by a former Berliner: "I took a lot of stuff from my classmates and from some of the teachers. There were two teachers in particular, Herr [X] and Herr [Y]. Herr [Y] looked like something out of a grade B World War II movie. He had a shaved head. He was very tall. . . . And he walked—strutted around in his SA uniform with a dagger. . . . You know, in this country people are worried that the kids will bring knives to school.

There the teachers brought knives to school. . . . And the principal of the school, Herr [Z]—he was a Party member with a . . . Party badge. And about once a month we got marched into the schoolyard . . . and we had to stand there, on parade at attention. . . . And then Herr [Y] and Herr [X] in their SA uniforms would strut up and down and salute each other, "Heil," and "Sieg Heil, Sieg Heil, Sieg Heil." And then the principal would harangue us about how the world was out to destroy Germany. . . . And, of course, the other kids used to come to school in uniforms and so on. I was beaten up rather regularly or at least harassed in one way or another."

The National Socialist-inspired harassment very much blindsided this interviewee because he had never thought of himself as a Jew. "I mean, kids would harass me. I knew nothing about any of this. My parents would try to shelter me. You know, by religion, we were not Jewish. . . . But of course [by] my ancestry, I'm completely Jewish."

Home

A major tool in the arsenal of oppression was the *Arisierung* of properties, the euphemism for a legal theft and robbery, ranging from the takeover of the apartments where the children lived with their families to that of the parents' offices, shops, and any other property, including forests and land. *Arisierung* was an experience that stuck with many of the children who had witnessed it. For example, ordinary civilians, even neighbors perhaps, could come into a home and demand that the family living there get out at once. As one of our interviewees recounted, "The son of the dairy store lady across the street, asked around where there were Jews living who had a nice apartment. . . . Well, he came up to see us, and said, 'I'd like you to move out.' And places were very hard to get. We had no choice because he held all of the cards. And so we moved into a very small flat which we shared with another couple, my piano teacher, and her husband. And that was trauma."

As was fairly common in the middle and upper-middle classes of that time, many of our participants' families employed maids, cooks, nannies, or other domestic help (who were virtually all non-Jewish). Some of those employees took advantage of the new situation in various treacherous ways. As the concept of private property no longer seemed to be in force for Jewish property, some domestic servants stole openly and unashamedly. For example, "My mother and my brother stored what was left . . . and at one point the maid took all our dishes. . . . And at that time even the maid, before she left, she would say goodbye to me and then would take dishes."

In a refreshing contrast to such treacherous behavior, there did exist some domestic employees who acted with loyalty and courage during the crisis, as some of our participants told us. "And that's another memory that sort of sticks in my mind. We had a wonderful, absolutely marvelous woman who really raised us, a *Kinderfräulein*, . . . who was enormously loyal and meant a lot to us children." Those interviewees also typically told us that they repaid their former employees' loyalty after the war through food packages and other forms of assistance.

Witnessing Persecution and Public Degradation

In addition to what the children experienced at school and at home, they witnessed how the whole fabric of society was being torn and the pieces were put back again in ways that left them with no rights, no means, and no dignity. Immensely traumatizing for the children and the whole family were the widespread roundups of Jews by the authorities. Fathers or other family members were arrested and put in jail or camps, and, in some cases, were even murdered there. Those who did get out were often scarred for life. One interviewee remembered, "[My father] was a beaten man when he came out [of Buchenwald concentration camp]." Another participant told us, ". . . Jewish men were arrested . . . and herded into a . . . public park . . . and badly beaten. In fact, my father never really recovered. He died at the age of 50." Here is a third example: "The synagogue was burning. [My father] rushed down and was picked up and then he was brought back to the house by two Gestapo men who asked him to pick up some clothing— we didn't know where he was going. . . . And then he was in Buchenwald for several months until early '39. We were able to get him a permit to go to England."[11]

The arrested men were often released under the condition that they leave the country within a short period of time after their release. The frantic efforts of the families to gain the necessary exit papers left them wide open for all kinds of extortions by corrupt officials—with the additional twist, that this kind of corruption was now hardly considered a crime any longer, but had almost become standard procedure. For instance, ". . . when the *Anschluss* came, we lost our house. We lost everything. Father relinquished all his property. The Nazis [said] essentially, 'If you don't give us your house, your pharmacy . . . —if you don't give it to us [you just don't get to leave]. . . . Give us everything you have and we'll let you go.' And my father knew that life was more important and he gave up everything he owned."

Amid the frequent suffering at the hands of various officials, some of our interviewees also recalled a few examples of decent officials. "So the police [chief] came to my father, 'Herr [X], you're under my protection.' And he said to him, 'I have the order to vandalize all Jewish homes. While I am police chief, nothing of that sort will be done.' And he took him home under police protection. . . ."

We should emphasize again that our participants' specific experiences and memories of concrete persons and their actions—how officials, teachers, domestic servants, other children treated them in the time of crisis—were crucial because these could have repercussions, later in life, for their attitudes toward the Germans or Austrians in general. Poignant memories of betrayal and mistreatment may have facilitated generalizations about the evil of the German or Austrian people, whereas individual acts of decency and loyalty, small as they may have been, may have provided the proof of existence of at least one "good" German or Austrian and thus may have counteracted such bleak generalizations.

Finally, frequently staged scenes of public humiliation powerfully symbolized the sea change of the National Socialist "revolution": a complete reversal of the Jews' social existence from a comfortable and respectable bourgeois status to that of a blatantly despised and oppressed Pariah class without rights. A haunting example was mentioned to us by a former refugee from Vienna: "Probably nothing shocked me more than to see middle-aged, elderly Jewish women being forced to get down on their knees and scrub the sidewalk while these howling young hoodlums stood around and made vile remarks about them. It's really just unforgettable."

Instant Adults

In those dramatic days, as the situation of the Jewish families was fast becoming untenable, as they rushed from one embassy or consulate to the next in a quest for the coveted visas, as Jews were persecuted by government officials as well as subjected to the whims of thugs and the cruelties of National Socialist mobs, were sown the seeds of a monumental and lasting transformation of many of the children. They used to be normal children, but not anymore. Because their fathers were in jail or in camps or hiding, or because youngsters aroused less suspicion than adults, many children became providers, managers, messengers, and information brokers in their family's struggle for survival. They took on responsibilities far beyond their years, becoming adults suddenly and at a young age. One former refugee wrote on the questionnaire: "Hitler robbed me of my childhood. They took our apartment, sent my father to Dachau [concentration camp]. . . . I was at age 12 the main force in my family, eventually I succeeded in freeing my father." Another former refugee told us in the interview, "She [mother] asked my brother and me about our opinion, even to the extent when it came to bribing the Gestapo to get airplane tickets to fly out. . . . She discussed it with us, although I was at the time 12 and my brother was 13. We discussed it like adults." Here is a third example for this experience that was widespread among the former refugees. "The truth of the matter is that after the Anschluss I really was never a kid again. I didn't think the way the kids think. I didn't play the way kids play. And for quite a spell . . . I was pretty much on my own. My mother was in no position to do anything. . . . My dad was totally out of the picture, and I had to become self-sufficient."

This instant growing up and the concomitant change it brought in the family structure are important themes that repeated themselves in the United States (in different variations for those who lived with their family in the new country and those who had been separated from it). As one of our participants who came alone to the United States said, "At age 13, I was alone in a strange country. I had to learn a new language and culture, learned to stand on my feet, make my own decisions; since I had no one to confide in, I learned to have confidence in myself. I had to become an adult; having been cheated out of my youth I could never be as gay and carefree as other young people."

Here, in this accelerated maturation process—both in Central Europe under the National Socialists and in the United States as refugees—we think, is rooted both the refugee cohort's eventual high achievement, on the whole, in socioeconomic and creative terms, and the psychological anguish we observed among many participants.

Destinations

The refugee movement started soon after Hitler seized power in Germany and lasted right through the war. In their often desperate and harried attempts to obtain visas for foreign countries that would take them in, or simply to escape the reach of the German authorities and their collaborators, refugees went where they could and scattered in many directions. The dramatic voyage of the ship *St. Louis* came to symbolize the plight of the refugees (Gellman 1971). The 900 passengers on the *St. Louis* were headed from Hamburg to Cuba in May 1939, but, to their great despair, the Cuban government cancelled their visas in the last minute and did not allow them to disembark. The ship steamed around in circles for a while, shadowed by the U.S. Coast Guard cutters to prevent the refugees from landing in the United States. In the end, four European countries (Britain, the Netherlands, Belgium, and France) agreed to take them in.

The participants in our survey managed to come to the United States in many different ways. For some, the journey was fairly straightforward—for instance, boarding a transatlantic steamer in Hamburg and disembarking in New York—but others had very protracted migrations, through several countries, before they finally arrived in the United States. Whereas for two-thirds (67 percent) of our survey participants, one month or less time elapsed between leaving Central Europe and arriving in the United States, the rest had longer and more contorted itineraries. These individuals, as many others, moved through several countries before they reached their final destination. Those, for instance, who had left the National Socialist Germany early on for its neighboring countries often had to flee again after Germany expanded its sphere of influence. Others, who were denied their preferred destination, later tried to move there from an intermediate place of refuge. Saenger (1941:78–9) found that those "experienced refugees" who came to the United States via other countries adapted better than those who came directly from Germany.

Here are a few samples of long itineraries, as reported by our participants:

- Berlin, Belgium, France, Spain, North Africa, Canary Island, New York
- Germany, France, Spain, Portugal, Casablanca, Azores, Bermuda, Cuba, San Domingo, Mexico, New York
- Austria, Belgium, France, Dominican Republic, Spain, Portugal, United States

Most refugees—again, both the older ones and the children—who endured an extended flight, moved westward, for instance, to England, or to France and later to Spain and Portugal, where they waited in port cities for the coveted passage to destinations in North, Central, or South America. A smaller group attempted the eastern route and went by train through Siberia as far as Shanghai and then to Kobe, Japan, with the North American West coast as their ultimate destination.

For instance, "Left Berlin during the war (November 1940) to flee to Shanghai, China, via then Soviet Russia, on the land route (the only way open!). Arrived Shanghai ca. three weeks later, with parents, at the age of 19." There were about 20,000 refugees in Shanghai.[12] The eastern route was also taken by a group of about 3,500 orthodox Jews, rabbis and yeshiva students, who had escaped from Poland to Lithuania (Zuroff 2000). Turkey became a major transit point to Palestine (Proudfoot 1957:60) as well as a temporary haven for refugees such as Hans Reichenbach, Richard von Mises, and Paul Hindemith.

The United States was the prime recipient of the refugee migration, and our project focuses on this subgroup of refugees. Yet other countries also received substantial numbers of immigrants. While most German Jews were not Zionists, the second largest refugee stream, consisting of Jews, went to

Table 1.2   Refugee Destinations (Other Than
United States)

France (incl. North Africa)	800,000
Palestine	150,000
Britain	140,000
Latin America	125,000
Italy	116,000
East African colonies	90,000
Switzerland	80,000
Sweden	44,000
Shanghai	20,000
Spain	18,000
Canada	6,000

Source: Davie 1947:14.

Palestine, where Jewish immigration had already been going on under less catastrophic conditions for decades, in accordance with the core belief of the Zionist movement that a national homeland for the Jews should be created in Palestine.

The estimates of refugee numbers vary widely, not least because many refugees went through one or more countries before reaching their final places of refuge. Davie's (1947:14) estimates of refugee numbers (Jewish and non-Jewish) to destinations other than the United States are presented in table 1.2. Transits as well as multiple immigrations may account for the inflated French figure. France is also the most prominent example of a country of mere temporary refuge. The first wave of refugees left France in 1940 in the wake of its defeat, and the second wave left in 1942 after Germany occupied all of France (Proudfoot 1957:56).

Although these numbers are anything but precise figures, they may well provide an approximate picture of the relative magnitude of the main refugee streams that poured out of Central Europe, starting from the time Hitler came to power and lasting right through the war.

Chapter 2

Advent

Situation in the United States and Official Policy

When the first refugees arrived in the United States soon after the change of government in Germany in January 1933, the country was still in the grip of the Great Depression that had started with the Black Friday of October 1929. Millions of Americans were out of work, and the popular sentiment was thoroughly unsympathetic to new immigrants. In addition to the restrictive attitudes and policies toward immigration in general (see below), anti-Semitism was strong, with "quotas" at universities, difficulty in entering many professions, or even housing—and the majority of the refugees were Jewish. These factors created an unfavorable situation for most of the refugees and would-be refugees.

American Jewry found itself in something of a dilemma. On one hand, of course, there was the ingrained obligation to help coreligionists in peril.[1] On the other, many American Jews shared the widespread perception that a substantial Jewish immigration from Central Europe at that time would fuel the flames of the already existing anti-Semitism and thus worsen the situation of American Jews (Neuringer 1980). This was also the view of American officials. In 1934, Colonel Daniel W. MacCormack, Commissioner of Immigration, reportedly told a Jewish leader bluntly that Jewish-Americans had to decide, whether they were more interested in protecting the nearly 5 million American Jews from the intensification of anti-Semitism that would result from an influx of refugees, or in aiding a relatively small number of German Jews to come (Szajkowski 1971:105). According to Arthur D. Morse (1968:383), "many [American] Jews were as disinterested as their Christian countrymen" in the unfolding catastrophe in Central Europe (cf. Brody 1956, Szajkowski 1971).

Over time, especially after the *Kristallnacht* of 1938, it became apparent that the situation of the Jews in Germany was deteriorating horrendously, and so the Jewish community increased its efforts to help their Central European coreligionists. Yet the Jewish community leaders were very reluctant to propose the abolition of the restrictive immigration quota system that they knew the huge majority of the American public supported (an April 1939 opinion poll showed 83 percent of the American people opposing any bill that would lead to a larger number of immigrants [Neuringer 1980:246]). They preferred to work toward easing the conditions for immigration strictly within the existing policy framework because they feared that any attempt at changing it might actually backfire. The failure of the Wagner-Rogers bill of 1939 that proposed to admit 20,000 refugee children outside of the quota (see below) served as a warning not to initiate any similar legislative proposals thereafter.

U.S. Policies

In an attempt to combat the Depression-induced mass unemployment, President Herbert Hoover, in 1930, had issued an Executive Order instructing the State Department's consular service to interpret the public charge provision of the Immigration Act of 1917 with the utmost strictness so as to minimize the number of successful visa applications (Neuringer 1980: 205–6). The Affidavit system (requiring a U.S. citizen to assume fiscal responsibility for a would-be immigrant), intended to make sure that the admitted immigrants would not become public charges, was a major weapon against large-scale immigration (Szajkowski 1971:113). Because of Hoover's Order, the number of admitted immigrants from 1931 on fell far short of the set immigration quota—even during the height of the refugee movement. The annual quota of 27,370 for persons born in Germany or Austria, for instance, was completely used up only in one year, that is 1939, and was almost exhausted only in 1940 (95.3 percent) (Davie 1947:29).

But upon the outbreak of World War II, the United States was the only country, with the exception of Palestine, that did not take immediate steps to restrict refugee immigration even further (Tartakower and Grossmann 1944:91–2). Instead, some bureaucratic measures implemented around this time facilitated refugee immigration, for instance, by pooling from July 1, 1939 all quota numbers for persons of the same national origin so that refugees could access their full national quota while residing in third countries, which had not been allowed earlier; and from December 1940 on, by "unblocking" the list of visa applicants so that applicants who were unable to emigrate could be skipped and a visa could be granted to the next person on the list without delay (Tartakower and Grossmann 1944:92). In contrast to these measures, there were also policies that in effect restricted immigration. On July 1, 1941, for instance, visa issuance became the responsibility of the Visa Division in the State Department (rather than of the local American consul), and this complicated and prolonged the bureaucratic process considerably (Tartakower and Grossmann 1944:93–4).

After Germany defeated France, the armistice agreement contained a clause that put political refugees in danger of being sent back from France to Germany. In view of this emergency, 200 political refugees were brought from France to the United States, first formally on visitors' visas that came to be recognized as a special category of emergency visa that could be extended as necessary (Tartakower and Grossmann 1944:90). Because this was clearly not sufficient, President Franklin D. Roosevelt in 1941 appointed the President's Advisory Committee on Political Refugees with the purpose of speeding the emigration of political activists and other leaders who were in immediate danger. This committee brought 2,000 political refugees to the United States (Davie 1947:114) and also provided special visitors' emergency visas for 1,200 orthodox scholars (Zuroff 2000:91–2).

When the United States entered the war after a Japanese surprise attack on Pearl Harbor, Hawaii, on December 7, 1941, measures were immediately taken to control the nationals of the enemy countries. Of the 5 million aliens in the United States registered in accordance with the Alien Registration Act of 1940, approximately 1,100,000 were classified as enemy aliens (Davie 1947:193). Ironically, most of the Central European refugees, including parents and children, thus became "enemy aliens" or—even more sinister—"alien enemies," as President Roosevelt's proclamation of December 8 actually called them (Tartakower and Grossmann 1944:109). Because this policy put the refugees in a grotesque situation, several bureaucratic twists and turns ensued to afford them a more appropriate status. For instance, persons who had been registered as Austrians or Austro-Hungarians under the 1940 Alien Registration Act were exempted in practice from the enemy alien regulations (Tartakower and Grossmann 1944:111). An Executive Order of March 20, 1942, extended on August 27, 1943, exempted those from enemy alien status whom an investigation found to be loyal, and allowed them to apply for naturalization (Davie 1947:194)— though most of the affected may not have known of that change. One of our study participants remembered, "We were Germans and some people did not understand that we left Germany for religious persecution reasons. Also, we were not allowed to travel outside our area. My father went skiing in New Hampshire—and was arrested."

In April 1943, the United States and British representatives met in Bermuda to discuss the refugee problem (Tartakower and Grossmann 1944:420–6). The Bermuda Conference, as it came to be known, accomplished little in terms of concrete outcomes and caused widespread disappointment among the pro-refugee activists. As public pressure for increasing refugee aid kept mounting, especially because, in the later phase of the war, the horrendous scale of the German atrocities was becoming more and more apparent, President Roosevelt created the United States War Refugee Board (headed by the Secretaries of State, War, and the Treasury) by Executive Order No. 9417 on January 22, 1944.[2] Tens of thousands of people were rescued by the efforts of this Board in collaboration with private relief agencies. For instance, 8,000 orphaned Jewish children were kept alive in France through American funds sent by way of Switzerland (Davie 1947:13). These children were hidden in convents, schools, and private homes. The board also succeeded in keeping the Hungarian government—a so-called puppet regime of Germany—from deporting many Hungarian Jews to extermination camps in Poland.

Whereas early accounts of the refugee problem (Davie 1947, Grossmann 1944, Tartakower and Saenger 1941) reported the American immigration policies of the time without much evaluation, some later scholarship took an explicitly and strongly critical stance. Book titles, such as *While Six Million Died: A Chronicle of American Apathy* (Morse 1968) and *The Abandonment of the Jews: America and the Holocaust, 1941–45* (Wyman 1984, cf. Wyman 1968) signaled the thrust of the argument made in these books: that the American government stood idly by while the European Jews were being oppressed and killed. It is primarily Assistant Secretary of State Breckinridge Long who is blamed for creating the bureaucratic red tape to slow down the immigration of the refugees.

Organizations and Individuals Who Helped

International Agencies

After World War I, a number of international agencies were created to deal with refugee crises, but their efforts usually had little success. The League of Nations appointed a High Commissioner for Refugees in 1921, initially to support Russian refugees, but the commissioner's mandate was later expanded to include other refugees. In 1933, the League created an autonomous Office of High Commissioner for Refugees Coming From Germany (Tartakower and Grossmann 1944:405). The American James G. McDonald was the first High Commissioner, but he resigned in frustration two years later, to be replaced by Sir Neill Malcolm, a high British official. In 1938, the two offices merged into the High Commissioner of the League of Nations for Refugees (regardless of where they came from), and Sir Herbert Emerson became its first incumbent (Tartakower and Grossmann 1944:408).

On the initiative of the American government, an international conference on the refugee problem was convened in Evian-les-Bains, France, on July 6, 1938, and established the Intergovernmental Committee on Refugees (IGCR). It aroused wild hopes, but had little tangible success in alleviating the plight of the refugees (Proudfoot 1957:30–1, Tartakower and Grossmann 1944:426–8).

Even during the war, it was recognized that a refugee problem of the greatest magnitude was looming on the horizon, in the postwar era.[3] After the war was over, vast numbers of displaced persons all across Europe needed to be repatriated or resettled. In addition to the mainly Eastern European surviving victims of German expansion, forced labor, and the Holocaust, now there were also German refugees, expelled from the eastern German provinces annexed by Poland, Czechoslovakia, and the Soviet Union, and other people who had become the casualties of the large-scale redrawing of the European map after the war.

For Europe's surviving Jews, Palestine/Israel—the state of Israel was proclaimed in May 1948—became the major destination. Between 1946 and the end of 1951, a total of 387,000 European Jews migrated to that land (Proudfoot 1957: 360). A smaller contingent of 166,000 went to other countries during about the same period (between 1946 and 1950). The United States received most of these (105,000), followed by Canada (20,000) (Proudfoot 1957:360).

Private-Sector Refugee Aid Organizations

While the American government involved itself in refugee rescue and aid hesitantly and relatively late, private organizations in the United States had been active from the start. Indeed, the story of refugee aid is primarily one of private welfare organizations, predominantly Jewish ones. Operating with donated funds, they supported both the transit of refugees to safety and their establishment in their new countries, and tried to mobilize public opinion as well as to influence the government in favor of the refugees.

Collectively, our survey participants mentioned a long and varied list of organizations, large and small, national and local, that helped them in some way. Here is just one of many examples: "The organization that helped me eventually, in the States, was HIAS, Hebrew Immigrant Aid Society. . . . In fact, after we arrived in the United States and lived with those people who had guaranteed our stay, they paid my brother's and my rent and board and keeping until we were eighteen years old. They also . . . sent me to summer camp . . . and we had yearly medical exams. And HIAS was very good to us." Of the former refugees in our survey, 38 percent said they received financial assistance from outside their immediate family during the first year after arrival. Among those who received such aid, 54 percent acknowledged the help of organizations, 34 percent said they were supported by distant relatives, 5 percent by friends, and the others mentioned combinations of these sources of financial assistance. From the questionnaire responses it becomes apparent that the refugees were supported in extraordinarily varied ways, including (in about 20 percent of the cases) by a web of charitable and philanthropic agencies of the private sector.[4] Besides the large and frequently mentioned national organizations, such as HIAS and the Joint Distribution Committee, the National Council of Jewish Women, and the American Friends Service Committee, our participants let us know about an abundance of local groups extending aid. Most of these were Jewish, but there were also a few others, such as the American Committee for Christian Refugees. (See note for a more systematic survey of the aid organizations.[5])

The reason for paying attention to this complicated and somewhat bewildering ecology of organizations is that it will play a major role in our explanation of the eventual socioeconomic success of many of the former refugees. These organizations epitomize the "opportunity structure"—a very useful concept pioneered by R. K. Merton (1996)—encountered by the young refugees upon arrival. It was an opportunity structure that opened the possibility of rapid mobility and success, that was highly decentralized with a large number of components, that, consequently, was somewhat disorganized and chaotic, and that provided many repeat chances. Some kinds of persons were better able than others to take advantage of this particular opportunity structure, and we are going to make the point, in a subsequent chapter, that the refugees, and especially certain kinds of refugees, found the opportunity structure they encountered congenial.

One might ask about the sociocultural conditions that allowed those nongovernmental organizations to flourish. Two key factors facilitated their enormous effort. One is a general feature of American civil society already described by Alexis de Tocqueville in the early nineteenth century. Americans tend to tackle problems through voluntary citizens' associations whereas other nations look to their governments for action. From early times, the immigrants to America generally followed this pattern. Most immigrant groups in America, from the Irish to the Chinese, tended to organize mutual aid associations along ethnic lines to help the newcomers and facilitate their adjustment to the new country. Subtle or not so subtle exclusions of ethnic minorities from the mainstream also reinforced this tendency toward subcultures of ethnic organizations (see Glazer and Moynihan 1963).

Second, what was characteristic of American society and of American immigrants in general, applied to an even greater extent to the Jews. When, in the middle of the seventeenth century, the first Jews were permitted to settle in what was then New Amsterdam, the Dutch West India Company decreed that the Jews themselves would have to take care of their poor (Cohen 1984:118). The symbolic significance of this stipulation has been enormous through the centuries. The old obligation was never allowed to be forgotten and became one of the planks for an extraordinarily strong tradition of generous Jewish-American philanthropy. From 1848 through 1869, for instance, there were in New York City 93 Jewish welfare associations, as compared with 96 non-Jewish ones, although less than 5 percent of New Yorkers were Jewish at that time (Kaganoff 1966:28–9).

Because the Jewish immigration from Eastern Europe (which peaked in the late nineteenth and early twentieth centuries) was to a considerable extent triggered by persecution, American Jewry and its aid organizations, such as the Hebrew Sheltering and Immigrant Aid Society (also known as Hebrew Immigrant Aid Society—HIAS) with its long and successful history of supporting Jewish immigrants and refugees,[6] were accustomed to dealing with emergency immigrations and with helping coreligionists fleeing from extreme peril. From the late nineteenth century, the Yiddish-speaking immigrants—many of whom settled in the East Side of New York City (Gartner 1964)—founded numerous *landsmanshaftn*, hometown associations, that provided both material benefits and social contacts for people who had come from the same hometown or region. In the late 1930s, a comprehensive survey of the *landsmanshaftn* in New York City, conducted by the Yiddish Writers' Group of the Federal Writers' Project concluded that about 3,000 such organizations existed among the Eastern European Jews of the city, with a total membership of over 400,000 (Soyer 1997:1).

When the refugees arrived in the United States, they could turn to as many as 110 different nongovernmental organizations, Jewish and non-Jewish, that were involved in helping the refugees, including children (Hirsch and Hirsch 1961:51)—a remarkable proof of the typically American tendency for private citizen action.

An important aspect was how the refugee issue was being framed and presented to the public. Because a substantial minority of the refugees did not consider themselves Jewish and also because there was a perceived danger of an anti-Semitic reaction, many organizations preferred portraying the refugee issue not as a Jewish problem, but as a general humanitarian one caused by an antidemocratic dictatorship. The Jewish leaders thus tried hard to enlist non-Jewish organizations in refugee aid, but funds from them were not forthcoming in adequate amounts. It even came to the point that, in 1939, the United Jewish Appeal granted $125,000 to the Federal Council of the Church of Christ for work with Protestant refugees, and the same amount to Bishop Bernard J. Sheil for the Catholic refugees (Szajkowski 1971:127).

Numerous specialized organizations devoted themselves to assisting specific groups of immigrants.[7] Of particular interest to our study are organizations that assisted refugee students. The International Student Service, founded in 1920 and headquartered in Geneva, Switzerland, played a major role in refugee assistance (Davie 1947:114, Tartakower and Grossmann 1944:89). The American Committee of the organization helped about 700 students. When this committee was disbanded in July 1943, a new organization called Student Service of America took its place (Davie 1947:114). Another organization, the Institute of International Education that also created the Emergency Committee in Aid of Displaced German (later: Foreign) Scholars supported more than 100 students through scholarships and other services (Davie 1947:114).

The Intercollegiate Committee to Aid Student Refugees secured scholarships for young refugees in about 300 colleges. It started in 1938, as a result of student activism at Harvard University, with the Harvard Committee to Aid German Student Refugees, then quickly mushroomed into a nationwide movement, and in 1939 merged with the International Student Service (Davie 1947:114–5, cf. Tartakower and Grossmann 1944:89). Among the other organizations that helped refugee students were B'nai B'rith, the Hillel Foundation, the American Friends Service Committee, the Educational Alliance, the American Christian Committee for Refugees that established the Refugee Scholar Fund, the Vocational Service for Juniors, and the numerous fraternities and sororities that gave room and board to refugee students. While some universities enthusiastically welcomed refugee students, others were lukewarm.[8] (We have been conducting a special study on this issue of refugee students and report on it separately [Sonnert and Holton 2006].)

Apart from the multitude of agencies providing assistance to refugees, the refugees themselves organized numerous self-help programs as well as other associations. They formed about 150 organizations, including congregations, two-thirds of them in New York City and most of them Jewish (Davie 1947:172, see Lowenstein 1989:101–31). The organizations fell into three large categories: mutual aid; trade and professional; and social, cultural, and recreational. Corresponding to the composition of the refugee group, most of these refugee associations were German, but the Austrians, Poles, and Russians, as well as a few smaller nationalities, also had their own organizations.

The three major mutual aid organizations, all nonsectarian, were: Selfhelp of Emigres from Central Europe, Inc. (founded in 1936 by professors of the New School for Social Research [Strauss 1981:258]); Help and Reconstruction; and the Blue Card that was affiliated with the New World Club. The Club was the largest refugee organization in New York City and a social hub for the refugees. Established by earlier German immigrants, it was taken over by the newcomers.[9] Under its umbrella flourished a host of activities—from two kindergartens to a philatelic group, from an employment office to the already mentioned Blue Card, to a cemetery association. The Club also sponsored a German-language newspaper called the *Aufbau*.[10] The New World Club had about 2,000 members, as did the Jewish Club of 1933 in Los Angeles (Davie 1947:176). Next to the New World Club, another major refugee organization was the Prospect Unity Club (Lowenstein 1989:104). There were also some *Landsmannschaften* of people coming from the same town or region. In concept, these German *Landsmannschaften* were identical with the already mentioned Yiddish *landsmanshaftn*.

About a dozen independent youth organizations were founded, but they typically did not last long because most of the young refugees aspired to enter the American mainstream as quickly as possible, and because many young men served in the armed services. The only organization that endured was the Austro-American Youth Council with about 200 members (Davie 1947:177).[11]

Finally, we should mention the kind-hearted humanitarian efforts of individuals. Many Americans provided the required "affidavits" of support for refugees in need, often for distant relatives, but sometimes even for unrelated persons. We know of cases where people who were not even particularly well-off went out of their way to give numerous affidavits.

Arriving in America

Fortunately for our present effort, the refugee phenomenon immediately attracted major social science research projects, on which we can draw. An early sociological examination was undertaken by Maurice R. Davie of Yale University and his collaborators (Davie 1947). Entitled *Refugees in America*, this large-scale empirical study was sponsored by five major refugee aid organizations. With the help of over 200 refugee service associations, the researchers distributed about 50,000 questionnaires and received 11,233 responses that could be used (Davie 1947:xii, xvi). Even earlier, Gerhart Saenger (1941), a refugee himself who was also a trained social scientist, carried out his own refugee study. Saenger examined a sample of immigrants mainly through informal interviews conducted by student assistants (Saenger 1941:xii). The book lacks precise information on how large his sample was. A major study of the Jewish migration out of Europe, entitled *The Jewish Refugee*, was conducted by Arieh Tartakower and Kurt R. Grossmann (1944) with the sponsorship of the Institute of Jewish Affairs of the American Jewish Congress and the World Jewish Congress.

Number of Refugees

We should first address the question of how many refugees there were in the target population of our study. The problems with an exact count of the American refugee population are obvious and have been recognized early on, for instance by Tartakower and Grossmann (1944:viii) and by Davie and his collaborators (Davie 1947). A key difficulty was that "refugee" was not a category used by the Immigration and Naturalization Service (INS). However, for the purpose of our project, we need only the rough size of the refugee population. Luckily, in the existing literature, we found a high degree of consensus about the approximate number.

Estimates by different agencies, organizations, and persons—such as the INS, INS Commissioner Earl G. Harrison, the Common Council for American Unity, and the National Refugee Service—all converged on about a quarter million as the number of refugees from National Socialism—both adults and children—entering the United States from all countries (Davie 1947:27, cf. Hirsch and Hirsch 1960:41, Tartakower and Grossmann 1944:102). In Davie's (1947:xvi) study, the total group of those refugees was estimated at roughly between 250,000 and 300,000. Thus, it is probably safe to take a quarter million as a robust estimate of the magnitude of the refugee immigration to the United States between 1933 and 1944 (with many in the late years having come via temporary shelters outside Europe). If one looks only at immigrants from Germany and Austria, the number is significantly smaller. Herbert A. Strauss (1987:292, cf. 1983:xxi) estimated that "between 129,000 and 132,000 German [including Austrian] refugees of all kinds reached the United States between 1933 and 1944."

The widely publicized claim of a total of 580,000 refugees by Assistant Secretary of State Breckinridge Long was an outlier because he actually referred to visas issued rather than to immigrants. The bureaucratic situation was complicated because the records of immigration visas were kept by the State Department, whereas the actual records of persons admitted to the

Table 2.1 Immigrant Arrivals in the United States, 1933–44

Year	From Europe	Refugees (Gross estimate)	Refugees (Refined estimate)
1933	14,400	11,869	1,919
1934	19,559	16,323	4,241
1935	25,346	21,915	5,436
1936	26,295	22,875	6,538
1937	35,812	31,537	12,012
1938	50,574	44,848	44,848
1939	68,198	61,882	61,882
1940	56,254	50,581	50,581
1941	36,989	30,808	30,808
1942	14,881	12,620	12,620
1943	8,953	6,629	6,629
1944	8,694	6,348	6,348
Total	365,955	318,235	243,862

Source: Davie 1947:24. The "refined" estimate was made by Davie by developing a more sophisticated algorithm for distinguishing refugees from other immigrants.

United States were handled by the INS of the Justice Department (Davie 1947:28).

Table 2.1 presents two of Davie's estimates. Refugees from Germany including Austria (129,582) accounted for more than half of the refined estimate total, followed by persons from Poland (27,158), Italy (21,672), and Czechoslovakia (12,016).

In addition to the quarter million of refugees admitted for permanent residence, about 200,000 were admitted for temporary stay, of whom 15,000 were still in the country at the close of fiscal year 1944 on extended permits (Davie 1947:27). This results in a total number of about 265,000 refugees. To this number, one needs to add the 1,000 refugees interned in a vacated Army camp, named Fort Ontario, at Oswego, New York. They were brought by the War Refugee Board from the wartime-liberated Southern Italy to the United States of America, outside of the regular immigration procedures (Tartakower and Grossmann 1944:106–7).

The question of how many Jews were among the refugees who fled from National Socialism to the United States is difficult to answer for several reasons. As already mentioned, "refugee" was not an official INS category and so this status has to be inferred from the country of origin, the date of immigration, and other information. The prime source of information of an immigrant's Jewishness is the INS classification "Hebrew." However, this was discontinued by INS in 1943 (Davie 1947:33). Moreover, whereas the European "Hebrew" immigrants of the period in question can reasonably be considered Jewish refugees, there was an additional group of uncertain size. It consisted of people who—although they were labeled and persecuted as Jews according to the National Socialists' racial laws—rejected this label and thus would not have declared themselves "Hebrew" to INS.

"The more closely the refugee group can be distinguished from other immigrants, the higher the proportion of Jews among them becomes." (Davie 1947:36). The Davie survey indicated that the proportion of Jews (those who checked "Jewish" on the question about religion included in Davie's questionnaire) among the refugees was as high as 80 percent (Davie 1947:36). The proportion of Jews among the refugees was highest among those coming from Poland and Rumania, followed by Germany. Among the non-Jewish refugees, Davie's (1947:36) survey found that Protestants outnumbered Catholics by three to two. According to the INS data, more than half of the 168,128 "Hebrew" immigrants from 1933 to 1943 were born in Germany, including Austria (57.9 percent). The second largest group hailed from Poland (17.2 percent), followed by the Czechoslovakian contingent (4.2 percent) (Davie 1947:35).

Our research project is particularly interested in the young immigrants. Out of the 1.6 million Jewish children in German-occupied Europe before the war, 1.5 million were killed (Tec 1993:276). The children's survival rate of less than 7 percent was very much lower than the general survival rate of all European Jews, which was 33 percent. A substantial part of the escaping and surviving Jewish children, as well as some non-Jewish refugee children, came to the United States. Davie (1947:39) made a gross estimate of 16.1 percent, and a refined estimate of 14.8 percent, for the percentage of children under 16 years among the refugee immigrants admitted from 1933 through 1944 (15 percent is the number given by Hirsch and Hirsch [1961:45]). In absolute numbers, these percentages translate to about 51,000 refugee children according to Davie's gross estimate, and 36,000 children according to the refined estimate. Davie (1947:204) himself quoted an approximate number of about 37,000 refugee children (under 16), but also gave a precise gender breakup (boys slightly outnumbered the girls, 19,041 vs. 18,206) that would set the actual number of Davie's refined estimate at 37,247. The target cohort of this project is slightly different from Davie's—especially because we focus mainly on those young refugees who were born in Germany and Austria. Our cohort comprises between 25,000 and 30,000 members and we will present detailed calculations later in this book.

Unusual Socio-Demographic Features of the Refugee Group as a Whole

The total group of refugees from Central Europe during the 1930s and 1940s differed in several crucial sociodemographic aspects from the customary immigrant pattern in the United States. As a group, the refugees were (1) more highly trained and educated; (2) included more families; (3) were older; and (4) included more women, compared with an average immigrant group (Davie 1947:37–8). The latter three characteristics were the result of this immigration wave having been set in motion by the persecution of a whole ethnic group. The first characteristic derived from the elevated socioeconomic status that Central European Jewry had collectively reached in a few generations after the eighteenth- and nineteenth-century emancipation.

When one compares the original socioeconomic status of all adult refugees entering the United States with the status breakup of the American labor force as a whole, one finds a disproportionately large number of refugees coming from the higher rungs of the occupational hierarchy. Table 2.2 compares three different estimates of the adult refugee group's (i.e., the "First Wave's") original occupational structure with that of the American labor force, as reported in the 1940 Census. The percentages omit those with no gainful occupation.

The estimated percentages for the refugee population are very similar for the three methods, perhaps with the exception of the skilled worker category where the refined estimate by "races" yields a substantially lower number than the other two estimates do. The main point is that, in comparison with the American workforce, professionals and business people were far more strongly represented among the adults in the arriving refugee group, whereas the larger representation of skilled workers seems somewhat less certain. Conversely, the immigrant group contained relatively few farmers and semi-skilled workers. The categories of clerks and of unskilled workers were also somewhat underrepresented, and Davie (1947:41) surmised that the reported percentage of the latter category (unskilled workers) was inflated so that the real underrepresentation may have been even more substantial. In short, this arriving group of refugees had an extraordinarily strong middle-class component, and those refugees who belonged to the working class tended to be concentrated in its upper rather than lower echelons.[12] Nonetheless, these data also relativize the predominant stereotype of the professional and scholarly "First Wave" refugee. That stereotype was certainly not true for all refugees as the refugee cohort contained individuals from all walks of life.

Table 2.2 Percent Distribution, by Socioeconomic Groups, of the Estimated (Adult) Refugee Arrivals, Fiscal Years Ended June 30, 1933–44, who had Gainful Occupations, Compared with that of Persons in the United States Labor Force in 1940

	U.S. Labor force (%) 1940	Refugee arrivals estimated by selected European "races" (INS term) (%) 1933–44		Refugee arrivals estimated by Europe as last place of permanent residence (%) 1993–44
		Gross estimate	Refined estimate	
Professional persons	6.5	17.5	18.3	17.5
Farm owners and tenants	10.1	3.3	3.5	3.1
Dealers, proprietors, managers, and officials	7.6	22.2	24.7	21.7
Clerks and kindred workers	17.2	11.5	12.4	11.5
Skilled workers and foremen	11.7	21.4	13.7	19.3
Semiskilled workers	21.0	6.0	7.1	6.4
Unskilled workers	25.9	18.1	20.3	20.5
Total	100.0	100.0	100.0	100.0

Source: Davie (1947:42)

For a more detailed view, based on INS data, of the adult immigrants (regardless of religion) who followed professional and commercial pursuits, one can turn to a table in the notes.[13] These data indicate that, among the (adult) middle-class refugees, the commercial wing (*Wirtschaftsbürgertum*) outnumbered the professionals (*Bildungsbürgertum*), but not by a large margin. Most numerous among the arriving professionals were physicians, followed by professors and teachers. A somewhat higher proportion of Christian than Jewish refugees were "university people" (Davie 1947:44).

By 1947, among the refugee group who had arrived as adults in the United States from Europe, there were 12 who had won the Nobel Prize, 103 persons listed in *Who's Who in America*, and 220 *American Men of Science* listees. According to Davie (1947:44–5), these lists were twice as long as one would have expected, given the relative size of the refugee group. Our own research on the *Who's Who* listees of the *Second* Wave revealed an even stronger representation, as will be shown in chapter 4.

The primary geographic concentration of refugees from all of Europe was found in New York City, where nine-tenths of them had arrived (Davie

1947:80–1, 157). Of the German and Austrian Jewish refugees, as many as 52 percent were settled in Washington Heights (Baumel 1990:176), ironically dubbed the "Fourth Reich,"[14] and another large group resided in midtown Manhattan between Central Park and the Hudson River. Smaller refugee groups were found in the Bronx, the Lower East Side, and in Queens, especially in its Jackson Heights, Forest Hills, and Kew Gardens areas. With the exception of the Lower East Side, where some of the poorest refugees lived, the others were all average or good neighborhoods. Some wealthier refugees could even afford choice residential areas near Central Park, on Riverside Drive, and on Long Island.

Next to New York City, Los Angeles and Chicago became centers of refugee settlement (Davie 1947:80). In Chicago, notable refugee communities grew especially in the Kenwood, Hyde Park, and South Shore areas on the South Side, and in the North Center, Lakeview, and Lincoln Park neighborhoods on the North Side.

One participant in our study of young refugees told us, "And it helped probably [that] there was a refugee community where we landed. . . . So there was a group suddenly where you had people who had some comparable experience, and I think at the beginning that was helpful. . . . [And] Travelers' Aid helped." Another interviewee reminisced about his life after arriving as a child in New York City: "Socially, of course, there were unbelievable numbers of people we had known or were related to people we had known. And the whole émigré situation in New York—also, our French relatives and our Italian relatives—they were all there. My family was spread all over, and so in New York one sort of met them all. It was like coming home almost." A third former young refugee (who had also come to New York City) commented, "The European influence continued in New York. I grew up in a community with many other German/Austrian refugees. Great emphasis on learning, education."

The refugee community, in the places where it was numerous enough, supported a vibrant cultural life, because the "First Wave" of adult refugees contained a rich crop of cultural and artistic luminaries, as well as a large proportion of people interested in matters of culture and the intellect. This influenced the children. An interviewee recalled, "When we were in New York, there used to be a wonderful German-language theater . . ., and all the good actors and actresses who were kicked out of Germany. I mean, we saw fantastic performances. And I [had seen] a similar thing in a really bombed-out neighborhood in London in the middle of the war. . . . You know, people were carrying their baggage and German culture with them."

A major concern of the agencies helping the refugees resettle in the United States was to prevent the refugees' geographical concentration in a few refugee neighborhoods and to spread them out all over the country.[15]

Our survey participants' initial geographical distribution reflected that concern to some extent. Whereas 40 percent of our participants settled in a neighborhood where there were no other refugees they knew about, 33 percent reported that at first they lived in a neighborhood with relatively few fellow refugees and 27 percent said fellow refugees were relatively numerous.

Chapter 3

Settling In

Several of our interviewees still vividly remembered the shock of the first day in an American school. As one put it, "When my parents sent me to school here, I was dressed in European clothes, short pants, wool stockings and a back pack. This caused quite a commotion." The newly arrived children, as well as the adult newcomers, experienced various instances and degrees of culture shock, a challenge common to most immigrants who are catapulted into what at first seems a strange and alien culture.[1]

The concept of "assimilation" has nowadays become rather suspect in some quarters, but it was, in the 1930s and 1940s, widely accepted as the goal for new immigrants. As the book title *Today's Refugees, Tomorrow's Citizens: A Story of Americanization* suggests, Saenger (1941:103) was indeed an unequivocal advocate of the refugees' rapid and complete assimilation into the American society, known as Americanization.[2] According to his findings, most immigrants agreed with the desirability of speedy Americanization and undertook extraordinary efforts to accomplish it as quickly as possible. Rapid Americanization was also the aim of the German-Jewish Children's Aid that sponsored unaccompanied children (Baumel 1990:103). Joining the military was a way for many refugees to show their loyalty to their host country and also to gain American citizenship fast. Of the whole group of male refugees of 18–44 years of age, 34 percent served in the armed forces (Davie 1947:197). In our sample of Second Wave refugees from Germany and Austria, 52 percent of the men (and 2 percent of the women) reported having done military service in World War II.

Although the speed and degree of assimilation may certainly have been higher among our young refugee group than among other immigrant groups, the expectation of total Americanization was probably too simplistic and unrealistic. Carried out decades later than the pioneering surveys,

Ruth Neubauer's (1966) study, though much smaller, cast some doubts on whether assimilation (of the children, let alone of the adults) was indeed as quick and thorough as particularly Saenger believed (also see Baumel 1990). Indeed, our study will serve to document in detail the limitations of Americanization for the Second Wave.

From Refugees to Americans

Here are some problems with which the refugees, young and old, had to struggle after their arrival and later on—in addition to the immediately pressing issue of economic survival. When the refugees came to United States of America, many suffered a disorientation that is typical for immigrants (Schütz 1944). They often knew little about America, and what knowledge they had was of dubious validity, because much of it consisted of stereotypes, such as those glanced from American movies. As the responses to our questionnaire showed, another (similarly unreliable) source of information or imagination, especially for the young males, was the "Wild West" books by German author Karl May. In America, the refugees were also often unpleasantly surprised by encountering anti-Semitic attitudes, with which they had been less familiar in the *pre*-National Socialist Germany or Austria (Saenger 1941:54–6, Davie 1947:63). If the refugees had family sponsors, relations with those sponsors were often difficult and conflict-ridden. The refugees tended to expect more help than some sponsors were willing to give; the sponsors often told them to start at the bottom and work their way up (Strauss 1981:243–4).

In Davie's (1947:89) survey, language was cited most frequently as the problem that presented the greatest obstacle to adjusting in the new country. The refugees, as a group, were very keen on acquiring the English language as quickly as possible. A special study of refugee families in Philadelphia, conducted as part of the Davie study, found that English was the only language commonly spoken in the home of 41.5 percent of the studied families (Davie 1947:167). Data from our study will show how quickly the young Second Wavers, as a group, acquired proficiency in English.

The transition to life in the new country was easier when the refugees had been able to bring some funds with them, which was the case among a few of the early immigrants. A minute, but very visible segment of the refugee group, the "café-society" of wealthy immigrants, became the target of antipathy from Americans who subscribed to the classical immigrant theme of starting at the bottom (Davie 1947:375–7).

Some First Wave refugees fell into the habit of constantly referencing their earlier elevated position and of going on about the inferiority of America (Saenger 1941:845), probably because they resented their loss of status or felt insecure in their existence. The *bei uns* (back home) type of complaints and jokes became somewhat notorious, named after the punch line that everything was once better *bei uns* in the old country (Davie 1947:384). Whereas Saenger (1941:15) made the point that "Traits such as rigidity, aggressiveness, traditionalism, a certain lack of humor, however, are resented by Americans and are considered as typically refugee behavior, while in reality they are typically German," Alfred Schütz (1944) thought that, sociologically speaking, these traits are typical for strangers in general. One might reasonably assume that the refugee experience certainly reinforced any preexisting proclivity toward the traits mentioned.

Of the respondents to Davie's questionnaire, almost half (47.6 percent) felt that by 1947 their living conditions were the same as they had been in Europe, and more than a quarter (26.6 percent) even said that they had improved. By contrast, only 11.9 percent said their *social status* had improved (49.2 percent thought it was the same) (Davie 1947:168–9). Not surprisingly, the refugees tended to feel that they lost more in terms of social than of economic status. On one hand, this sentiment to some degree derived from the benefits of the higher material standard of living that generally existed in the United States. On the other, the elevated social status that many refugees had enjoyed was particularly hard to transfer, partly because in the United States many newcomers were unable to obtain social positions commensurate with their erstwhile status in their home countries, at least initially; and partly because their status was based upon the European system of social hierarchy that differed from the American one.

Whereas in America status was primarily determined by economic success and money, the Central Europeans attached enormous respect to *Bildung* (loosely corresponding to "liberal arts education"). In their social universe, titles were important. Being a *Herr Doktor*, for instance, conveyed high social distinction, and it was considered bad form not to address such a person by his proper title. At least among themselves the refugees tried to maintain these standards that made them look somewhat supercilious in the American eyes. "The social stratification of the refugee group, which the outsider is likely to consider a unit, is in fact a replica of that of the countries from which they have come" (Saenger 1941:158–9).

Psychological issues were perhaps even more intractable than the social ones. As Davie (1947:170) remarked, "The psychological problems of the refugee will be solved long after his economic and social problems, if indeed, except for the young children, they can be solved at all. In many cases the tragedy of the refugee's experience will be stamped upon his soul to the end." Especially note how, in this passage, potential psychological aftereffects were downplayed for the children. Our study will show that this expectation must be revised. Nonetheless, some individuals responded to the crisis with resourcefulness, courage, and endurance, particularly when they realized that others depended on them.[3]

Family Dynamics

Life, even for those who were fortunate enough to come to the new country with their family members, was usually very different, especially in the initial phase. The sometimes drastic decline in the family's fortune and status after they arrived in the United States as refugees was painfully obvious even to the children. As one former young refugee recalled, "Living in a very small apartment. I mean, from living in total comfort to more or less living in poverty, going from . . . riches to rags, so to speak . . . it was a matter of survival, and it's all I remember." Another interviewee's father went from being a manager to "working as a chauffeur. . . . And so our lifestyle really changed rather drastically. We went from upper middle class, where I was in a private school, and Dad had a plane and all that, to probably something below working-class level."

A third interviewee said, "The one thing I do remember, when my mother was cleaning the house, I couldn't imagine her doing that because we had about three people working for us, just doing the house and cooking and taking care of us. . . . So that was a shocker. . . . She worked all week and then on weekends, you know, had to do the cleaning . . . and the cooking because my father, being the old European type, he was not much help. He worked very hard, too."

In some cases, as one might expect, these hardships created a lot of tension for the married couple and for the whole family. "There was a tremendous amount of stress. My father worried about being able to support his family from the time we got here until he died. . . . It was always hard. My mother worked at very menial kinds of jobs, and she had gone to law school. . . . My father was [depressed] to some extent . . . because he never probably achieved what he thought he should have." Or, in a more severe case, "With the strains between my parents . . . I lived in the streets . . . but that was hard. [My family] was dysfunctional."

At least in the early years after arrival, women often were active in providing for the family, for instance, by acquiring skills in demand on the labor market or by working menial jobs (the only ones available to them). This had marked consequences for the hierarchy within the family. When a man was supported by his wife and children, "a practical reversal of the

traditional family pattern occur[red]" (Saenger 1941:174). It was obvious
to observers that "The male head of the family has tended to lose authority and status, and the women and children have experienced something
approaching an emancipation" (Davie 1947:147). On average, women
adjusted better to life in America than men did, as many of the men were
more demoralized and paralyzed by the substantial loss of social status they
had to endure.[4] We found ample evidence for such a gender difference also
in our study. Several of our participants observed that, among the adult
refugees, women tended to settle in more easily than men did. As one
summarized, "My father didn't adjust. I think the men adjusted less well
than the women." Here is an example from another interviewee: "My
father and mother were very different people. My father, I think, felt that
he had been sort of sabotaged, had his legs cut off, or something like that.
He was—you know, he came from a well-to-do family . . . and he sort of
never really faced the hard facts of life, which is one of the reasons why he
sort of wanted to make sure that we did. He sort of felt shortchanged in
some way when he came over here, figured he had a duty to perform to see
that his children grew up. . . . And my mother was much more positive
and outgoing."

Two more instances of the same pattern:"My mother took to it like a fish
to water. She didn't know English before. She learned it very quickly. She
was very adaptive, enjoyed, accepted things here. . . . [My father] never
became that fluent . . . and he always remained very critical of this country,
never really accepted being here." And, "She [mother] really took it very
well, and you know, she just pitched right in. It was my dad who was the
worrier always, you know, about money, about everything. But [mother]
really worked hard. . . . My father was very dependent on my mother."

When the women took on a more active and responsible role in many
aspects of life, this was partly precipitated by the necessities inherent in the
refugee situation. Partly, however, they moved toward a standard to which
American women had already grown accustomed. One of our interviewees
noted that his mother enjoyed the greater level of independence that she
experienced in America. "My mother certainly was one of those [who] felt
a perverse sort of gratitude toward Adolf Hitler for having gotten us the hell
out of Europe, period. And [for] my mother, it manifested itself in sort of
the anonymity and freedom of the big city. . . . She had a very confined
way, a bourgeois constraint [in Central Europe], so [she] felt liberated here
in the U.S. . . . My father was less happy."[5]

The refugee group, however, also contained some avant-garde socialist
intellectuals from the metropolitan centers who (at least in theory) espoused
equality between the genders, a precursor model to the ideas that were to
enter the American mainstream much later in the 1970s. In these circles,

women often worked in high-level careers, and they were thus used to assuming work responsibilities as warranted by the refugee situation.

But there was of course a wide range of individual reactions to the refugee life among the adults, and, in some cases we were told, women did not adjust well. "Well, my mother felt like a victim. We had no car. She had to go shopping with a shopping bag, and she had to work. She'd never worked before. We had 5 servants. We had a gardener, we had a nanny, and we had an upstairs maid. We had a downstairs maid, and we had a cook. And my mother had never had to work before. All of the sudden she had to shop and cook, and she felt very sorry for herself, and I'm afraid she made life hard for my father. You know, she just simply wasn't being supportive." On the other hand, we also heard of fathers who were able to adjust quickly and successfully. For instance, "So he [father] made a living within a week of coming to the United States. And once he got promoted, he got more money, and then became part of management. Life was pretty comfortable, I think."

The Children's Experience

The drastic changes in life circumstances of the immigrant families often placed a heavier burden not only on the wives, but—and this is most important for our study—also on many children who, at a young age, had to take on much larger responsibilities than is usual. Children tended to rise to the challenge, as Saenger (1941:44) observed in his early study. "Children, under pressure of oppression, developed a maturity and initiative far beyond their years. . . . Young people, particularly, not only became more mature and more serious, but proved to be able to live up to the exigencies of the time. The necessity to adjust resulted in greater initiative and versatility among these victims of oppression." This early statement about the children turned out to be quite prophetic. Our study will document its plentiful corroboration in the high level of eventual socioeconomic achievement, on average, of our group of former refugees. We heard numerous stories about the young refugees' early maturity and responsibility in the early years of immigration, and, because we think this is a central point in many Second Wavers' experience, we now give several examples from different individuals. A mere 14-year-old girl on arrival, for instance, would become the de-facto manager of the family. "I adjusted much more quickly [than the parents]. . . . I took over the household, and I did the cooking and shopping [and income tax]. . . . When we were ready to find an apartment, I went out and looked for apartments. I went all over town and knew what our price range could possibly be, and I would go to the super, and I would look at it and ask the proper questions, and so on."

Another participant told us, "I was the only breadwinner of the family. . . . And I was very proud of the fact that I was the only one who was earning money and all that." An interviewee who was 19 years old when arriving in the United States, after having spent some time without his family in England, said, "I think the family dynamics really had already changed before this, in England, when I was [sending] advice to my parents as to what to do and what visas were available. I really knew more than they did about these things. . . . I knew English . . . so I became sort of an advisor. . . . I did really so much in terms of finding an apartment, signing a lease and all of that sort of thing." Finally, another interviewee poignantly summarized that shift in family dynamics in one sentence: "And I think in a way I was the parent and they were the children."

As has been observed in many immigrant groups, the difference in the degree of acculturation between the generations can cause some strain within the families. The older generation tended to hang on more tightly to the values and norms of their original culture, but the children were more in tune with American culture. In view of the typically more authoritarian child-rearing practices in Europe (Saenger 1941:176), the fathers' loss of authority, in many cases, after the transfer to America, was all the more dramatic. Young refugee children "will sometimes feel embarrassed" (Saenger 1941:181, see Neubauer 1966:153) at their parents' broken English and at their old-country habits and attitudes, yet often the refugee situation in which the family members had to rely on each other may have also created closer bonds between children and parents. Religion seemed to play an important role here. In the case of orthodox Jewish families, because of being distanced from the American mainstream, the family members drew closer together, and thus the estrangement between the generations was lower among the orthodox groups than among the nonorthodox groups in Neubauer's (1966:163–7) study.

Strauss (1981:245, orig. in German) observed that, in the long run, the refugee children experienced less of psychological alienation from their parents than is usual among immigrant groups: "In contrast with immigrant groups that have different social and cultural structures, the younger and second generation of the Jewish immigrants of the National Socialist period appears to exhibit none of the social pathologies that traditionally are associated with the 'alienation' of a generation from the parents' culture, e.g., crime, violence, dropping out of school, or other symptoms of *anomie*."

The noted role reversal between children and parents, among many Second Wavers, created a protective attitude, almost a quasi-parental attitude, toward their own parents. Although, in some cases, the relationship with the parents was problematic or disturbed,[6] it was the quasi-parental attitude that predominated. The following quotes will illustrate the strong desire to save and protect one's parents from harm and destitution, from disappointment and worry.

"My sister and I always, and even to this day, always tried very hard to do our best. . . . I think partly it was because we didn't want to impose additional worries on our parents. . . . We felt that would be one way of perhaps making life a bit easier for them."

"I know one thing. We were all very ambitious. We were looking for a better future, and also we were very concerned about our parents not having enough money. We were trying to help them as much as possible, and trying to earn our own keep. . . . I worked during the day and went to college at night, which was really very difficult."

"And I was very close to my mother, but more in terms of feeling the responsibility to support her rather than feeling that I needed the support."

In other cases, the parents were role models for overcoming adversity through hard work. "I saw my father work so hard and struggle so hard to make life work in this second life, and I think that I modeled myself [on my father]. I sort of took for granted you worked 130 hours a week."

There were of course some instances of youthful rebellion against the parents, but this tended to be mild and limited. An interviewee, who described himself as rebellious in his early years, said that, when push came to shove, "We wanted to do what we needed to do, and it may have been related to all this background stuff, because we knew what the circumstances were and we knew what had happened. And we knew we had to do certain things. And I didn't want to do things that my parents didn't approve of. Or worry them."

In most cases, parents seemed to be able to keep children with a deviant streak in line. One of our participants remembered that, as a youngster, he was somewhat on the cusp. "I also got arrested when I was about nine. . . . I was throwing . . . mud balls at the cars, you know." He thought he would have become a juvenile delinquent, "if it hadn't been for my mother." "But the point is I always had very good role models." The parental influence appeared strong enough—and a peer-dominated culture of deviance weak enough or absent—to keep most of the somewhat marginal children on a straight path.

Unaccompanied Children

We now turn to the challenges that the so-called unaccompanied refugee children faced.[7] Persecution and flight tore many families apart. Indeed,

"Among refugees it is *usual* to be separated, husband from wife, children from parents; it is *unusual* for a whole family to be together." (Davie 1947:145). A special program was instituted in the United States for admitting unaccompanied children who had no possibility of obtaining a sponsor (Baumel 1990, Jason and Posner 2004). The privately organized European-Jewish Children's Aid (at first called German-Jewish Children's Aid) was founded in 1934. It reached an agreement with the immigration authorities that unaccompanied refugee children under the age of 16 could be admitted on a corporate affidavit from the European-Jewish Children's Aid organization, guaranteeing that the children would not become public charges (Davie 1947:208). In the early years funding for this program came from a variety of foundations and individuals. From 1938 through 1941, the National Council of Jewish Women financed the program, and thereafter the National Refugee Service took financial responsibility. As long as the immigration quota was not filled, this program worked well, but in 1938 applications began to exceed the quota, and because of the large number of adults' applications, only a small proportion of the children's applications was granted.

To help the backlogged children, as noted, the Wagner-Rogers Bill that was introduced in Congress in 1939 proposed to admit, within a two-year period, a maximum of 20,000 refugee children of all faiths under the age 14 *outside the quota restrictions*. Named after its sponsors, Senator Robert Wagner from New York and Representative Edith Nourse Rogers from Massachusetts, this bill encountered massive opposition and failed already at the committee stage (Davie 1947:209).[8] The total number of unaccompanied children admitted from 1934 through 1944 was 1,035. The greatest worry for those who arrived in America on their own was the fate of the relatives left behind, and they focused all their energies on helping and rescuing them. It is said that, once these young refugees learned that some or many of their loved ones had in fact perished, they were often burdened by survivor's guilt. For many unaccompanied children, the dreaded orphan status became eventually a harsh reality; but some were lucky enough to be reunited with parents who had escaped or survived the Holocaust. In our survey, 46 percent of the former refugees reported that they had migrated without father or mother. Of those who were separated from both parents when fleeing from Central Europe, 49 percent were reunited with both, 38 percent were reunited with neither, and the rest with one parent. However, rarely were these reunions the hoped-for instant happy endings, because the years of separation and hardships had often created rifts that took some time to be closed.

The figures in table 3.1 indicate an initial peak in the early years of the Hitler government in Germany and the main peak in 1940 and 1941. The American entry into the war made rescuing children more difficult.

Table   3.1 Admissions   of
Unaccompanied   Children,   by
Year of Arrival

1934	53
1935	106
1936	76
1937	92
1938	74
1939	32
1940	118
1941	260
1942	88
1943	127
1944	9
Total	1,035

Source: Davie (1947:211).

A relatively large group of children arrived as late as 1943, but their numbers dropped drastically thereafter.

Nearly two-thirds of the total group of unaccompanied children were of German extraction, and a quarter of Polish parentage (Davie 1947:210–1). There were also 57 Austrians and smaller numbers of several other European nationalities. The children came from middle-class and lower middle-class families, and their fathers were most typically engaged in business or commercial pursuits. Boys outnumbered girls (627 against 408), and this gender imbalance was most pronounced in the early years. One might speculate that, in the early years of the Hitler government, many families anticipated discrimination in educational opportunities and in the professional and business arenas, but not physical annihilation. Given the then prevailing notions of gender roles, the parents—or perhaps the selecting agency—might have considered it more important for the boys than for the girls to circumvent the presumed career obstacles within the National Socialist regime. Or, perhaps the thought of sending away girls alone was simply too abhorrent for many. A particularly moving segment of the documentary film "Into the Arms of Strangers," for instance, tells the story of a father pulling his young daughter from the train as it had already begun moving (see the following section on the *Kindertransport*).

Other Countries' Rescue Efforts for Children

Compared with the efforts of other countries, the United States' rescue of 1,035 unaccompanied children was relatively modest in size. In Britain, a large-scale *Kindertransport* (children's transport) for refugee children from Germany, Austria, and Czechoslovakia up to 17 years and as young as 3 years was organized through the Movement for the Care of Children from Germany, also known as Refugee Children's Movement (an umbrella organization of several voluntary agencies that had merged with the earlier established Inter-Aid Committee for Children from Germany) (Turner 1991:46). It was made possible by action of Parliament, following a memorable, magnificent address by Philip Noel Baker soon after the outrage of *Kristallnacht* and its aftermath became known.[9] In the nine months from December 1938 to the outbreak of World War II, a total of 9,354 rescued children were registered with the Movement that was headquartered at Bloomsbury House in London.[10] Estimates of the percentage of Jews among the children vary from almost 90 percent (Gottlieb 1998:125) to 72 percent (Tartakower and Grossmann 1944:220–1) and a rough estimate of more than 60 percent (Davie 1947:209). Several hundred other children brought to Britain by the Movement for the Care of Children from Germany were sponsored by independent agencies and not registered by the Movement (Gottlieb 1998:125). A small trickle of escapees entered Britain after the outbreak of the war. The total number of refugee children in Britain was given as nearly 20,000 by Tartakower and Grossmann (1944:221) and Davie (1947:209 [apparently based on Tartakower and Grossmann]). Both accounts mention the nearly 10,000 children rescued by the Movement and an additional 10,000 children whom a legal loophole permitted entry into Britain on the condition that they would leave the country after reaching their majority. About 2,000 of the 10,000 *Kindertransport* children eventually migrated to the United States.[11]

The Netherlands offered a haven for 1,850 unaccompanied children, Belgium for 800, France for 700, and Switzerland for 300 (Hansen-Schaberg 1998:83). Through Youth Aliya, 4,800 children went to Palestine by November 1938. Conceived by Recha Freier, Youth Aliya was a Zionist youth organization that prepared young persons for immigration to Palestine through camps that taught them agricultural and other practical skills. During the war, about 12,000 children went to Palestine (Hansen-Schaberg 1998:83).[12]

In France the efforts to rescue children were spearheaded by the Oeuvre de Secour aux Enfants (OSE) under Ernst Papanek (1975, 1980). Starting in February 1939, children were brought from Germany and other nations to four boarding schools at Montmorency, north of Paris. By the spring of 1940, OSE took care of 1,600 children living in 11 boarding schools that were run according to progressive and socialist principles of education. The children came from varied backgrounds——not only from political activist families, but also from orthodox Jewish and from nonpolitical homes[13] (Papanek 1975, 1998:230). When the German military defeated the French, the children escaped to unoccupied France.[14] The plan was to emigrate to the United States from there, but red tape and conflicts among and within aid organizations prevented a timely departure of the whole group. While some of the Jewish children were deported to Germany and murdered, OSE succeeded in rescuing others to the safety of the United States.[15] Upon the children's arrival there, Ernst Papanek was unable to reinstitute his boarding school concept because the European-Jewish Children's Aid insisted on placing the children in foster homes (Baumel 1990:93–4, Hansen-Schaberg 1998:85, Papanek 1975).

Separation from Parents

The children who came unaccompanied had to deal with the separation from their parents. The younger among the earlier arrivals did not understand the reasons well, and this affected their emotional adjustment; the later ones worried about their parents (Davie 1947:217). "Sometimes children seemed to wish to draw a veil over the early part of their lives, and seldom mentioned their parents, yet nonetheless missed them. . . . Occasionally some child who for years had given the appearance of having become happily reconciled to the parting would break down and blurt out a story of loneliness and heartache which he had long tried to mask" (Davie 1947:219). Interestingly, placements in foster homes had slightly higher rates of what was considered "good adjustments" than placements in relatives' homes did (Davie 1947:221).

How did the separation from, and in many cases loss of, their parents affect the young refugees who came to the United States? The psychological situation must have been rather complex and ambivalent. For instance, at the start, some of the *Kindertransport* children reported they were excited and pleased when they boarded the train for the journey to England via Holland. Mixed feelings were, of course, more prevalent. Several former refugees described a shifting mélange of feelings of adventure and loss.

The trauma of separation weighed heavily on other children. As one of our interviewees summarized, "We were put on the *Kindertransport*, and that was probably the most horrible night of my life. Nothing has ever— nothing before or since even comes close." To some children, being sent away by their parents might have appeared as some kind of abandonment. "[That feeling of abandonment] is forever. It's still there today."

The children who entered the United States in the *early* years of the refugee movement were, according to the contemporary reports, generally optimistic and thrilled. The 1939–40 arrivals, marking the end of that early phase, already foreshadowed what was to come later. These children were more upset, and many of them were reported to have suffered from "hyperactivity, aggressiveness, voracious eating, bed-wetting, suspiciousness, and fearfulness (Davie 1947:215–16)," yet on the whole even these children appeared "amazingly normal" (Davie 1947:216).

The children who arrived in 1941 or later were more like "pathetic waifs" (Davie 1947:215) and had often undergone extremely harrowing experiences. "Sad-eyed and serious, having struggled for long to maintain life itself, they had to learn how to play and be children again. But the recuperative power of children is extraordinary." (Davie 1947:216). The unaccompanied Austrians, as a group, did not adjust as well as the others, which Davie (1947:231) attributed to the rapidity with which the National Socialists had overtaken Austria. The severely disturbed individuals among the child refugees were placed in American homes (mostly in Vermont, but also in Pennsylvania, New Jersey, and New York) over the summer under the leadership of Dorothy Canfield Fisher (Saenger 1941:126).

At the positive end of the spectrum, some unaccompanied children reveled in the new opportunities and described their experience as upbeat throughout. As one participant who came to the United States alone said, "I had everything. Even when I was living with [foster parents] I did skiing and skating and tennis playing and everything . . . horseback riding. . . . I had a wonderful childhood and I had a wonderful time when I came over here." Another one was full of praise for the amenities of the Jewish orphanage he attended on arrival in the United States, "It was . . . really a fantastic place. They had their own gymnasium, they had tennis courts, they had a woodshop, machine shop. Kids that wanted music lessons got them. I mean, it was really a fantastic place."[15]

At the other extreme, there were also reports of uncaring and exploitative situations that children had to endure with foster families—being treated as cheap servants, rather than as family members. "And I cleaned this whole damn house. I worked in the greenhouses. I worked in the orchards. I learned to make marmalade. I leaned to skin chickens. I did everything. . . . I was a slave. But worst of it was that they didn't pay me for over two years."

Of our survey participants who, during or after their migration, lived outside their immediate family, 71 percent described their experience as "very positive," "positive," or "somewhat positive."[16] The others gave negative ratings. We found a substantial gender difference. Only 22 percent of the males, but 39 percent of the females said their experience was, to some degree, negative. One might surmise that this difference, at least in part, was caused by quite a few foster parents having had some gender-stereotypical "refugee girl = domestic servant" or "refugee girl = future housewife in training" equations in their heads.

As mentioned, of those separated from both parents, 49 percent were reunited with both, 38 percent were reunited with neither, and the rest with one parent. In a sense, one would assume, being reunited with one's parents' refreshed and revitalized the young immigrant's Central European socialization and thus would boost European tendencies. As one participant put it, "I cannot readily distinguish between the European influences that came from my early upbringing and later ones, since I was fortunate enough to be re-united with my parents who were European and continued to educate me. . . . Through my parents I continued to meet European refugees, and through their friends I found work with a rare book dealer who was a refugee from Austria, and there I worked (and became friends) with other employees who came from Europe." This passage also illustrates how, for the Second Wavers, networking within the refugee community was facilitated by the parent generation.

However, some participants also reported additional emotional upheaval associated with reunification.[17] For instance, "Being separated from my parents to be sent to England, becoming attached to the woman who took care of my brother and me, and then being sent to the USA to be reunited with my parents. [This] left me with very little trust and extremely insecure."

"It [reuniting with parents after 7-year absence] was, you know, kind of like not a very close emotional relationship . . . . I think it was easier for my brother. But I never did really feel very close to my parents until . . . almost a couple of years before Mother died. It was very difficult for me to exhibit love and so forth. Primarily because, I think, deep psychologically, . . . when you're sent away from home at the age of five, it has an emotional impact to the extent that, see, you're being rejected by parents. . . . You're being abandoned. . . . Intellectually, as you grew older, you realize that if it hadn't been for that, we probably wouldn't be alive today. . . . And, quite frankly, I've always felt that my emotional maturity is that of a six-year-old when it comes to family life, because that's when . . . it stopped. . . . And so your emotional maturity . . . kind of comes to a screeching halt. And I presume that that's had an impact upon my . . . makeup and the way I turned out, in some respects anyway."

A woman who was seventeen when she was reunited with her parents remembered, "I had no feeling anymore for my mother; we had been apart for so long, and I had sort of outlived my childhood." And she further said, "my mother was so changed to me, in my eyes, that I didn't know her. And it must have absolutely killed her, but I was just not an adorable little girl anymore."

In the following instance, a girl's transition from the foster family back to the original family went smoothly, thanks to the gradual approach devised by a wise foster mother. When the young refugee's parents arrived in United States, her much beloved foster mother "didn't want to separate me from the life I had led the past year and three months [with the foster parents]. I went to school [where I had been living] five days a week, and on the weekend she would drive me . . . to spend the weekend with my parents [who had just arrived]." After a while, the living arrangement changed, but contact was maintained. She now "lived with my mom and dad and sister, but on the weekends [my foster mother] would come and get me [so I could] spend time with them [the foster parents] and with the kids."

The Children's Adjustment

Although the initial conditions were less than ideal—for both the unaccompanied young refugees and the others—many children thrived. There were an "unusual number of outstanding students at all levels of education" (Davie 1947:226, see Gates 1955 and Neubauer 1966). For example, a 15-year-old refugee girl in New York City won a citywide high school contest for her essay, "What it means to me to be an American," and another refugee girl even received the first prize of a nationwide competition for her essay, "Why national unity is important to my country" (Baumel 1990:97). Most parents considered the German or Austrian educational system vastly superior, and this belief was bound to be challenged by their children who went through the American system and felt happy in it. In any case, the parents understood the importance of a good education for their children's future and tended to pressure their children to succeed academically (in line with both their own middle-class background and American-Jewish behavior) (Strauss 1981:245). Hirsch and Hirsch (1961:56) observed that the "young generation" went disproportionately into academe. We shall provide a detailed quantitative analysis of the former refugees' educational achievements, as a group, in a subsequent chapter.[18]

Two Hypotheses

Overall, the early accounts of the refugee movement that were available and that we were privileged to be able to draw on in this chapter, typically subscribed to the view that, compared with the adults' travails, the children's problems were mild to negligible. This view contains two hypotheses, the first cultural and the second psychological: (1) The children would quickly become Americanized; and (2) they would get over their earlier ordeals quickly and without any lasting adverse effects. The following passages from the Davie-Report exemplify the first hypothesis.

"It might be stated as a rule that the adjustment of immigrants in their personal and social relations with Americans varies inversely with age. Children, because they are still in the formative stage, adjust most readily to life in a new environment and soon become practically indistinguishable from the native children. They learn English rapidly, associate freely with other children, and present no social problem. Having few or no ties to the European background, they do not know or long for any other life, as their parents may. They cannot therefore think of their future apart from America" (Davie 1947:143, cf. 224–5). The younger ones were also found to acquire the English language without accent. "Only those above elementary school age on arrival had difficulty in losing their accent" (Davie 1947:225, see Baumel 1990:101). This finding corresponds with the observation, universally made by linguists, that the age at which one is exposed to a new language determines whether one retains an accent or not.

Saenger's (1941:128) view was even more extreme: "Experience, however, shows that practically all refugee children are completely Americanized within a year or two after their arrival." Whereas Saenger both observed and celebrated rapid Americanization in general, and of the children in particular, Ruth Neubauer (1966:2), who studied a small group of immigrant families in the 1960s, found much less assimilation among the children (let alone the parents). "The children of this study group, however, were not so fully assimilated as one might expect," with the orthodox children the least and the religiously unaffiliated children the most assimilated. Almost a third of Neubauer's subjects who arrived as children said that, even after living about 30 years in the country, they still felt either slightly or strongly different from their American cohorts. Most of those "mentioned that they were socially inhibited, too serious, and less given to enjoyment of life. Many replied that they were less independent, too careful, fastidious, frugal, ambitious and achievement-oriented. They often mentioned being choosy in friendships and making fewer but closer friends" (Neubauer 1966:138). Our results will parallel and amplify these findings.

Those who had arrived as children in Neubauer's (1966:155) study also gave very mixed evaluations of how their background affected their subsequent life; some considered it a handicap, others a strength, while the largest group saw aspects of both. Neubauer (1966:219–20) concluded that ". . . where parents unobtrusively held on to their own values and just lived by them, the children seemed to accept these values as their own. If, however, parents downgraded what they termed 'American values,' the children became critical of their parents' attitudes and tended to disregard or even fight the parents' ideas, customs, and values. Unable to throw off their background completely, such individuals seemed uprooted and doubtful as to which group they really belonged, the more so if they did not feel fully accepted by the indigenous group." Similarly, Judith Tydor Baumel (1990:140) found among former unaccompanied refugee children a common "feeling of being a stranger in their own country," which has not abated over time.

The second original hypothesis concerned the overcoming of psychological trauma. In general, although Jewish children at the minimum suffered insults and humiliation, and often were subjected to much more severe trauma, under the National Socialist regime, in school and by their peers (Saenger 1941:27–8, 125, Krist 2001, Wetzel 1992), contemporary observers thought these maltreatments had caused no permanent damage to the children. These early investigators typically emphasized the resilience of the children, who despite their ordeals appeared "amazingly normal," to quote Davie (1947: 216) again.

A very different view emerged from authors, often with a clinical psychological background, who focused on the long-lasting psychological scars that the early events had left on some of the former refugee children (e.g., Fogelman 1993, Marks 1993, Tec 1993, cf. Keilson 1992, Zander 1992). In this view, many children were indeed deeply traumatized, even if they did not show it on the outside, and this trauma was likely to come out into the open at some point, even after long periods of repression. The Freudian school of psychology, in particular, has traditionally attached much importance to a person's childhood experiences. From a psychodynamic perspective, thus, one would expect anything but smooth sailing for the refugee children in their later lives. Former "hidden children," who survived the Holocaust in hideouts or under a false identity, went through particularly severe traumata in their childhood (Delpard 1994, Friedländer 1979, Marks 1993). Psychologists found them to have fears of abandonment (in some cases caused by a double separation, both from the birth parents and from rescuing parents), identity confusion, a fundamental distrust of the outside world, and, most importantly, incomplete mourning and unacknowledged anger about the childhood losses (Fogelman 1993, Kestenberg and Brenner 1996, Kestenberg and Kahn 1998).[19]

Scholars interested in psychological trauma will tend to rely on samples of subjects who suffer from that very trauma. Random samples are useful to put findings from such specifically selected samples in context. For instance, in his study of mostly adult individuals who survived the Holocaust in Europe before coming to America, William Helmreich (1996:220–1) pointed out that his random sample of survivors was actually less likely than a comparison group of American Jews to have been treated, in America, by a psychiatrist, psychologist, or social worker.[20] While not denying the difficulties and challenges his subjects faced, Helmreich's (1996) book *Against All Odds* emphasized the successes of his group as a whole. Similarly, Martin Gilbert's (1996) study of Polish labor camp and death camp survivors who came to Britain after the war, entitled *The Boys: Triumph over Adversity*, also accentuated the positive outcomes.

In our own study, to a considerable extent, the story of the young refugees is one of an amazing resilience.[21] Nonetheless, in many cases, these childhood psychological events left some residue in our participants, even after so many years and even though some coping and compensation mechanisms were in place. The assumptions in some early studies of the refugee children's quick and total Americanization as well as of their quick and total psychological recovery were obviously too simplistic, and, in the following chapters, we shall present a more complex picture.

Chapter 4

Socioeconomic Achievements

The former refugee children can now look back on more than five decades of life in their new country. Based on anecdotal evidence and individual cases, most people would assume that the former refugees did very well in terms of socioeconomic status, but, to our knowledge, no quantitative assessment of their success, as a group, to date, exists. In this chapter, we will present such a quantitative picture, drawing on large representative samples, such as those of the United States Census and the National Jewish Population Survey, as well as on the *Who's Who* and our own survey.

We readily acknowledge that this focus on describing collective socioeconomic achievements from large, representative data sets, for now leaves out other, vastly important, dimensions of success, for instance, personal growth, emotional health, and creativity. These aspects can be better assessed in a more personalized and in-depth approach, such as we adopted in our interviews.

The Success of Former Refugees: An Analysis using *Who's Who*

The unusually good odds for members of the refugee group to be awarded the Nobel Prize (we calculated that a member of our refugee group had about a 1 in 5,500 chance of winning the Nobel Prize, whereas that chance for the American-born comparison group was roughly 1 in 650,000) make for a flashy statistic, but their meaning is somewhat limited because the award of a Nobel Prize is such an unlikely event that one is dealing here with very small numbers and, consequently, a high impact of randomness.

We therefore turn to examine a much larger group of high achievers (in all career fields)—those listed in the *Who's Who*—where statistical comparisons are on a more solid ground. Here again the former refugees shone, compared with the entire American population of the same age bracket. To preview the two major results of this analysis: First, there were about *15 times* as many former young refugees in the pages of the *Who's Who* as one would expect from the size of the group. Second, these young refugees found their pathway to success particularly in the fields of science and engineering. In another chapter, we shall go beyond the data that follow, to supplement them by hypotheses and testimonies that might, if not explain, at least illuminate the data.

Defining Success

Because a major interest of Project Second Wave was to study former refugee children who came to lead unusually productive lives, we inquired into a way to define success, and to identify successful individuals, in a nonarbitrary and systematic fashion. Success is, for most people, a very meaningful and momentous concept, intimately connected to feelings of self-worth, to self-image, and even happiness. It is also a very personal and idiosyncratic notion—one person's definition of what constitutes success is likely to vary from the next person's.

For our sociological study of the life paths of a large group of people, we needed a uniform and readily available measure of success that, though may be regarded by some as somewhat limited, holds at least a certain degree of real-world validity. One such operational definition of success is a person's listing in the Marquis *Who's Who in America* database. That measure has three major advantages[1]:

1. The *Who's Who* is a relatively large database. *The Complete Marquis Who's Who on CD-ROM* (Winter 2002–2003) that includes 20 volumes of Marquis *Who's Who* since 1985, lists the biographies of more than 768,000 people, active, retired, or deceased.
2. The *Who's Who* documents accomplished individuals in every major field.
3. The *Who's Who* uses certain criteria of excellence for a person's inclusion (i.e., one cannot simply buy one's way in—though one might of course opt out).

Our analysis focused on both the overall size and the internal composition of the group of refugee listees. In terms of group size, it revealed how well the former refugees were represented at the high rungs of career success that warranted inclusion in the *Who's Who*. In terms of the internal composition of the refugee group, it showed that the breakdown by occupation among the listees of our refugee cohort differed substantially from the occupational breakdown of the other individuals accepted into *Who's Who*. (Details of our sample selection and method are described in the "Samples and Methods" Appendix.)

High Achievements

To determine how well the group of former refugees was represented among the *Who's Who* listees, we used data from the 1970 U.S. Census that showed the size of the overall U.S. population in the relevant age bracket (born 1918 through 1935) to be 41,728,400, and the size of the group in the same age range who immigrated to the United States from Germany or Austria from 1935 through 1944 to be 26,600. Of course, that Census category (covering the decade from 1935 to 1944) did not completely coincide with the time span in which we were interested (1933–45). We therefore had to make some adjustments that resulted in our estimating the size of the immigrant cohort (1933–45) as 28,090.[2]

The corresponding number of *Who's Who* listees was 71,082 overall, and 713 for the former young refugee cohort.[3] Therefore, in the entire American population of the relevant age group (41,728,400), about 0.17 percent—or *less than 2 in 1,000*—made it into the pages of *Who's Who*. But 2.54 percent—or *more than 25 in 1,000*—did so among the former refugees. A random member of this cohort was thus about *15 times* more likely than a random member of the American population to achieve *Who's Who*-level success. Another way of illustrating this remarkable eventual achievement of the young refugees, as a group, is to note that, if the former young refugees were proportionately represented in the *Who's Who*, one would expect only about 48 refugee listees; but in actuality, there were 713 (i.e., 15 times as many).

If one looks at the genders separately, one finds that 4.6 percent of the male former refugees were listed in *Who's Who*, an astounding percentage that is more than 15 times as large as the percentage of listees among all American men of the same age group (0.29 percent). The female former refugees (0.49 percent) also had a much higher representation than all American women (0.046 percent) and, what is more remarkable is that they were listed even at a higher rate than all American men (whose percentage, as seen, was 0.29 percent). Here we find the "glass half-full or half-empty" quandary of the cohort of women who came from Central Europe. As a group, they did extremely well when compared with other women or even American-born men, but their collective achievement lagged greatly behind that of their male fellow immigrants.

The *Who's Who* database contains a scheme of occupational categories that allowed us to break the entries down by occupation (multiple classifications for one individual were possible), and then to group the listees into eight large occupational fields[4]: (1) Science, Engineering, Architecture; (2) Humanities; (3) Education; (4) Health; (5) Law, Government, Military; (6) Public Sector, Communications, Religion; (7) Business, Industry, Athletics, Agriculture; (8) Arts. We found that the former refugees were not spread evenly across the *Who's Who* listees' career fields, but that they tended to cluster in some fields more than in others—even though there were still more than eight times as many former refugees as expected in education, the field with the relatively lowest representation of this group. Science, engineering, and architecture, by contrast, had the strongest showing of former refugees; in this field, the pages of the *Who's Who* contain no less than about 28 times as many former young refugees as one would expect (see table 4.1).

Another way of examining differences by field is to compare the occupational breakdown of the group of former refugees mentioned in *Who's Who* with the overall occupational breakdown of all listees in that publication. The field of science and engineering was by far the most frequent avenue to career success for the immigrants. More than a third (37 percent) of the former refugees listed in *Who's Who* had careers in science, engineering, or architecture—a proportion almost twice as large as the corresponding

Table 4.1   Former Young Refugees' Relative Representation Factors in *Who's Who* (Compared with All Americans of the Same Age) by Field

Education	8.4
Law, Government, Military	8.6
Public sector, Communication, Religion	9.6
Business, Industry, etc.	10.3
Arts	14.3
Health	14.4
Humanities	20.8
Science, Engineering, Architecture	28.2

Note: A factor of 1 would indicate that, in the given field, the *Who's Who* lists just as many former refugees as one would expect from the size of the refugee cohort. A factor of 10.3, for instance, indicates that, in this particular field, more than ten times as many former refugees as expected were present.

proportion among all listees (20 percent). The humanities sector was also somewhat larger among the former refugees than among the overall group of listees (8 percent vs. 6 percent). Conversely, relatively few of the former refugees were listed in the fields of law, government, and military; the percentage of former refugees in those fields was little more than half that of all listees (9 percent vs. 16 percent). Education was another field with proportionately fewer refugees (3 percent vs. 6 percent). Similarly, listees in the fields of business and industry were relatively rare in the immigrant group; the percentage of former refugees in business, industry, athletics, or agriculture was only about two-thirds of the corresponding percentage of all listees (15 percent vs. 22 percent).

When we look at the genders separately, we find that the occupational breakdowns of all male listees and of the listed male former refugees were similar to the overall breakdowns just described (because about 86 percent of all listees and 91 percent of all listed refugees were men). The formerly Central European young women listed in the *Who's Who* tended to cluster in the field of arts (26 percent; whereas the corresponding percentage for all listed women was 19 percent), and in science, engineering, and architecture, where their percentage was more than twice as much as that of all listed women (19 percent; all women: 8 percent). By contrast, the pages of the *Who's Who* contain relatively few women of Central European origin in the fields of education (4 percent; all women: 15 percent) and business and industry (2 percent; all women: 12 percent).

Compared with their male counterparts, a much larger proportion of the women from Central Europe who were listed in *Who's Who* made their careers in the field of arts (as noted above, 26 percent of the women, but only 7 percent of the male former refugees, were in this field), and in the public sector, communications, and religion (19 percent; male former refugees: 5 percent). On the other hand, relatively few women were in business and industry (2 percent; male former refugees: 16 percent).

Because the occupational breakdown of the listed former young refugees differs so sharply from that of all listees, one might speculate that the former refugees' overall strong showing would at least in part be explained by a "field effect." If the *Who's Who* had a field bias (i.e., practitioners in one field had much better odds of being listed than did practitioners in another field), and if the refugees were overproportionately clustered in fields with favorable odds, their overall overrepresentation might to some extent be an artifact of differential field choice. A quick argument to address this concern is the following: Assuming a pure field effect, every overrepresentation of the refugee group in favored fields is balanced by its *underrepresentation* in disfavored fields. This property could be used for a "worst case scenario" argument in the presence of an unspecified field effect. However, even in the refugees' weakest field in terms of representation—education—the former refugees were *over*represented by a factor of 8.4, whereas, under a pure field effect regime, one would expect a factor that is smaller than 1. Hence, the observed pattern cannot be sufficiently explained simply by differential field choice.

We looked into this issue more deeply by drawing on the 1970 U.S. Census data that showed the occupational breakdowns (in the approximate *Who's Who* occupational categories) of the entire American population in the relevant age bracket and of the former young refugees. This allowed us to calculate, for the former refugees and for all others within that age group, the respective percentages of *Who's Who* listees among practitioners of certain occupational fields (see table, panel a, in note 5). These numbers are imprecise, because the relatively small sample of former refugees available in the 1970 Census data resulted in a rather large uncertainty about the real number of former refugees in those occupational fields (or, technically speaking, in relatively large standard errors—with a magnitude of up to 3 percent, as shown in table 4.4). Even with this proviso, however, the data clearly refute the hypothetical scenario that the strong representation of the immigrants in the pages of the *Who's Who* was caused merely by their clustering in "*Who's Who*-prone" fields. The immigrants' numbers exceeded those for the rest of the population in every category.[6]

In the field of health, for instance, 43 percent of the male immigrant practitioners ended up in the *Who's Who*, but only 3 percent of the other male practitioners did. This enormous difference bears out the observation made by one of our interviewees working in the medical field: "I'm thinking back on my medical school class and actually on my brother's medical school class to a certain extent, because I think that the émigrés carried with them this idea that they need to continue to strive. And they don't know how to stop, I guess, whereas I look at a lot of my medical school classmates who didn't come from European backgrounds—once they got out of medical school reached a certain plateau and then never moved beyond that. . . . But if I look at my [European] colleagues, . . . I find many of them actually just keep on working as much as they can and trying to improve and trying to strive."

If we look only at Harvard Medical School as an example, we encounter several of the former refugees who have brilliantly served the medical science. Eugene Braunwald has been an exceptional contributor to the treatment of heart disease. The late Edgar Haber made great advances in cardiology. Edward Lowenstein has greatly influenced the management of anesthesia, and Kurt Bloch is a distinguished researcher in the fields of allergy and immunology.

In sum, the *Who's Who* analyses confirmed and quantified what had been anecdotally suspected about the socioeconomic success of the former young refugees, as a group. Overall, there were about 15 times as many refugees in the pages of *Who's Who* as one would have expected. Furthermore, the areas of science and engineering were shown to be prime pathways to distinction for the young refugees; more than a third of the former refugees who were listed owed their prominence to those areas. The immigrant women, as a group, were highly successful, compared with American women and even compared with American men, although much less successful than their male fellow immigrants.

The Big Picture: Representative Data About Our Immigrant Cohort From the United States Census

Within the framework of Project Second Wave, basic statistical information about our cohort of immigrants is important for at least two major reasons. First, the information gained in this way will let us gauge the representativeness of our own survey and its results. Second, only representative and sufficiently large data sets allow us to determine how our immigrant group fared as a whole. It has become increasingly popular, especially in the realm of political rhetoric, to "prove" general points by selected individual case examples, but the validity of this approach is rather limited. For us, an important question is how typical certain achievements are, and what the outcomes have been for the group as a whole. While one focus of this project is on the stories and experiences of individuals, we also wish to know the bigger picture; hence our use of statistical information about our cohort as a whole.

The first part of this undertaking was our analysis of the U.S. Census data; the next part was an examination of the National Jewish Population Survey data set, to be presented in the section Refugees from Central Europe and American-born Jews: A National Jewish Population Survey Analysis. Fortuitously, the 1970 Census and the 1970/71 National Jewish Population Survey (NJPS), which both contain the most relevant data for our purposes, were conducted almost simultaneously at a near ideal time in terms of our cohort's life course, more than two or three decades after they had arrived as youngsters. After presenting the findings from those representative sources, we shall reach deeper—into the findings from our questionnaires and interviews. First, however, we explore our cohort's size, its demographic features, and its position in terms of the three traditional indicators of socioeconomic stratification: level of income, education, and type of occupation, all as of 1970, by which time their careers were in place.

Group Size

A crucial first question that Census data are able to answer, at least approximately, is How large is our cohort of former Central European immigrants?
Note that we were dealing here with a 3 percent sample of the Census
population (as described in the "Samples and Methods" Appendix). Hence,
to estimate the population size of a group of people from its sample size, the
number found in the sample has to be multiplied by 33 1/3.

Our 3 percent 1970 Census sample contained 798 persons (392 men,
406 women) who were born between 1918 and 1935 in Central Europe
(Germany, Austria[7] and immigrated to the United States between 1935 and
1944. Multiplication by 33 1/3 yields an estimate of 26,600 individuals for
the total size of this immigrant group.[8] This definition of the refugee group
will be used in the following analysis. (If one wanted to have a more precise
estimate of the refugee cohort, using a method described earlier[9] to include
the immigration years 1933, 1934, and 1945, the number is 28,090.)

The total number of individuals in our Census sample—people who fit
our target age range, regardless of birthplace—was 1,251,851, corresponding to a population of more than 40 million (41,728,367). Numerically,
our cohort of immigrants from Central Europe thus constitutes but a tiny
fraction of the whole population of that age cohort (six hundredths of
1 percent). By determining the approximate size of the refugee cohort, we
have gained a denominator for calculating various proportions describing
the achievements and contributions of our immigrant group, and we are further able to compare these proportions with the corresponding proportions
found in suitable comparison groups.

In the following, thus, we compare this immigrant group with their
contemporaries who were born in the United States. However, one needs to
be aware of the limitations of what such a comparison can mean, because
the respective aggregations of the two groups are vastly disproportionate.[10]
To be sure, the group of former refugees differs from the general population
in many characteristics, and a number of those can reasonably be expected
to have contributed to any observed differences in socioeconomic outcomes. Nonetheless, comparisons with the native population provide an
obvious first, rough benchmark. In addition, we made some comparisons
with immigrants from Eastern Europe (including USSR) who arrived at the
same time, as well as with immigrants originating from the same area
(Central Europe) who arrived in the United States at a different time
(1945–49). This latter cohort is very diverse: it contains refugees who
waited out the war in other countries and then came to the United States,
people who survived concentration camps, in hiding, or were Displaced
Persons (though most individuals in this category of survivors would,

because of their birth place, not be contained in this cohort, but in the Eastern European post–war immigration cohort), individuals from Central Europe who had never been refugees from National Socialism but migrated for other reasons, and, most of all, women. Whereas, in the 1935–44 immigration cohort—the one on which we focus in this project—there was essentially gender parity (women: 50.9 percent), in the immediate postwar years (1945–49), the proportion of women jumped to 80.2 percent.[11] A plausible explanation for the overrepresentation of Central European women is that their ranks were swelled by the many "GI brides" whom American military personnel had met while serving in Germany or Austria.

Demographic Features

The Census asked about a host of basic demographic variables, such as marital status, age at first marriage, and the number of children born. Results for these three variables are given in note 12. Suffice it to summarize here some differences between the refugee cohort and their American-born counterparts. Slightly larger percentages of former refugees than of the American-born group were married in 1970. On average, the former refugees, both men and women, were older than the American-born individuals when they got married for the first time; and the former refugee women, as a group, had fewer children than did the American-born women—already foreshadowing differences particularly in the women's educational and career achievement, because, for women, lower fertility tends to correlate with higher levels of education and career-orientation. This conjecture is indeed clearly borne out in the analysis of income differentials to which we turn now.

Income

According to the 1970 Census, the annual income of the Central Europeans who had arrived as children and youths between 1935 and 1944 by far exceeded the average income of the corresponding American-born population (see figure 4.1).[13] On average, they received 185 percent of the income of the American-born individuals, and their income was also substantially higher than that of the Eastern European immigrants of the same age cohort who entered the United States during the same period.

For comparative reasons, it may be interesting to look also at a subsequent immigration cohort (who came to the United States later, but were of the same age cohort [born between 1918 and 1935] as the earlier

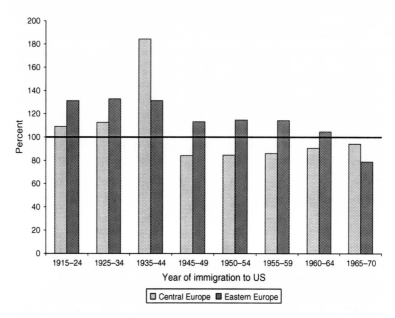

Figure 4.1 Total Annual Income in 1970 (100% = Average of American-Born Population)

immigrant group). We found a huge difference in average incomes between Central Europeans from our 1935–44 immigration cohort and those from a 1945–49 cohort, whose average income was dramatically lower than that of their predecessors, and even lower than that of the American-born persons. The spectacular shift in gender composition mentioned above (from virtual parity to 80 percent women), in combination with a substantial gender gap in income, explains this finding.[14]

Even when controlling for the impact of gender by looking at male and female immigrants from Central Europe separately, one finds that the 1935–1944 cohort was exceptionally successful with respect to reported income in 1970. In that year, the average income of the men who had arrived between 1935 and 1944 was almost twice (192 percent) as high as that of the American-born men of that age group. However, the men among the postwar arrivals earned "only" 142.4 percent of the American-born men's income. To some extent, this difference may be a function of age at arrival in the United States, with latecomers having less time to establish themselves and reach elevated positions, not to speak of the possibility that members of this group had a more severely traumatizing experience before arriving in the United States. The Central European women of the 1935–44 immigration cohort, on average, earned 149.2 percent of the income of American-born women, whereas the women of the following immigration cohort earned only 118.5 percent. We should note here that, in light of the particular circumstances of refugees' migration, the income advantage enjoyed by our 1935–1944 immigration cohort in 1970 cannot, in most cases, be attributed, to any considerable extent, to the transfer of familial wealth already accumulated in Central Europe.

Of the American-born contemporaries of our cohort, 6.7 percent of the men, and 10.0 percent of the women were at or below poverty level according to the 1970 Census.[15] The corresponding numbers are substantially lower for the Central European immigrants who arrived from 1935 through 1944. Only 0.8 percent of the men and 1.7 percent of the women were considered poor in 1970. The figures for the Eastern Europeans were slightly higher, but still markedly below the level of the indigenous population. In terms of income, the immigrants, overall, were clearly very successful in achieving the "American Dream." When looking for reasons for these income disparities in favor of the former refugees, we first turn to one of the most powerful predictors of income, namely educational achievement. As mentioned earlier, education is also traditionally considered one of the three core dimensions of socioeconomic status, along with income and occupational prestige (to which we shall turn in the following section).

Education

As early as 1961, a chapter in the book celebrating the twentieth anniversary of the American Federation of Jews From Central Europe proudly extolled the exceptional educational achievements of the "young generation" (Hirsch and Hirsch 1961). The authors reported that most parents of the young refugees had tried hard to put at least their sons through college. "We suppose, furthermore, that there is no [social] group in which the percentage of those with Master's Degrees and Ph.D.s is as large as particularly in our young generation. . . ." (Hirsch and Hirsch 1961:61, orig. in German). When we check these claims against the Census record of 1970, we indeed find a good deal of supporting evidence (table 4.2).

It is one of our most remarkable findings that almost half of the men (48.2 percent) among the former young refugees from Central Europe who came in 1935 through 1944 had by 1970 achieved four years or more of higher education in the United States, with almost a third of the Central European men (32.4 percent) having gone on to receive also postcollege education. Considering their original situation on arrival, this collective achievement is nothing short of amazing. No other group of men came even close

Table 4.2 Educational Attainment (in Percentage) as Reported in the 1970 U.S. Census

	8th grade or less	9th to 12th grade	Some college	4 years college	Over 4 years higher education
American-born men	21.4	52.2	11.1	7.8	7.5
(n = 573,334) *s.e.*	*.08*	*.09*	*.05*	*.05*	*.05*
American-born women	17.3	64.1	10.6	5.3	2.8
(n = 610,074) *s.e.*	*.07*	*.09*	*.05*	*.04*	*.03*
1935–44 Immigration cohort					
Central European men	5.1	30.1	16.6	15.8	32.4
(n = 392) *s.e.*	*1.2*	*2.4*	*2.0*	*2.0*	*2.5*
Central European women	12.3	52.2	17.0	9.4	9.1
(n = 406) *s.e.*	*1.8*	*2.7*	*2.0*	*1.6*	*1.5*
Eastern European men	24.1	34.8	12.3	12.8	16.0
(n = 187) *s.e.*	*3.2*	*3.6*	*2.5*	*2.5*	*2.8*
Eastern European women	27.2	50.0	10.4	5.9	6.4
(n = 202) *s.e.*	*3.2*	*3.7*	*2.2*	*1.7*	*1.8*
1945–49 Immigration cohort					
Central European men	22.5	39.6	10.7	11.2	16.0
(n = 187) *s.e.*	*3.1*	*3.7*	*2.3*	*2.4*	*2.8*
Central European women	21.0	53.8	18.6	3.7	2.9
(n = 758) *s.e.*	*1.5*	*1.8*	*1.4*	*0.7*	*0.6*
Eastern European men	32.8	32.8	15.5	5.7	13.2
(n = 795) *s.e.*	*1.7*	*1.7*	*1.3*	*0.8*	*1.2*
Eastern European women	33.6	44.8	11.4	6.0	4.2
(n = 949) *s.e.*	*1.6*	*1.7*	*1.1*	*0.8*	*0.7*

Note: Standard errors (s.e.) are in italics. They were calculated from Table B available at the IPUMS website and adjusted for a 3 percent sample. Additional adjustments were not necessary (adjustment factor was given as 1.0 for this variable).

to that record, not the former Eastern Europeans of the same immigration cohort, neither the former Central nor Eastern Europeans who arrived after the war, and most significantly, not the American-born men, for whom the corresponding percentages were 15.3 percent (four years or more of higher education) and 7.5 percent (post college education)—that is, *over three times less in the first case, and more than four times less in the second.* (Some hypotheses about the reasons for these disparities will be presented in chapter 6.)

As one might expect, gender made a huge difference: In our cohort, men, in general, had more education than the women did (see figure 4.2). However, the women of the Central European group, on the whole, also fared exceptionally well. The collective educational level of the Central European women who had arrived between 1935 and 1944 was higher than

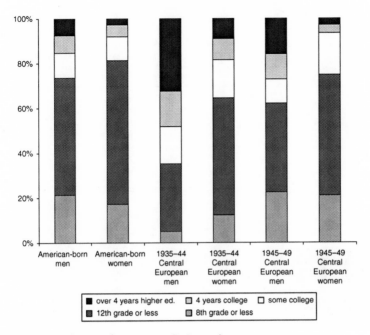

Figure 4.2 Educational Attainment (in Percent)

that of the women who had arrived from Central Europe at other times, higher than that of the American-born women, and *even higher than that of the American-born men*. For instance, of this group of Central European women, almost a fifth (18.5 percent) had four years of college or more, as compared with 15.3 percent of the American-born men. That proportion compares even more favorably to the 8.1 percent for the American-born women, and only 6.6 percent for the Central European women arriving after the war.

Yet, the former Central European women lagged behind the Central European men, and that gender gap was even larger than the corresponding gap between the American-born men and women. That finding reiterates the already mentioned quandary for the formerly Central European women: On the one hand, some might be happy with educational achievements that exceeded those of the typical American woman; on the other, some might be disappointed at seeing their ambitions thwarted in comparison with the relatively much more successful Central European men.

Table 4.3   1970 Census Occupational Groups (in Percentage)

	American-born		Central European-born		Eastern European-born	
	Men	Women	Men	Women	Men	Women
Professionals	14.5	13.9	40.8	25.6	25.7	22.3
			2.9	*2.8*	*3.6*	*4.0*
Managers	13.6	4.0	26.4	6.1	20.8	2.9
			2.6	*1.5*	*3.4*	*1.6*
Sales workers	6.7	8.1	11.1	14.1	10.4	11.5
			1.9	*2.3*	*1.8*	*3.0*
Clerical workers	6.7	32.4	3.6	32.3	4.9	30.9
			1.1	*3.0*	*1.8*	*4.4*
Craftsmen	23.5	2.0	11.1	1.7	19.1	1.4
			1.9		*3.3*	
Operatives	12.5	16.3	2.3	6.4	6.0	13.0
			0.9	*1.6*	*2.0*	*3.2*
Transport Operators	6.6	0.6	1.3	0.3	3.8	0.0
Laborers	5.4	1.1	0.5	0.0	1.6	1.4
Farmers	2.9	0.3	0.5	0.0	0.5	0.0
Farm workers	1.3	1.0	0.3	0.0	0.0	0.0
Service workers	6.3	16.8	2.1	11.8	7.1	15.8
			0.9	*2.1*	*2.1*	*3.5*
Household workers	0.1	3.6	0.0	1.7	0.0	0.7
N	552,224	425,006	387	297	187	139

Note: The immigrants are of the 1935–44 immigration cohort. Standard errors are given where appropriate (in italics).

Occupation

The differences in income and education we reported above strongly suggest corresponding differences in occupational status. Indeed, as table 4.3 shows, the relatively larger representation of the former Central Europeans among the upper rungs of the socioeconomic spectrum is astounding. Central European women were almost twice as likely, and men were almost three times as likely as their American-born counterparts to be in the top category of the Census ("Professionals").

The unusually high success under this occupational heading by the former young refugees stands out when one compares this refugee group with earlier and later immigrants from Central Europe of the same age cohort, as well as when one compares them with the former Eastern Europeans, again of the same age cohort, who themselves also generally were represented in relatively larger numbers in the professional ranks. Because belonging to the

Table 4.4   1970 Census Subgroups of Professionals and Managers (in Percentage)

	American-born		Central European		Eastern European	
	Men	Women	Men	Women	Men	Women
Arts	2.4	2.9	3.9	7.5	3.6	2.9
			1.4	*3.1*	*2.3*	
Education	8.6	36.2	4.3	34.4	8.4	55.9
			1.4	*5.6*	*3.4*	
Engineering	16.9	2.0	11.3	0.0	16.9	5.9
			2.3		*4.6*	
Humanities	2.6	2.7	3.9	3.2	2.4	2.9
			1.4	*2.0*	*1.9*	
Industry and business	50.4	25.2	43.8	19.4	43.4	11.8
			3.5	*4.6*	*6.1*	
Professional	8.1	22.5	16.4	23.7	10.8	8.8
			2.6	*5.0*	*3.8*	
Public sector	5.2	5.9	5.9	5.4	3.6	5.9
			1.7	*2.7*	*2.3*	
Science	5.9	2.7	10.6	6.5	10.8	5.9
			2.2	*2.9*	*3.8*	
N	151,801	72,819	256	93	83	34

Note: The immigrants are of the 1935–44 immigration cohort. Standard errors are given where appropriate (in italics).

top two socioeconomic groups turned out to be so much more typical for the former Central European immigrants (as of 1970) than for the comparison groups, it should be also interesting to examine the more detailed occupational structure in these ranks. However, any such breakdown of the professional and managerial categories[16] into smaller subgroups cannot go into very fine detail, because of the relatively small numbers of the immigrant groups in the Census sample.

If we distinguish eight broad fields, the substantial gender disparities again immediately catch the eye. Nearly half the men in the top two occupational categories (to whom table 4.4 refers) worked in industry and business, whereas that proportion was much lower for the women. But the women of all groups were very strongly represented in education.[17]

The Central Europeans, both men and women, were slightly less drawn to business and industry careers, but went disproportionately into the sciences. Whereas among the women professionals and managers of Central

European extraction, 6.5 percent were scientists, only 2.7 percent of the American-born women in these occupational categories were in science by 1970. The proportion of formerly Central European women who were scientists in 1970 at least equaled that of the American-born men. The Central European men who belonged to the top two occupational categories were almost twice as likely as their American-born counterparts to have gone into science. Moreover, both men and women of Eastern European extraction resembled the Central Europeans in their penchant for scientific careers. One of reasons that those careers were particularly attractive to former refugees was surely that any initial language difficulty was less of a handicap in the sciences than it would be, say, in the humanities or in law. Furthermore, some of the Central Europeans may have arrived with a relatively solid preparation in the sciences that they received from European schooling.

Measures of Socioeconomic Status

Having a single indicator variable that assigns scores to all occupations facilitates summarizing and comparing occupational achievement. The Census provides two such measures, one called Occupational Income Score (OIS) and the other called Duncan Socioeconomic Index (SEI). The OIS reflects the relative economic standing (in terms of income) of occupations in 1950. In constructing the SEI, median income and educational levels for men in 1950 were used to predict prestige assessments of a select group of occupations. The resulting statistical model then served to create scores for all occupations (Duncan 1961). The two measures correlate strongly in our Census sample ($r = .7$).

On the OIS, both Central European men (OIS score of 37.5) and Eastern European men (33.1) of the 1935–44 immigration cohort surpassed American-born men (29.1), with the Central European men scoring especially high. The immigrant women of that cohort had scores similar to those of the American-born women (Central European women: 24.7, Eastern European women: 23.5, American-born women: 22.0).[18]

The Central European men (63.5), and to a smaller degree the Eastern European men (51.7), of the 1935–44 immigration cohort substantially outdid the American-born men (39.7) also on the SEI. The immigrant women of that cohort also did better than the American-born women, on average, although the differences were smaller here (Central European women: 49.3, Eastern European women: 43.6, American-born women: 38.9).[19]

Income by Education and Occupation

We now revisit the respective income data (see above) in light of the educational and occupational structure. We found that, at every level of educational achievement, the average income reported in 1970 by our immigrant cohort was higher than that of their American-born contemporaries. This applied to both men and women; however, the differences in income were much more pronounced for the men than for the women.

A similar picture emerges when we look at the subgroup of people within the top two occupational categories, and consider income by profession. In every professional category (i.e., the eight subcategories of the top two occupational categories, see table 4.4), the immigrant men had a higher average income than the American-born men did. The immigrant women's average income exceeded the American-born women's in six of the eight professional categories, the exceptions being the ones called "education" and "professional."

These findings strengthen the result that, on the usual socioeconomic measures, our immigrant group had been successful in America by 1970. We already knew that they succeeded in entering higher socioeconomic positions in relatively large numbers, and now their higher average incomes within those positions suggest that, in addition, they were particularly successful in their chosen fields—a result that is consistent with the *Who's Who* analysis reported earlier.

Conclusion

On the whole, the group of former Central European young immigrants who had arrived between 1935 and 1944 had done exceedingly well socioeconomically in the United States by 1970. The Census data confirm the popular notion about the exceptional success of our cohort, on average, by providing a quantitative picture of its extent, as determined from the analysis of a representative database.

To be sure, as mentioned, the comparison of a specific immigrant group with the indigenous population as a whole has obvious limitations. To deal with one aspect of those limitations, we re-did the above analyses, using as comparison group only the white indigenous population. Thus the effects of the well-known, considerable educational and socioeconomic discrimination against the non-white population in America at that time were removed. Although the achievement gaps tended to become slightly smaller, as was expected, these analyses confirmed the general findings. The big picture remained the same, whether we compared the immigrants with the indigenous population as a whole or only with the indigenous white population.

Further analysis in the following section will yield additional insights into the extent to which our immigrant cohort's achievements were unique, by using more specifically selected comparison groups (e.g., by examining the National Jewish Population Survey). Further down the road, we will also look more closely into the different avenues and career paths to success and will use testimonies from our interviews and questionnaires to illuminate the crucial finding from both Census and *Who's Who* data that, in comparison with their American-born contemporaries, the immigrants were less drawn to careers in business and industry, and more to careers in science. Finally, one major issue for further investigation in our study will be the degree to which parental socioeconomic status was associated with the immigrants' achievements.

Refugees From Central Europe and American-Born Jews: A National Jewish Population Survey Analysis

The U.S. Census data of 1970 (Long Form 1) allowed us to compare the immigrants from Central Europe with their American-born contemporaries. This comparison yielded empirical data to support and quantify the often-heard conjecture that these immigrants, on average, became remarkably successful in the United States. However, while the indigenous population is perhaps the most obvious first choice of a comparison group for the immigrants, the drawback of such a comparison is that the indigenous population is an aggregate of a multitude of vastly dissimilar groups. Therefore, analytic precision may be gained by comparing our immigrant group with a better-matched subsection of the American-born individuals, that is, with an American-born group that shares with the immigrants some sociocultural background characteristics that are considered relevant.

Because the vast majority of the young immigrants in our study were of Jewish ancestry, we thought it instructive to compare the immigrants with American-born Jews of the same age group (i.e., born between 1918 and 1935). The 1970 National Jewish Population Survey (NJPS) enabled us to make such a comparison, although the relatively small number (84) of Central European immigrants in that survey limited the possibilities of statistical analysis, which had been less of a problem with the U.S. Census data. (For details on data and methods, see the "Samples and Methods" Appendix.)

It is well known that the Jewish ethnic group in America has, on average, been quite successful in terms of educational and socioeconomic achievements. This part of our study started with the question of how our group of Central European refugees (predominantly of Jewish background)—with all their initial handicaps—turned out collectively in comparison to American-born Jews of the same age cohort. If the former refugees were found to have done better, on average, than that comparison group, our initial result of the exceptional nature of the immigrants' accomplishments as a group would be strengthened, and further investigations would be warranted. On the other hand, the former Central Europeans, though more successful than the general population, might be found not to have exceeded the collective achievements of the American-born Jews. If the former Central Europeans' achievements were indistinguishable from those of the American-born Jews, their Central European background, or any other factor specifically associated with that group, would seem less likely to have exerted a major influence over their later life paths. In that case, traits shared by both the former Central European and the American-born Jews—general Jewish background characteristics perhaps— or an immediate and complete merger of the former Central Europeans into the group of "American Jews" would appear to be a more straightforward explanation of the immigrants' achievements.

In the following, we shall compare the basic socioeconomic variables we already used for our Census analysis; but first, we turn to the geographic distribution and historic mobility patterns.

A technical note: Because, in the following, we essentially repeat, on a different data set, the type of analysis we already conducted with Census data, we moved the statistical tables to the notes section, so as to unburden the narrative while still enabling interested readers to view the data tables.

Geographic Distribution

The 1970 U.S. Census indicated that a much higher proportion of our refugee cohort than of the U.S.-born population as a whole lived in the Northeast region. The National Jewish Population Survey afforded a more fine-grained breakdown. According to the NJPS of 1970, which gave residence by state, New York state was home to 24 percent of the Central European immigrants. This geographical concentration was shared with the American-born Jews, of whom a similar percentage (27 percent) resided in the state of New York. Yet we also found divergences in the geographical settlement patterns. The proportion of former young Central Europeans living in California (when the 1970 NJPS was taken) was twice that of American-born Jews (23 percent vs. 11 percent).

Historic Mobility Within Families of U.S.-Born Jews and of Former Central European Jews

Because the NJPS survey asked not only for the respondents' birthplace, but also for their parents' and even grandparents' birthplaces, we could gain some insight into the historic mobility patterns of our groups.

Whereas most of the NJPS participants in the relevant age range (birth years 1918 through 1935) were born in the United States (86 percent), many of those were the children, and almost all of them were grandchildren, of immigrants. More than half (53 percent) of the American-born participants said that their father was born in Eastern Europe, while only 33 percent had a father who was also born in the United States. The mothers, however, were slightly more likely than the fathers to have been born in the United States (42 percent born in United States vs. 46 percent born in Eastern Europe). This observed difference appears to illustrate a common tendency for male immigrants to marry "ethnic Americans" of their own group (i.e., Jewish-American wives, in this case).

Less than 8 percent of the U.S.-born individuals' maternal grandmothers were born in the United States, and the numbers for the other grandparents were even slightly lower. Less than 3 percent of the American-born Jews had both parents and all four grandparents born in the United States. Around two-thirds of the grandparents (of U.S.-born respondents) had been born in Eastern Europe, whereas less than 10 percent had been born in Central Europe.

In sum, these data indicate that the bulk of the American-born cohort under study is one generation or two generations removed from immigration. Most trace their roots to the massive immigration from Eastern Europe in the late nineteenth and early twentieth centuries.

Turning now to our cohort of Central European immigrants, about three quarters of their parents were also born in Central Europe (fathers: 79 percent, mothers: 74 percent). Most of the other parents came from Eastern Europe, as part of the intra-European Jewish migration movement from East to West. More than two-thirds of the Central European respondents' grandparents were themselves born in Central Europe. This is in marked contrast with the American-born Jews because the vast majority of them had immigrant grandparents of mostly Eastern European extraction.

Education

According to the 1970 NJPS, the men who immigrated in 1933–44 from Central Europe collectively had achieved higher educational levels than the

American-born men of the same age group did: 67 percent of those former Central Europeans in the NJPS had at least four years of higher education, as compared to 54 percent of the American-born men (see table in note 20). Higher education beyond four years was obtained by 56 percent of the male former Central Europeans, as compared with 36 percent of those born in the United States—a more substantial difference. In respect to having at least four years of higher education, the women of that immigrant cohort from Central Europe also may have done slightly better than their American-born counterparts, but it was a statistical tie (35 percent vs. 32 percent). If we look only at those with post-college education, however, the difference is more pronounced (Central European women: 30 percent; American-born women: 16 percent). Furthermore, when, in the NJPS dataset, we compare the 1933–44 immigration cohort with the postwar immigration, we generally find that the former did much better in terms of collective educational achievement.

Occupation

We now come to the next fundamental measure of success in terms of socioeconomic status, as traditionally defined in sociological research. We found that, at the time of the 1970 NJPS, a strikingly large proportion of the Central European 1933–44 immigrant cohort—both men (59 percent) and women (61 percent)—worked in the top category ("professionals") of the broad occupational classification, as defined by the U.S. Census (see table in note 21). Their American-born contemporaries did so in much smaller percentages (men: 34 percent, women: 33 percent). Conversely, however, a relatively higher number of American-born respondents worked in the second category ("managers"). This result confirmed the relative tendency among the Central European immigrants away from economic pursuits, and toward other careers within the two top occupational categories.

The next step would be to look at a more fine-grained occupational structure at the two highest categories, but the relatively small numbers of the immigrant groups in NJPS limit the trustworthiness of any such results. Nonetheless, the difference in the popularity of science careers among the men (22 percent of Central Europeans versus 4 percent of American-born participants) was so huge that it reached statistical significance even with a small sample of immigrants in the NJPS. The Central European women were also represented strongly in the sciences. Again, "industry and business" is the category in which American-born Jews clustered much more strongly than the immigrants did.

The relative dearth of our refugee cohort in the managerial category flies in the face of a particular, but stereotypical version of the immigrants'

"American Dream," according to which newcomers work their way up in the economic and entrepreneurial fields to achieve success in America—from the proverbial dish washer to the self-made millionaire. A glance at the male Jewish immigrants from Eastern Europe, who were as strongly represented in the managerial category as the American-born Jews were, certainly suggests that this group was more inclined to follow that pathway (although that group of Eastern European immigrants is too small to make meaningful statistical comparisons). At least two causes may have contributed to our cohort of young refugees from Central Europe deviating from that pattern: the large proportion of those coming from a highly educated and professional family background, and a general tendency, enshrined as a core value of the Central European culture and transmitted to the young refugees, to value education and professional pursuits as much as, if not more than, monetary success.

Income

In the NJPS, income is not strictly a continuous variable, but is represented in intervals of varying range. We converted this variable into a quasi-continuous variable by assigning the respective approximate interval midpoint to each person. Because the income variable reports *household* income, there is very little difference between the genders.

When the NJPS was conducted in 1970, the average income of the Central European 1933–44 immigrants was slightly lower than that of the U.S.-born Jews, but this small difference was far from being statistically significant. In the U.S. Census sample, we had examined income by education and occupation, but the small size of the immigrant group in the NJPS made this not very meaningful statistically. However, a glimpse at the numbers gave no indication at all that the pattern found in the U.S. Census (i.e., the Central European immigrants collectively having higher income levels than their American-born counterparts even after controlling for education and occupation) would be replicated in the comparison between former Central European and American-born Jews. In other words, the former Central Europeans and the American-born Jews, on average, had achieved a fairly similar level of income in 1970, according to the NJPS.

Differences Among American-Born Jews

As a related issue, we explored whether, within the group of American-born Jews, it made a difference how far back in the family history the immigration occurred. We divided the American-born NJPS respondents (who were of the same age range as our refugee cohort) into three groups—those with both parents born in the Unites States; those with one parent born in the Unites States; and those with neither of the parents born in the United States—and examined to what extent these groups differed on the usual socioeconomic variables.

In terms of educational achievement, those with two foreign-born parents collectively did worst, those with two American-born parents did best, and the others were in the middle. Interestingly, this difference was not reflected in the occupational distribution that looked fairly similar for all three groups. The only exceptions were a slightly elevated percentage of managers among the men with two American-born parents (47 percent vs. 40 percent [one American-born parent] vs. 42 percent [no American-born parent]), and a relative dearth of professionals and a corresponding abundance of clerical workers among the women with two foreign-born parents. The breakdown of the top two broader occupational categories also showed an overall picture of similarity of all three groups. When it came to household income, the group with two American-born parents had the highest, and those with two foreign-born parents had the lowest average, but the differences were so slight that they did not rise to statistical significance.

In sum, the overall finding for our comparisons within the group of American-born Jews is one of general homogeneity. Within this group, differences in their family's immigration history were not associated with major socioeconomic differences. Those who were closer to immigration may have started from a disadvantageous position in terms of formal education, but then seemed to have been able to compensate and catch up in terms of occupation.

Conclusion

The NJPS permitted a comparison, as of 1970, of the former young refugee group with a more closely matched group (American-born Jews), even though the small numbers of former refugees in the NJPS limited the power of statistical analyses. The former refugees' educational attainment was higher, on average, and the former refugees were more likely to work as professionals (and less likely to work as managers) than the American-born Jews, although these differences were not as large as the corresponding differences between the refugee group and the American-born population in general. No differences were found in terms of reported income levels. In sum, while the refugee group was certainly more similar to American-born Jews than to the American-born population in general, in terms of broad socioeconomic indicators, Jewish ancestry by itself is not a sufficient explanation of their achievements.

Socioeconomic Status: Our Sample

Our analyses of large representative databases, such as the United States Census and the National Jewish Population Survey, have allowed us to establish a broad and basic picture of what happened to our group of young refugees in their new country. We discovered a picture of remarkable and unexpected success, by the conventional measures, for the former refugees, as a group. These large databases were, however, limited in addressing the detailed and specific other questions that we considered important for our study. We now turn to the analysis of our *own* questionnaire survey, which we could tailor to the questions we were interested in, and which adds valuable information that would otherwise be unavailable. Our analyses of existing large databases (i.e., what social scientists call secondary data analysis) and our own survey thus methodologically complement each other.

First of all, doing a survey of our own allowed us to distribute it more precisely to the target population of interest: former refugees. After the end of the war, the immigrants from Central Europe were a very complex group, including some former refugees, but many others who were not refugees. In our secondary analyses of existing databases, we therefore reported the entire postwar immigration cohort separately and compared it with the pre-1945 refugee cohort. In our survey, we were also able to include among the refugees those whose route took them to the United States in the early postwar years, that is, from 1945 through 1949. Many of those are former participants of the *Kindertransport* to Britain, while others had spent the war years in other countries.

The question of how many of our survey participants were Jewish has no singular answer; it depends, of course, on how Jewishness is defined. In the pre-National Socialist era in Central Europe, Judaism was predominantly viewed as a religion. The National Socialists, however, in their "Nuremberg Laws," used a mainly racial definition as the basis for their persecution of the Jews, which depended on how many Jewish grandparents one had.[22] Obviously, this National Socialist classification, even if not considered legitimate and meaningful by the individuals themselves—for instance, if they had been brought up as Catholics or Protestants—had a greatly adverse real-life significance for those so classified by the regime. In our survey, we asked questions about the grandparents' religion, and this allowed us to see to whom, among our participants, the National Socialist definition of

Jewishness would apply. Among the former refugees in our questionnaire survey, 69 percent said they were of the Jewish religion.[23] An additional 23 percent (who did not indicate they considered themselves Jewish by religion) would have been so-called *Volljuden* by the National Socialist criteria, and 5 percent so-called *Halbjuden*, according to the reported religions of their grandparents.

When we examine the socioeconomic status of our own survey participants,[24] we again turn to the three dimensions that have been traditionally considered its three main components: occupation, education, and income.

Occupation

For reasons of consistency and comparability, we coded the questionnaire respondents' reported occupations with the three-digit system of the United States Census that had also been used in our analysis of large representative data sets (the 1970 United States Census and the 1970 National Jewish Population Survey). We then examined the occupational breakdown of the male and female former refugees who participated in our survey in terms of the broad occupational categories that summarize the three-digit codes (see table in note 25).[26]

Among the men, almost two-thirds (63 percent) had reached the position of professionals, and 29 percent were managers; only very few were in any of the lower occupational categories distinguished by the United States Census. Among the women almost half (49 percent) were professionals, and 18 percent were managers. A sizable percentage (23 percent) of the women was made up of clerical workers.

We now turn to a more detailed analysis of only the first two broad occupational categories (i.e., professionals and managers) that contained the majority of former refugees (see table in note 27). Particularly striking was the gender disparity in the field of education, where 21 percent of the women, but only 4 percent of the men worked. Women further were more strongly represented than men in the fields of health (11 percent vs. 1 percent), arts (8 percent vs. 2 percent), and associations and organizations (5 percent vs. 0 percent). In the other fields, women were either represented about equally as were men, or they were underrepresented. The relative dearth of women was most pronounced in physics (0 percent vs. 6 percent), mathematics and computer sciences (2 percent vs. 10 percent), other natural sciences (3 percent vs. 10 percent) and medicine (2 percent vs. 9 percent). On the whole, the gender disparities found among the former refugees mirror those found in the American society at large, where, for instance, teaching and nursing traditionally have been stereotypically female pursuits, whereas the "hard" sciences have historically been stereo-typically male.

In the following section, we reduced the occupational fields to a smaller number of more comprehensive groupings (see table in note 28). About a third of our former refugees were in business and industry (men: 34 per-cent; women: 31 percent). Another third of the men (35 percent) had chosen careers in some field of science, compared to only 9 percent of the women. But remember that, by general standards, this is a high percentage for science careers among women. The women's relative overrepresentation in education and in the arts showed up again identically, because these categories remained unchanged.

Here are some explanations, offered by our participants, of the former refugees' tendency to choose science careers. The dominant theme was that the universality and objectivity of science would transcend national and social particularities. "Is it perhaps that science gives you a more neutral and stronger foothold in terms of outlook on life, a stability . . . which is more fixed, more rigid in a way than, let's say, social sciences or businesses? . . . Or does it provide a certain security maybe . . . in terms of knowledge? These things are fixed. I mean, they are established. They're not subject to whims of historical or political events . . . . [The scientific laws] are universal. You know, I communicate with somebody no matter where in the world . . . . It broadens your horizon, I think, more than anything else."

"It may be because the sciences are universal . . . . It may get back to this feeling that whatever it is that you can learn, nobody can take it from you, and you can do it anywhere. And whether that's explicit or implicit, I don't know, but I would suspect that is part of the reason."

Other participants mentioned reasons of a more practical kind. Science was attractive to newcomers with limited English because it did not require language skills to the extent that other fields did. And the participants who had been schooled in the *Gymnasien* often said that they felt they had received a solid grounding in the sciences.

The statistics provided on the occupation of the participants are likely to be skewed toward the top two broad occupational categories, and especially toward scientific professions, owing to our systematic inclusion of former refugees listed in *American Men and Women of Science*, *Who's Who*, and *Who's Who in American Jewry*. (We might in shorthand call these participants the "elite samples" for our purposes.) We therefore performed a parallel set of analyses from which the listees of those compilations were *excluded*. (For tables of results, see note 29.) The heavy emphasis on professionals and scientists was attenuated as expected, yet the broad picture remained the same. The percentages changed more for the men than for the women, because the elite samples contained predominantly men.

Comparing these results of our own survey with the results of a representative sample of the refugee group from the U.S. Census allows us to gauge the participation biases in our survey. The men in our survey (leaving aside the elite samples) were somewhat more likely to be professionals (48 percent vs. 41 percent) and managers (38 percent vs. 26 percent) than the men in the Census refugee cohort. For the women, the differences were more pronounced. Almost half the women in our own nonelite survey (46 percent) were professionals, but only 26 percent of the Census refugee cohort were; and 18 percent of our female survey participants, but only 6 percent of the women former refugees in the Census cohort were managers. By contrast, the female refugee population, according to Census data, contained more clerical workers (32 percent vs. 25 percent), sales workers (14 percent vs. 5 percent), and service workers (12 percent vs. 2 percent). In sum, thus, our survey sample (even when disregarding the elite participants we recruited from the pages of *American Men and Women of Science, Who's Who*, and *Who's Who in American Jewry*) was skewed toward the top two occupational categories. Whereas this was true to a moderate extent for the men, the divergence was more pronounced for women. Compared with the Census data, our survey had a clearly smaller segment of female former refugees who worked outside of the top two occupational categories.[30]

Comparisons

Among our survey participants, we compared the former refugees who had made it into *Who's Who, Who's Who in American Jewry*, and *American Men and Women of Science* with the control group of American-born listees. This allowed us to ascertain to what degree the former young refugees have chosen different avenues toward excellence (see table in note 31).

We found that, for the former refugees, the path to excellence led through science and engineering more often than for their American-born counterparts. The only exception to this general pattern was the life sciences, in which 10 percent of the American-born, but only 6 percent of the former refugees worked.[32] This emphasis on science among the high-achieving former refugees who participated in our survey dovetails nicely with similar results of our analyses of the *Who's Who* population and of the Census.

We also looked specifically only at the scientists in our database who were listed in *American Men and Women in Science* and compared their fields with the fields in which their American-born counterparts worked. Overall, the field distributions were similar, but it was noticeable that there were proportionately fewer life scientists among the scientists who had come initially as children from Central Europe (9 percent vs. 19 percent), and proportionately more physicists (17 percent vs. 8 percent) (see table in note 33).

Furthermore, among the listees in *American Men and Women of Science*, we could compare our former refugees with non-refugee immigrants from Central Europe of the same age cohort. We found that, neither for the broad nor for the detailed occupational categories, did the breakdowns differ in a statistically significant way between the former refugees and the non-refugee immigrants.

Education

Here, in our survey data, we again encounter the strikingly high educational achievement of the former refugees as a group—educational achievement measured here as the participants' highest educational level attained (regardless of when and in what country this occurred), as reported in the questionnaires. (See tables in note 34.)

Our findings are analogous to, and consistent with, those on occupation. Even when looking only at our "nonelite" sample, the men in our survey, as a group, had achieved a somewhat higher level of education, compared with the refugee group of the representative U.S. Census sample; but our female survey participants had substantially elevated levels of education. For instance, whereas only 9 percent of the female former refugees in the 1970 Census had more than four years of higher education, 28 percent of our female survey participants reported such an educational level.

Income

We also asked our survey participants to indicate the approximate current annual household income (see tables in note 35). (If they were retired, we asked for the income for their last year of employment.) Even excluding the elite samples, more than half of the male former refugees (56 percent) reported on their questionnaire to have had an annual income of $90,000 or more at that time. The women, by contrast, reported significantly lower income levels.

Chapter 5

Partial Assimilation—Complex Identities

In his classic conceptualization of the stage sequence of assimilation of immigrants, Milton Gordon (1964) maintained that acculturation usually preceded structural assimilation (that entails entrance into the social structures and institutions of the host society). Gordon's model in a sense formalizes the stereotypical American Dream: Immigrants would start at the bottom rung of society while acquiring language skills and culturally becoming Americans. Once this was accomplished, they, and especially their offspring, would be able to enter fully into the civic and social life of America and to obtain elevated socioeconomic positions.

For our former refugees, we have just documented that structural assimilation was accomplished with enormous success. At the same time—and contrary to expectations by early observers—these former refugee children did not assimilate completely in most cases, and we will now examine the contours of this partial assimilation. We will show the retention of formative cultural elements from Central Europe, and we will survey how their particular origin and history gave rise to complexities in their collective identity. This chapter prepares the ground for a key argument to be made in the following chapter: that the former refugees' great socioeconomic success, as a group, did not so much occur in spite of their often incomplete assimilation, as it occurred *because* of that incomplete assimilation. Many former refugees, we will argue, benefited from their Central European origins. In other words, retaining their distinctiveness in particular aspects gave them an edge, a *distinctiveness advantage*.

We start with an area in which our cohort of former refugees did assimilate rapidly and thoroughly: the area of language (see Espenshade and Fu 1997, and Pozetta 1991).

Language Acquisition

The first purpose of this section is to point out the language skills that the young refugees possessed when they arrived in this country. The second is to demonstrate the facility with which this group acquired a proficiency in English.[1] The third purpose is to introduce the theme of assimilation and identity, which will be carried on in the following section.

Our participants were a truly polyglot bunch. When asked which languages they knew while still in Europe *in addition* to their native language (which in virtually all cases was German), only about a third (35 percent) said they did not know any.[2] Among the others, one could find, at least at school level, Latin, Greek, English, and French, Hebrew mostly from religious instruction, and/or languages picked up on the European refugee trail, such as English, French, Dutch, or Spanish. To know three foreign languages, at least to some degree, was not unusual in this group. Among the most impressive linguists was a person who noted "French, Hebrew, Spanish, Latin, Welsh" in addition to his native German (and his English).

For most, mastering English upon arrival as a child or youth in the United States (or in another English-speaking country) was not a problem. More than half (53 percent) of the former refugees reported they had found learning English very easy, and 41 percent said it was easy. Only the small remainder reported that it was hard or very hard for them. A large majority (70 percent) of the former refugees said that they achieved age-appropriate proficiency in English within less than a year of arrival. A quarter (24 percent) said it took them one to two years, and only a few reported longer periods.

The Effect of Age on Language Acquisition

It is generally believed that age strongly influences various aspects of language acquisition. In our group, age had a very strong effect in terms of accent (R^2 = 24.5 percent). Of those who arrived at age six or younger, 95 percent said they speak English without any foreign accent; of those who arrived at age 19 or older, only 18 percent said so. In addition to the generally declining trend of accent-free English with increasing age at arrival, we found a particularly precipitous fall between the age groups of 10–12 years and 13–15 years (see figure 5.1)—data that are in line with the usual findings on this topic.

One should also expect that, among the refugee cohort, younger children found learning English easier and were quicker in picking it up

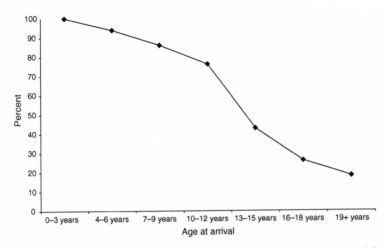

Figure 5.1 Percentage of Former Refugees Who Report Speaking English Without Foreign Accent, Plotted by Their Age at Arrival

than were older children. Such effects could indeed be identified, but they were not as strong as the age effect on accents mentioned earlier. Of those (relatively few) who arrived in the United States at age six or younger, 74 percent said learning English was very easy for them, but only 39 percent of those who were older than 18 at arrival gave that response. Of those younger arrivals, 72 percent also reported that it took them less than a year to reach age-appropriate proficiency in English, whereas only 64 percent of the older group said so. In regression models, age at arrival was a significant predictor in both cases, but explained little variance ($R^2 = 2.9$ percent for perceived difficulty, and $R^2 = 0.8$ percent for time to proficiency). Perhaps older individuals were more determined, or also more skilled through their earlier multilingual experiences, so that they compensated well for what might have been an age handicap. In essence, their doing very well diminished the size of any advantage that the younger children could possibly have had (ceiling effect).

A further important determinant of the ease and speed of language acquisition, one might surmise, was whether, and for how long, the arriving youngsters lived in a German-speaking household (which, in turn, was of course related to the young persons' age at arrival, $R^2 = 11.2$ percent). The young persons' living situation, however, did not affect the perceived ease of learning English, when controlling for age at arrival. Living in a German-speaking household did have small effects (in addition to the age effect) in terms of prolonging the time to English proficiency and in terms of increasing the likelihood of speaking accented English. Overall, however, outside influences, such as the schools or peers, appeared to have ensured a relatively quick and smooth linguistic assimilation even of those who spoke German at home.

Current Use of Native Language

How strongly are the former refugees today in touch with their native language? The largest group (69 percent) said they rarely spoke it; 16 percent reported that they never spoke it, whereas 15 percent noted that they frequently did so. Reading in the native language was, overall, even less frequent than speaking it; and, in addition, women were less likely than men to read German. Of the men 25 percent and of the women 40 percent reported they were not reading German at all; about half of each gender group read it rarely; and 21 percent of the men, but only 10 percent of the women, read frequently in their native language. An explanation for this gender difference may be that the men's professional careers resulted in higher exposure to German reading.

Name Changes

Of the former refugees, 22 percent noted that their last name was changed or anglicized. This often involved dropping umlauts, the last n in "-mann" (e.g., Kaufmann to Kaufman), or the c in "sch" (e.g., Fischer to Fisher) for a more English-looking appearance. In other cases, an entirely different name was selected. Sometimes, our participants wrote, this was done to get rid of an obvious Jewish name to avoid anti-Semitism that was rather widespread in the United States at the time of their arrival. One participant explained the choice of an Anglo-Saxon last name in the following way: "Father for business. Brother to get into medical school," indicating two of the areas in which Jews were likely to face particular obstacles.

As one might expect, the percentage of last name changes was virtually identical for men and women, because that decision was usually made by the parents or guardians and often applied to a whole family. Naturalization, or the initial step of "first papers," was frequently the occasion to make such a change in last names, but it also presented an opportunity to change one's first name. In fact, the immigrants were often—some even on arrival— invited by immigration and naturalization officials to pick new American names (both first and last names), as this was a long-standing and pervasive practice in the United States as a nation of immigrants. Such suggestions by administrative authority figures were quite persuasive for newly arriving youngsters, and many went along. But, of course, not all, as in the following instance recalled by one of our participants. "At Ellis Island . . . they said, 'Hans, you should change [your name] to John.' I said, 'No way. I was born Hans; I'm going to stay Hans. That's me.' "

As to first names, most Germanic, Biblical, or Classical names that the Central European youngsters carried had close English equivalents. Names like Robert, Barbara, or Peter required no spelling change at all and only slight adjustments in pronunciation; others, like Bernhard (Bernard) or Josef (Joseph), could be made to look English with but minor changes; in a few cases, though, (e.g., Hans/John) the correspondence was not quite so obvious. Thus, common strategies included the use of the English equivalent, a name that sounded similar, or a name that had at least the same initial. Sometimes switching first and middle names helped to create the desired effect (e.g., Helmut Ernst to Ernest H.). In a few instances, a name changed more than once, reflecting the escape route. One participant noted, for instance, "[my name] was changed 3 times—into French, then Hebrew, then English." Among other multiple transmutations we encountered was one from Heinrich to Henri to Henry; and a Liese became Lisette and finally Elizabeth.

The change of first names was more common than the change of last names, and here we found an intriguing gender difference. Almost half (48 percent) of the men, but only 31 percent of the women, reported changing or anglicizing their first name. Our participants' descriptions of the circumstances allow us to venture some hypotheses about the general motivations behind their first name changes, as well as about the reasons why males were more likely than females to change their names.

The main motivation behind the name change was assimilation, that is to become American. One participant bluntly explained the change thus, "Shortly on arrival in 1941, to ensure better Americanization." An equally important motive was not to broadcast one's German origins, for displaying any connection with Germany would, of course, have been disadvantageous during the war. For instance, "My first name was changed within 6 months of arrival in US. I had a very strong desire to get rid of any Austrian/German association or label."

Another motivation was simply the desire to make things easier and to avoid mispronunciations. Our sample highlighted the plight of several Renates who suffered from acute mispronunciation. "Renate was pronounced Renat, so I changed it to Renata in self-defense." Another Renate wrote, "I found that school teachers mispronounced Renate. So I changed it to Renee which they found easier." A participant originally named Inge noted, "No American can pronounce my name 'Inge' correctly. I chose 'Ingrid,' its Swedish version, because of Ingrid Bergman."

Whereas the above considerations applied to boys and girls, we now turn to possible explanations of the observed gender difference. First, being teased for having "exotic" names might have been much more intense for boys than for girls. In other words, there may have been a greater cultural and social leeway for the acceptance of unusual girls' names, whereas there was more pressure for boys' names to belong to a shorter list of "approved" names. Mostly boys gave the avoidance of "teasing" as a reason for the name change. For instance, as one participant feared, " 'Wolfgang' would be source of too much teasing." The popular German name Heinz was another likely candidate for being dropped because of the Ketchup connection and its inherent teasing potential. Then there was the predicament of the Hellmuts. "My name in Europe was Hellmut. When it came time to go to high school, [the principal] asked my name. Well, Hellmut! Looked at me for a while, then said 'Hellmut nothing!! You'll go home and pick another name.' So we went home that evening, sat around for a while and finally decided on Hugh. It was later told to me, [the principal] did not want a Hellish dog (hell mutt) running around in his school."

Second, an explanation applying more specifically to this group of Central European immigrants would be that, during war time, bearers of "enemy names"—and these typically were male names—were likely to be ostracized. The most obvious example would be the following. "When I lived in England, my host family requested that I take on a more appropriate first name, as my legal name was Adolf and that would subject me to 'hazing' in school." Apparently, the American public also considered the names Hans and Fritz (as well as Heinz, mentioned earlier) archetypal German names that would trigger some hostility. "When I arrived at my host family, the relative suggested that Hans was a no-no. She suggested I become Harry. And that has stuck." Several Hanses and Fritzes related similar stories.

Finally, joining the military was frequently reported as a concrete incentive for a name change. One of the male participants, for instance, wrote about his name change: "During U.S. Army service in 1944, it was suggested that 'Gunter' should be changed to George."

In their combination, these last three circumstances may at least partly explain why, in our refugee group, males were more likely than females to change their first names.

Elements of Distinctiveness

Whereas, linguistically, our group of former refugees adjusted quickly and thoroughly to life in the United States, they also remained influenced by their Central European upbringing and maintained various levels of distinctiveness in several dimensions that we are now going to survey.

Ties with the Past

Among the women 80 percent and among the men 71 percent said that they thought about their life in Europe from time to time or more often.[3] Similarly, large majorities of women (84 percent) and men (75 percent) think of their migration experiences from time to time or more often.[4] Of those who have children, half (53 percent) said they have talked with them about their origins and early-life events from time to time, and 32 percent said they have done so frequently.[5] (Only 1 percent reported to have never talked with their children about this topic.) A majority of the former refugees (69 percent) think that their early upbringing in Europe influenced their later life considerably, strongly, or decisively.[6] Among women 67 percent and among men 60 percent think their migration experience influenced their later life considerably, strongly, or decisively.[7]

One of our participants expressed a common sentiment, "Well, I think even though it was only for 13 years, I think . . . the importance of the cultural part of your life, and work ethics, and just good moral fiber was definitely instilled by the parents. And that, I think, has persisted throughout."

Of the participants 43 percent said they maintained a special interest in their country of childhood.[8] Some of our participants swore to themselves that they would never again set foot in the country that had mistreated them so severely. One interviewee said, "I made the promise . . . that I would never step on the soil of that accursed country ever. And I kept it." But the participants who followed such a rule were in the distinct minority. A total of 89 percent of the former refugees who participated in our survey had returned, at least once, to the country they had left.[9] While 19 percent had been back exactly once, 18 percent had been back twice; 30 percent said they had gone back three to five times, and 22 percent had made even more frequent trips. Among those with children 53 percent had taken them on a trip to the country of their origin.[10] Among the participants 41 percent intended to make a trip to that country sometime in the future.[11] On all these questions, the men showed a stronger interest, involvement or more frequent contacts with their country of origin. A special interest in, and frequent contacts with, the former homeland correlated with the strength of German, Austrian, and European identities, and they correlated inversely with the participant's Jewish identity.

Visits to the former homeland, especially if they were first visits after a long absence, usually stirred up quite a lot of anxiety and mixed feelings in the former refugees and created a great alertness toward the nuances of the treatment they received. In Germany, official programs exist by which former refugees are invited back to their old hometowns, and most of our participants who had been in such programs said that they came back from those trips with an overall positive feeling, as those trips appear to succeed in providing some element of closure. While many of the people who told us about visits to their homeland—officially sponsored or not—said that they were pleasantly surprised by the younger (postwar) generation whom they had met and who had seemed earnestly interested in preventing any reoccurrence of a Hitler-type regime; however, they were suspicious of people of their own generation and older. "What did they do in the Hitler regime?" was a question that, in one way or another, was reported to have frequently entered the minds of the former refugees, as they again walked the streets of their former hometowns and encountered those older people. The experience varied somewhat between the former Germans and former Austrians. The latter were likely to encounter the attitude that the Austrians themselves were innocent victims of the National Socialist transgressions (their so-called *Opfertheorie*), whereas the former were more likely to find, among the Germans, an acknowledgment of the German responsibility for the wrongdoings.

In the typical case, sentimentality toward one's place of childhood and youth (*Heimweh*, as it is called in German) is strongly tied to the people of that place, but some of the refugees clearly separated the place from the people. They said they felt elated at seeing again the architecture and natural sites with which they had grown up, at listening to familiar sounds and eating familiar dishes. But they were far less enthusiastic about the inhabitants. As one interviewee recounted, "I have been back, and it was very alien to me and unpleasant. You know, people [say]: 'Oh, the scenery is so beautiful. It's such a lovely country, and the music,' and this and that. Okay, that's true. But as far as a place to live and to feel accepted and comfortable, no." Another one wrote about Vienna: "I still love the city of my childhood, but not its people. The sadism I encountered . . . has left a scar that will last forever."

Another interviewee described a much more positive and satisfying return visit. "And so I [spent a semester in Vienna] and it just turned out to be a good experience for me. . . . And what made it a good experience? First of all, I have to say I did not encounter any anti-Semitism personally. . . . But a lot of the important things were—the way I kind of encapsulate it is by saying that I discovered two things, both of which were very important—how much of Vienna is still in me and how much of me is still in Vienna."

Many refugees naturally wanted to see once more the house where they had grown up. Large parts of some German cities were destroyed during the war so that this was not possible in all cases; but if the old house still existed, a typical and memorable encounter ensued between the returning refugee and the current occupants. "Probably in the mid-sixties, I went back to the house where I had been brought up, this huge house in my memory. And it was still there; it had been turned into various apartments, and looked pretty shabby. . . . I was not allowed [to go inside]. I asked [and the people said], 'I am sorry, but we don't let anybody in'. . . . They were not very friendly, so there was nothing much I could do." Others told of more pleasant interactions with the current inhabitants. For instance, "I went to see my old flat. . . . I remembered the name on the door, and looked it up in the Vienna phone book. I wrote her a very nice letter telling her who I was, and that I had to leave the place for reasons well known in 1938, and it would be very meaningful to me to be able to show my sons the rooms where I grew up. And she wrote me back a very nice letter [and said] 'just come on ahead.' . . . And there were some changes, but it was the same thing, so we spent an afternoon there." Others never actually summoned up the courage to make contact. "I went to visit the apartment where we had lived—went to see the outside. . . . And I didn't have the guts to knock on the door to go in. I don't know if I could have handled it. I was by myself, and it was very hard to do."

It was understandably difficult to hold onto and appreciate the valuable aspects of one's German heritage in view of the horrible events, but many of the First Wavers insisted that it had to be done. This was brought home to one of our Second Wave interviewees, then a pubescent teenager, in dramatic fashion.

"I'll tell you a story and then you'll understand my relationship to Germany. . . . It was during the war, probably a couple of American flags flying. And I said, 'Mom, I hate being a German.' And she laid back and gave me a slap on my ear. . . . You know, 'You'll never say that again.' And suddenly—my mother almost never hit us. I mean, a little bit here and there, you know. . . . Say, 'Holy sh . . . ! Well what—what was that all about?' And I realized that no matter what the Germans have done, whether it's the Holocaust or [killing] people in Auschwitz, that there's still a terrific heritage there, genetic and everything else, that I should be proud of. And, you know, Hitler and Nazis and all that—my mother gave me that blessing that I think that was. . . . I don't know if there was a discussion or whether I cried or anything. I don't remember that. I just remember that my ear still rings today because the old lady . . . took a step and she said, 'My son's not going to get away with that.' And she took a step and it impregnated in me—made me think about that for the rest of my life."

Cultural Remnants

We examine the issue of collective identities by first looking at cultural remnants from the native lands. Our group constitutes a strategic research site, as Robert Merton would call it, for studying the assimilation processes that immigrants undergo in the United States. The pressures toward assimilation were particularly high for several reasons that bear repeating: The refugees entered at a time when the immigration stream was severely restricted, when immigrants were unpopular and eyed with suspicion, when, at war time, any trace of Germanness could easily lead to their being mistaken for enemies (also see their official classification as "enemy aliens"), and when the predominant doctrine proclaimed the desirability of rapid and thorough Americanization. Moreover, except for the smaller groups of "exiles," the immigrants themselves, having been dispossessed of their national identity by the National Socialist government would usually be less than enthusiastic in clinging on to this identity. Whatever level of cultural remnants these immigrants retained under those circumstances thus might, compared with other immigrant groups, mark an extreme low, that is, a nadir of biculturalist tendencies. It would also mark the limits of the assimilation process, contrary to the expectations of the observers in the 1930s and 1940s who thought the refugee children would assimilate completely.

In our study, we found that these expectations need revision and refinement. On the surface, no doubt, the acculturation of this group was rapid, thorough, and enthusiastically desired by themselves. The area of language we just visited is a testament to that. Multiple sources supported them in their acculturation effort. When asked who the most important person was in introducing them to American culture, the responses varied widely. Some mentioned a teacher (20 percent), others a friend (17 percent), or a relative (14 percent). Smaller groups mentioned their spouse (8 percent) or a colleague (3 percent).[12] More than a third (38 percent) noted other influences, often combining several of the above categories. Yet if one looks more closely at the outcomes, a more complex picture than that of complete assimilation emerges. One participant spoke for many: "[I] Don't feel fully assimilated, but appear to be." The typical refugees' situation is that of cultural ambiguity, and not only implies both potential difficulties and challenges, but also often the chance to thrive. In fact, our refugee cohort will provide a case example of distinctiveness advantage of an incomplete assimilation that is conducive to positive socioeconomic outcomes.

In the survey, we asked in which areas of life our participants retained European ways. Large proportions of the former refugees indeed told us that they retained some cultural elements. The choices were—in order of the frequency by which they were mentioned—food and cultural interests

Table 5.1 Percentage of Former Refugees Mentioning Retention of European Ways in Various Areas

Food	57
Cultural interests	57
Tastes/preferences	50
Values	47
Outlook on life	32
Customs	28
Other behaviors	22

(these two categories tied), tastes/preferences, values, outlook on life, customs, and other behaviors (see table 5.1).[13]

Culture has a tremendous span, from the most abstract ideas and ideals to behaviors, routines, and clothes, to bodily reactions and preferences, such as retaining a life-long attachment to certain foods of one's youth. Scholars who are conditioned to focus on the realm of ideas may sometimes underestimate how very salient an element of culture food can be.

In the category of food, tied for first place, an opulent litany of favorite dishes emerged from our questionnaires—evidence of strong memories of, and allegiance to, the comfort food of youth. For instance, "[I] definitely enjoy and seek out foods I was accustomed to as a child—e.g., breads, meats, pastries." Or, "I still make some of the old family recipes: plum torte, marble Teig [dough], herring salad." Another participant simply wrote, "I'd walk a mile for a correctly prepared Wiener Schnitzel." But health concerns about their native cuisine were also occasionally heard: "Typical Viennese/Jewish cooking (mostly abandoned now because it's so unhealthy)."

Cultural interests, general preferences, and tastes ran in the direction of understatement and conservatism and toward what is considered classic. One participant spoke of a "Pretty reserved style of dress and décor, don't like glitzy, tend to like intellectual activities." In a typical response, a participant described the preferences thus, "Classical tastes in music, literature, poetry. Enthusiasm for learning many foreign languages, traveling all over the world and exploring cultures different from my own. A love of natural beauty—being outdoors for its own sake, not for sport or health."

In terms of outlook, some participants told us that their goal was to abandon their roots as quickly as possible, so as to become American. "I tried very hard to stay away from the damn immigrants. I wanted to be identified as an American." However, other participants said they were drawn to the familiarity of their own refugee group and sought the nearness of fellow immigrants. For instance, "I feel more comfortable with people who are European immigrants than with native-born Americans. All of my best friends have been immigrants, with a similar background to mine." Others emphasized that they had an unusually broad and flexible outlook, for example, "Cosmopolitan, multicultural. Ease in adjusting to different national, cultural and language environments." Or, "Well, a European background is an advantage, being here in this country, which the Americans don't have. . . . I would say we had a better understanding of the world as it is than the Americans had because of the history of Europe. . . . Our approach to life was different and our way of thinking was influenced accordingly. . . . [Because of negative experiences] we were at an advantage because we knew what life was all about."

New York City was seen as a natural environment for fostering this latter kind of attitude. "The city of New York . . . made me feel comfortable. The fact that it had a library, and I could do anything I wanted, and I would never be bored. It was the fact that the city was such an open place and so interesting and so easy to get to different parts of it. . . . I played hooky a lot and would go to the Met. I'd go to the Philharmonic. I'd go to museums. . . . It's an absolutely wonderful place to grow up."

"[My migration experience] gave me a sort of cosmopolitanism, an outlook of breadth, some knowledge of languages and the culture that goes with the languages that I would not have had. . . . I think it gave me a much broader base of experience, knowledge, and a kind of confidence that comes out of having that background."

As a residual of their Central European origins, many participants professed a preference for inner, spiritual, and permanent values and said that they shunned fleeting flashiness and superficial attention seeking as well as crass materialism. They portrayed themselves as serious, responsible, punctual, reserved, and well mannered. Here is an assortment of quotes in which the former refugees expressed these traits: "Manners, importance of education. Reserve about personal feelings and happenings."—"Honesty, punctuality"—"Being on time always, being 'straight laced' "—"A certain seriousness; rejection of superficialities"—"Have not been able to accept materialism and waste as a way of life."—"Willing to explore complex situations and defer 'instant' gratification for a long term goal."—"I am uncomfortable with affluence and its manifestations and critical of conspicuous consumption. I dress conservatively and shy away from casting attention on myself."—"More conservative dress"—"Interested in fairness, equality, honest business practices and honesty in politics"—"trying to be more philosophical, less dedicated to the immediate present." Good manners were also mentioned frequently. "I always feel I must do the 'correct' thing, write thank-you notes or phone, pay bills promptly, and reply to mail quickly, don't procrastinate."

The experience of poverty and want in their youth enforced a thrifty lifestyle later in life for many. "Make do with what we have. Repair and extend the life of goods that others throw away." Great emphasis was also placed on the family, for example, "Fostering strong family ties—put great value on having children & grandchildren near." Often, a desire for stability was palpable, for example, "After terrible upheaval during my adolescence, I have a strong desire for stability and financial security." This desire often expressed itself in a certain reluctance to move (by American mobility standards). Among our interviewees, many had lived in the same house for decades. A former refugee who had lived in the same house since 1959 explained this tendency, "I think because in those early years . . . there was so much change from day to day, week to week, month to month . . . you value stability."

A dominant outlook was pessimism and a tendency to worry that was sometimes contrasted with a more optimistic American attitude and traced back to the refugees' childhood experiences. "I see the glass as half empty. I tend to worry a lot. . . . it might be also some of the fears from those early years. . . ."—"I am not always as optimistic and easy going as Americans born here."—"Worry about future"—"Tend to be 'pessimistic,' tearful, overly worried."

"You know, there are two of us at home now, and if you walk into my pantry you'd think there are a dozen people living there. Can't help it. There may be a war tomorrow, you know?"

Occasionally, we found a tendency of being disillusioned bordering on the cynical. "I tend to decide each issue on its individual merits. I doubt if I have ever voted straight ticket, expect both management and labor to lie, both political parties to lie, and any orthodox religion to do more evil than good." One participant described the following determinants of his worldview: "Concern with justice (a Jewish trait). Horror of violence, mass actions (reminiscence of Nazi years). The old, adolescent dream of a fairer, better society just refuses to die. And yet: pervasive cynicism concerning the 'goodness' of human nature." Another respondent echoed this deep-seated skepticism by describing himself as "Most pessimistic about life ('realistic' might be better word)."[14]

In contrast with the prevailing pessimism, there were a few voices that said the exact opposite, for example, "More positive than my American son, friends." Or, "I'm totally American. I feel very good about being an American. . . . I feel that probably I have led a life that's been very rewarding. Life's been great and has allowed me to do things I probably would not have been able to do if I hadn't been an American." And a third participant said, "I have a different attitude to life, of not being scared of things. It might have to do with, what can happen to me that hasn't happened already, really? . . . So let's say I'm more fatalistic."

In each cultural category, the women's percentage of affirming that they had retained European ways was higher than was the men's, although this gender difference reached statistical significance only in the areas of values (p < .05) and customs (p < .01).[15] By adding the responses to all seven areas (see table 5.2), we constructed an index of cultural retention (ranging from 0 [no retention of European ways] to 7 [retention of European ways in all seven categories]). The women had a somewhat higher average on this index than did the men (3.1 vs. 2.8; p < .05).

Further Dimensions of Assimilation and Distinctiveness

Political Views

While Saenger (1941:48–50) observed, among the First Wave refugees, a growth of interest in politics (as well as in religion), Strauss (1981:254) noted that the refugees as a group had little to contribute to tackling the big political problems of postwar America (in particular, Strauss listed the issues of race, equality, mass migrations, and women's rights). These two statements do not necessarily contradict each other. Saenger looked at the refugees during the immediate time of their persecution and immigration and Strauss took a much more long-term view. It is a plausible scenario that many immigrants, once they established themselves in the new country, jettisoned some their crisis-induced political alertness and reverted to their earlier state of relative political acquiescence. In our project, we were specifically interested in the political involvement of the younger refugees. Were they really as politically abstinent as Strauss observed for the whole group? We looked into various aspects and areas of political involvement within this generation, and we did find some political activists among our participants. Often this political activism flowed directly from the experience of being oppressed and driven from their homes. But most of these individuals acted not as representatives and in the name of a Central European immigrant community, but as American citizens. Such a pattern might reinforce the false impression of a politically dormant community.

In our survey, the former refugees typically reported to be politically on the left of the American spectrum, which resulted in the incongruence (by American standards) of being "Probably more conservative in living style and more liberal (socialistic) than most Americans," as one participant aptly put it.

More than one-third (36 percent) described their political views as Democrat, 22 percent said liberal, and 18 percent said "middle of the road." Only small minorities labeled their views as conservative (3 percent),

Republican (3 percent), or socialist (1 percent). Fifteen percent chose various other terms. On the whole, our participants were decidedly slanted toward the left. Women were more likely than men to identify themselves as Democrats, whereas men leaned more towards the liberal, "middle-of-the-road," and (rarely) Republican categories.

The majority (60 percent) said that their early-life background and experiences had influenced their political views considerably, strongly, or even decisively. Only 13 percent thought that, for them, there was no such influence at all. On one hand, the former refugees' political views were influenced by their European political environment, in which the allegiance to left-wing parties (e.g., *Sozialdemokratie*) was a common occurrence. On the other their refugee experience was often described as sensitizing them to the dangers of a dictatorship and totalitarianism, and elevating their level of vigilance for the survival of a free and democratic society that they take much less for granted than does the average native-born American, because they always remember what happened in Germany and Austria.

On the whole, the former refugees were a politically unusually active group. Because of their early experiences under a tyranny, and because of their gratitude for being provided a safe haven, most participants developed a deep appreciation of the American constitutional system that allows for freedom and opportunity. As one said, "I saw first hand what persecution had been for my family—being chased from our home, refused schooling, cafés. My father, who was a physician, lost his practice. I can appreciate the freedom from fear in the US." Those early experiences also provided a strong incentive to oppose dictatorship, discrimination, and anti-Semitism. A person wrote, "I do not believe in dictatorship, do not approve of any discrimination. I would like to see all children have an equal opportunity to attend higher education." And another said, "I am conscious of my Judaism and sensitive to all signs of anti-Semitism." Some felt that, given the privilege of a democratic society, they should make the most of it. "I am (very) active politically. I write letters to my representatives, do volunteer work to that end, and give monetary aid of a modest nature. I support certain groups that favor my point of view. I have presented my story to some 8th grade classes." Or in the words of another participant, "I am strongly aware of those in need & help whenever I can. I have always been active in community & liberal causes."

Here are three more examples: "[My European upbringing] has strongly influenced me in fighting prejudice wherever I've encountered it."—"My choice in 1964 to seek training as a clinical worker very likely had to do with my search for social justice, and empathy for 'the underdog' and people who are in pain emotionally and otherwise."—"Some of my sensitivities to civil liberties issues and things of that kind, certainly the European origin, made the difference."

Some participants generalized the historical experience of the 1930s and 1940s into a fundamental conclusion—that any attempt at appeasing aggressors is disastrous. This may lead to a "hawkish" stance on security matters, which is evident in the following quote. "[The immigration influence] has led to a lifelong sense of American patriotism that pervades damn near everything I do. . . . My wife . . . calls it my refugee complex, but I have an enormous debt of gratitude to this country. . . . So defending the United States of America is enormously important to me and tends to make me somewhat more hawkish than one otherwise might be. So I think it is the single and most explicit and obvious consequence of [my immigration]." Here is an extreme quote of the same type. "They [my experiences] have given me a strong dislike of goyim and of idiot-liberal Jews who believe we can get along with Arabs and others who want to kill all Jews. I particularly dislike the ACLU since they defended the Nazi march through Skokie, as well as the left wing parties in Israel who want to help the Palestinians. My philosophy is somewhere to the right of the Likud."

In the following passage, the commitment to civil liberties and equality led to a wider, cosmopolitan focus. "I am strongly against discrimination of any sort, devoted to protective civil liberties; a dedicated internationalist, contrary to our current president, I do not consider America to be the 'greatest country in the world.' It is a great country but there are many other 'great' ones, including Peru, Pakistan, Israel, Germany, France and Tanzania, etc. We are all citizens of the world and good people are everywhere. We just need more of them."

A connection between early experiences and an involvement in the women's movement was also made in some cases. One female former refugee said, "My escape from the Holocaust was one of three factors in my life that left me with the feeling that my life had been saved because there was a contribution to the world I was to make. I later became one of the founders of the second wave of women's movement in the U.S." Another one said, "Even at the age of four I was aware of how the Nazis treated us. It also influenced my involvement with obtaining equal rights for women."

Religion

Whereas the former refugees who participated in our survey were strongly involved in the political system, they had unusually weak links to religion. A third (33 percent) of the former refugees said they considered themselves not at all religious, 46 percent said they were somewhat religious, and the rest professed stronger religious ties.[16] The women, on average, were more religious than the men. Among those participants with a religious affiliation, 91 percent reported themselves to be Jewish, 6 percent were Protestant,

1 percent Catholic, and the others mentioned a variety of religious group-ings. A religious conversion had occurred in 6 percent of the cases, and 39 percent experienced an increase or a decrease in the intensity of their religious feelings over their lifetime.

Among the parents' generation, the level of religiousness was reported to have been higher. Only 25 percent of the fathers, and 22 percent of the mothers were described as not at all religious. The father's and the mother's levels of religiousness correlated strongly with each other (r = .73), and less strongly with the Second Waver's religiousness (r = .45 for father, r = .44 for mother). As one might expect, the level of religiousness correlated with the intensity of the reported Jewish (r = .47) and Christian (r = .40) identities (for details on the identity issue, see below).

Membership in Organizations

The former refugees, as a group, were well integrated in American civil society, if one takes membership in voluntary organizations as an indicator.[17] In Gordon's (1964) scheme, as mentioned, such membership is an element of structural assimilation. At the same time, many former refugees were active in organizations of their specific ethnic or religious communities. Forty-three percent participated actively in trade or professional organiza-tions, 42 percent in religious organizations, 42 percent in community organizations, 37 percent in cultural organizations, 30 percent in social or recreational organizations, and 9 percent in fraternal and mutual aid organizations. A larger percentage of men than of women noted being members of trade and professional organizations; conversely, women were more strongly represented in cultural and social/recreational organizations. When asked specifically about refugee organizations, 20 percent of the participants acknowledged such a membership.[18] Half of the former refugees also said that they have regular contact with former refugees or are members in refugee organizations. The others reported either no contact at all or only accidental contacts.[19]

Spouse

In immigration studies, the choice of a spouse from one's own ethnic group vs. a spouse from outside one's group (endogamy vs. exogamy) has been considered an important marker of assimilation processes.[20] High rates of endogamy tend to preserve a group's distinctness, whereas high rates of exogamy tend to augur a blending into the American mainstream. Within the category of immigrants' endogamy, it may be useful further to distin-guish between a spouse who is a fellow immigrant and a spouse who is of the same ethnic background but American-born. In our case, the latter means marrying into American Jewry (which, however, had its predominant root in Eastern, not in Central Europe).

In our survey, the questions "was spouse born in Europe" and "is spouse of same religion" allowed us to gain an approximate overview of endogamy and exogamy patterns among the former refugees.[21] Almost all among the former young refugees who responded to our survey eventually got married (97 percent). In nearly half the cases (46 percent), the married survey participants chose a fellow refugee as their spouse (in their first marriage). An almost equally large group (42 percent) married non-European-born coreligionists (i.e., married into American Jewry), and a small group married outside (12 percent). Exogamy was more pronounced among the men; 16 percent of them entered an exogamous marriage, as opposed to 5 percent of the women—whereas a larger percentage of women (58 percent) than of men (39 percent) married a fellow refugee.[22]

Having a spouse of an endogamous background clearly helped the stability of the marriage. Only 9 percent of the first marriages in which the participant had married a fellow refugee ended in divorce, whereas 15 percent of the first marriages with non-European-born coreligionists and 33 percent of the exogamous first marriages were terminated by a divorce. These data can be compared, at least in a rough approximation, with national data reported by the Census Bureau: In 1996, 24.4% of the American men born between 1925 and 1934, and 23.7% of the American women in the same cohort, were divorced at least once by the time they reached age 60 (Kreider and Fields 2002: Table 1). On the whole, the endogamous marriages of the former refugees thus appear to have been more durable than the national average, whereas the opposite was the case for the exogamous marriages.

We also looked at those participants who entered a second marriage. Second time around, were they more likely to venture out into exogamy, or was there an opposite tendency to return to the fold? We found that, of those who reported a second marriage (N = 227), a third (33 percent) chose exogamy, only a quarter (24 percent) married a fellow immigrant, and the rest married non-European-born coreligionists.[23] These overall results appeared to support the first pattern (increase in exogamy), but they were not conclusive—an ecological fallacy might apply here.[24] We therefore examined the individuals' marriage histories. More than half (53 percent) married the *same* kind of spouse (fellow immigrant, non-European-born coreligionist, or non-European-born individual of a different religion) they had in their first marriage, 31 percent moved in the direction of exogamy, and 16 percent moved in the opposite direction. Thus, there was indeed a trend toward exogamy. If we consider a dichotomous variable that only distinguishes endogamy and exogamy (grouping the two variants of endogamy together), we find that 19 percent moved into, and only 9 percent moved out of exogamy, while the rest stuck with their type of marriage. This general pattern also applied to either gender separately. The marriage succession thus predominantly followed the first hypothesis (increase in exogamy).

We now turn to a detailed quantitative picture of the former refugees' traits and how they differed from those of American-born persons of the same age.

Attitudinal Profile

"Outgoing," "punctual," "watch television," "listen to classical music," "shy with strangers" were only a few items of an extensive list of 39 traits that we submitted on our questionnaires to the survey participants, asking them to rate the extent to which they possessed each of these traits in comparison with what they considered the average American of their age. The choices offered to them were "much less," "less," "slightly less," "same," "slightly more," "more," and "much more."

A statistical analysis of these data follows. In it, we focus not only on the group of former refugees as a whole, but we look at the genders separately, and we further compare the former refugees with a group of people born in the United States as well as with a group of non-refugee immigrants from Central Europe (mainly scientists who had arrived after the war to avail themselves of career opportunities).

Traits of Male and Female Former Refugees

The first table presents an ordered list of these traits reported by our cohort of former refugees, as perceived by those participants (table 5.2). Traits that they, as a group, thought they possessed to the highest degree are at the top. Note that the above-mentioned choice labels were mapped onto a numerical scale, with "4" representing "same (as the average American of your age)," so that averages above 4 represent various degrees of "more," and those below 4, various degrees of "less."

We see that "listen to classical music" is the top-rated trait, followed by "interested in learning" and "punctual." The eleven top traits (those that received an average rating above 5) paint the picture of a group with a strong work ethic, a strong will to achieve, and an interest in what might be called high culture. There can be little surprise that these traits ended up on top, because, as already reported, many of our participants' qualitative

Table 5.2 Self-Rated Traits among Former Refugees—for the Whole Cohort, and by Gender

	N	Mean	Std Dev	t-Test for Difference	Men's Rank	Women's Rank
Listen to classical music	1486	5.76	1.30	Men	1	2
Interested in learning	1464	5.73	1.12	Men	2	3
Punctual	1490	5.65	1.24	n.s.	4	1
Disciplined in work	1448	5.61	1.13	Men	3	4
Like to read	1465	5.43	1.32	n.s.	6	5
Hardworking	1459	5.42	1.22	Men	5	6
Organized	1466	5.29	1.31	n.s.	7	8
Interested in the arts	1463	5.21	1.37	n.s.	9	10
Thrifty	1468	5.20	1.23	n.s.	10	9
Family-oriented	1484	5.16	1.33	Women	11	7
Achievement-oriented	1446	5.08	1.43	Men	8	13
Serious with close friends	1454	4.91	1.24	Women	13	11
Ambitious	1450	4.88	1.35	Men	12	14
Like to write	1448	4.62	1.68	Men	14	18
Like the outdoors	1476	4.60	1.44	Women	15	12
Involved in charities	1462	4.43	1.51	n.s.	16	16
Interested in food	1451	4.39	1.40	n.s.	17	19
Friendly with strangers	1460	4.31	1.25	n.s.	18	17
Emotional when frustrated	1443	4.21	1.40	Women	19	20
Do volunteer work	1448	4.15	1.81	Women	22	15
Active in philanthropy	1399	4.08	1.72	n.s.	20	24
Active in community	1474	4.06	1.57	n.s.	21	22
Interested in socializing	1467	3.92	1.35	Women	26	21
Like to have a good time	1458	3.91	1.19	Women	23	25
Outgoing	1466	3.89	1.48	Women	25	23
Active in politics	1444	3.80	1.61	n.s.	24	29
Shy with strangers	1467	3.79	1.43	n.s.	28	26
Lenient with children	1444	3.78	1.35	n.s.	27	27
Easygoing	1457	3.61	1.39	n.s.	29	31
Interested in movies	1465	3.41	1.53	Women	30	30
Religious	1473	3.26	1.77	Women	31	32
Wear fashionable clothes	1465	3.21	1.56	Women	33	28
Like to play music	1352	3.08	1.97	n.s.	32	33
Watch television	1490	2.98	1.49	Women	34	34
Active in sports/athletics	1423	2.80	1.66	n.s	35	35
Follow sports events	1474	2.57	1.68	Men	36	39
Listen to popular music	1460	2.48	1.45	Women	37	36
Like to paint	1381	2.43	1.67	Women	38	37
Interested in celebrities	1461	2.09	1.24	Women	39	38

Note: The Ns fluctuate slightly from item to item because of varying numbers of "missing values" (i.e., of questionnaires where the respective item was left blank). A t-test is a statistical method that allows us to infer, from the difference found in a sample between the averages of two groups, how likely it is that the averages of these two groups are in fact different in the whole population from which the sample was drawn. If the averages for men and women did not differ at a statistically significant (p < .05) level, "n.s." appears in the t-test for difference column. If the averages differed at least at the p < .05 level, the gender with the *higher* average score was entered.

responses vividly testified to the importance of these traits. Classical music, for instance, was frequently reported to have played a strong and formative role in the households where many Second Wavers grew up.

The bottom traits (those that received an average rating below 3) constitute the very opposite: leisure in the style of the American popular culture, for example, "watch television," "listen to popular music," and "interested in celebrities."

In addition, the table indicates the differences between men and women. Obviously, the overall pattern did not differ much by gender.[25] Because of the large sample sizes, the tests had a great deal of statistical power so that even quite small differences were found statistically different. The table shows the traits for which statistically significant gender differences occurred. Some of those gender differences could be considered typical, as they conform to prevailing gender roles. Compared with the men, women, on average, described themselves as more family-oriented (5.3 vs. 5.1), less achievement-oriented (4.7 vs. 5.3), being more strongly involved in volunteer work (4.5 vs. 4.0), less active in politics (3.7 vs. 3.9), more likely to wear fashionable clothes (3.7 vs. 2.9), and less likely to follow sports events (2.2 vs. 2.8). They also described themselves as more interested in socializing (4.2 vs. 3.8). Men's self-ratings covered a wider range, their high scoring traits receiving higher averages and their low scoring traits, lower averages, whereas the women's extremes strayed less far from the middle (i.e., the "same" category[26]).

Another way of looking at gender differences is comparing the rankings the individual traits received by men and women. To nobody's surprise, the largest difference in rank (seven ranks, in each case) occurred for "do volunteer work" and for "wear fashionable clothes." In both cases, these traits ranked higher for the women than for the men. A five-rank difference was found for being "achievement-oriented," "active in politics," and "interested in socializing." On the first two, the men had higher ranks; on the third, the women. Family-orientation was four ranks higher for the women than for the men, whereas the same rank difference in the opposite direction was found for "like to write" and for "active in philanthropy."

Comparison Between Former Refugees and American-Born Persons

Our survey database includes American-born listees also in the *Who's Who*, *Who's Who in American Jewry*, and *American Men and Women of Science*. In the following, we compare them with the former refugees listed in those same publications. We are dealing here of course with two elite groups— those listed in various compilations of high achievers. The ratings of the

American-born reflect their perception of how they differ from the population norm. In a sense, these ratings show how an indigenous American elite
group believes itself to differ from the general American population. (These
perceived differences, therefore, are a function of socioeconomic position,
not of cultural background.)

Examining the t-test results for comparing average ratings by the former
refugees and by the American-born on each of the 39 traits, we find that differences between these two groups predominate over similarities. Only 8 of
the 39 traits do *not* show a statistically significant difference (at the $p < .05$
level). These are "active in politics," "interested in movies," "interested in
food," "thrifty," "emotional when frustrated," "like to write," "like to
paint," and "like to play music." Whereas, in most of the other 31 cases, the
average ratings were higher for the American-born than for the former
refugees, the refugees rated themselves higher on three traits: "listen to
classical music," "interested in the arts," and "shy with strangers."

The former refugees rated themselves even lower than did the American-
born on traits they thought they possessed to a low extent, such as
"interested in celebrities," "listen to popular music," "follow sports events,"
"active in sports/athletics," and "watch television," and so forth. But the
former refugees also rated themselves slightly lower than did the American-
born on many traits that they (the refugees) thought they had to a high
degree, such as "interested in learning," "punctual," "disciplined in work,"
"like to read," "hardworking," and so on (see table 5.3).

Especially in view of the higher overall level of the ratings by the
American-born, a comparison of the relative rankings of the traits might be
more telling than a comparison of means. In table 5.3, the traits are ordered
by the refugees rankings, and the rankings of the American-born are given
in the right most column. This method lets us realize a pattern of overall
similarity (Spearman rank correlation coefficient = .92), although the
following pronounced differences might be worth mentioning. The traits
"listen to classical music" and "interested in the arts," which, as reported,
received higher ratings from the refugees than from the America-born, were
also much higher on the refugees' ranked list than on that of their counterparts (ranks 2 vs. 11, and 7 vs. 14, respectively). "Shy with strangers" ranked
ten places higher for the refugees than for the American-born (22 vs. 32).
"Emotional when frustrated" and "active in politics" also received higher
relative rankings from the former refugees (20 vs. 29, and 21 vs. 28, respectively). By contrast, the rankings of the American-born placed "family-oriented" (7 vs. 13), "outgoing" (18 vs. 27), "easygoing" (23 vs. 29), "religious"
(27 vs. 34), and "follow sports events" (30 vs. 37) higher than did the
former refugees' rankings.

Table 5.3 Self-Rated Traits of Listees in *Who's Who, Who's Who in American Jewry,* and *American Men and Women of Science,* Comparing Former Refugees and American-Born

	Refugees		American-born		Rank/ refugees	Rank/ Am. born
	N	Mean	N	Mean		
Interested in learning	411	6.11	528	6.31	1	1
Listen to classical music	416	6.01	536	5.25	2	11
Disciplined in work	407	5.69	535	5.86	3	4
Like to read	409	5.67	535	5.98	4	2
Hardworking	407	5.49	532	5.88	5	3
Punctual	411	5.48	537	5.69	6	6
Interested in the arts	410	5.44	537	5.02	7	14
Achievement-oriented	412	5.42	532	5.80	8	5
Organized	403	5.19	538	5.52	9	8
Like to write	406	5.08	533	5.28	10	10
Thrifty	411	5.07	536	5.00	11	15
Ambitious	407	4.96	531	5.47	12	9
Family-oriented	408	4.85	539	5.53	13	7
Serious with close friends	399	4.75	528	5.03	14	13
Like the outdoors	405	4.54	530	5.25	15	12
Interested in food	406	4.44	536	4.46	16	19
Involved in charities	408	4.22	536	4.76	17	17
Active in philanthropy	399	4.11	528	4.37	18	21
Friendly with strangers	409	4.06	537	4.82	19	16
Emotional when frustrated	404	3.95	529	3.81	20	29
Active in politics	408	3.91	535	3.82	21	28
Shy with strangers	410	3.86	540	3.34	22	32
Active in community	413	3.85	535	4.36	23	22
Like to have a good time	402	3.70	531	4.40	24	20
Lenient with children	401	3.70	530	4.21	25	26
Do volunteer work	407	3.68	531	4.31	26	24
Outgoing	407	3.56	533	4.63	27	18
Interested in socializing	408	3.54	532	4.25	28	25
Easygoing	409	3.34	539	4.31	29	23
Interested in movies	410	3.19	534	3.09	30	35
Like to play music	380	3.10	520	3.15	31	34
Active in sports/athletics	408	2.71	529	3.27	32	33
Wear fashionable clothes	405	2.62	532	3.38	33	31
Religious	412	2.61	533	4.12	34	27
Watch television	413	2.51	535	3.00	35	36
Like to paint	391	2.40	521	2.46	36	38
Follow sports events	413	2.38	533	3.65	37	30
Listen to popular music	410	1.95	534	2.83	38	37
Interested in celebrities	411	1.85	529	2.18	39	39

Comparison Between Former Refugees and
Non-Refugee Immigrants

We further compare the former refugees listed in *American Men and Women of Science* with listees of the same age group who were also born in Germany or Austria, but had immigrated to America not as refugees, but for other reasons. A few of these non-refugee immigrants from Germany and Austria had arrived before 1933; the bulk had arrived after the war, mainly to take advantage of scientific career opportunities. The members of this group of non-refugee immigrants typically were non-Jewish.

As seen in table 5.4, very similar pictures of the self-rated traits emerged for these two groups. Only 8 of the 39 traits showed significant differences in the t-tests ($p < .05$). These were: The former refugees were more strongly "involved in charities," they were more "lenient with children," more "active in politics," more "interested in the arts," more "interested in movies," more "active in the community," more "interested in food," and more "emotional when frustrated." We can only speculate about the reasons for these differences. Perhaps their typically longer exposure to American culture made them more "American," compared to the non-refugee immigrants, in some instances (e.g., food, movies, child-rearing); perhaps there were after-effects of the refugee experience (e.g., politics, charity, emotion); and perhaps there were influences reaching back to the former refugees' particular sub-cultures in which they grew up in Central Europe (e.g., politics, charity, arts).

The rankings of the traits support the overall impression of great similarity (Spearman rank correlation coefficient = .97). In addition to rank differences in the traits already mentioned, the refugees ranked "easy-going," "like to have a good time," and "friendly with strangers" lower than did the non-refugee immigrants (ranks 29 vs. 23, 25 vs. 19, and 20 vs. 16, respectively). The latter differences, expressing a heightened tendency of being on guard vis-à-vis others, might be lasting after-effects of the former refugees' turbulent and often traumatic childhood experiences.

In sum, we found our group of refugees to describe themselves, on average, as being oriented toward high achievement, as being conscientious hard workers, and as gravitating toward a particular kind of high culture and away from certain aspects of American popular culture. (In these respects, there were hardly any differences by gender.) A comparison between the former refugees listed in *American Men and Women of Science* and the Central European non-refugee immigrants also listed in that compilation showed that these two immigrant groups were very similar in their traits. Another comparison, between the former refugees listed in *American Men and Women of Science*, *Who's Who*, or *Who's Who in American Jewry* and

Table 5.4 Self-Rated Traits of Listees in *American Men and Women of Science*, Comparing Former Refugees and Other, Later Immigrants from Germany and Austria

	Euro. refugees		Euro. immigrants		Refugee rank	Immigrants rank
	N	Mean	N	Mean		
Interested in learning	243	6.16	60	6.12	1	1
Listen to classical music	248	6.09	59	6.05	2	2
Disciplined in work	239	5.66	61	5.79	3	3
Like to read	242	5.57	60	5.75	4	4
Punctual	244	5.42	59	5.73	5	5
Hardworking	241	5.41	59	5.44	6	6
Interested in the arts	244	5.35	61	4.97	7	11
Achievement-oriented	244	5.31	60	5.32	8	8
Organized	240	5.27	60	5.28	9	9
Thrifty	243	5.19	59	5.41	10	7
Like to write	242	4.93	59	5.05	11	10
Family-oriented	241	4.83	60	4.92	12	12
Ambitious	240	4.82	60	4.72	13	14
Like the outdoors	241	4.69	60	4.85	14	13
Serious with close friends	235	4.68	60	4.43	15	15
Interested in food	239	4.47	61	3.89	16	18
Involved in charities	242	4.09	61	3.41	17	22
Emotional when frustrated	238	4.06	60	3.52	18	21
Shy with strangers	243	4.04	59	3.95	19	17
Friendly with strangers	244	4.01	61	4.15	20	16
Active in philanthropy	236	3.90	59	3.53	21	20
Active in politics	242	3.73	60	2.70	22	31
Lenient with children	239	3.72	61	3.05	23	29
Active in community	245	3.63	61	3.11	24	28
Like to have a good time	238	3.63	60	3.58	25	19
Do volunteer work	240	3.55	61	3.18	26	27
Interested in socializing	244	3.39	59	3.27	27	25
Outgoing	241	3.39	61	3.33	28	24
Easygoing	244	3.37	61	3.36	29	23
Like to play music	228	3.22	57	3.21	30	26
Interested in movies	243	2.96	61	2.54	31	33
Active in sports/athletics	241	2.66	59	3.00	32	30
Religious	245	2.46	60	2.55	33	32
Watch television	245	2.44	61	2.31	34	35
Wear fashionable clothes	239	2.29	60	2.50	35	34
Like to paint	233	2.27	58	2.12	36	36
Follow sports events	245	2.23	61	2.11	37	37
Listen to popular music	243	1.84	61	1.92	38	38
Interested in celebrities	244	1.72	60	1.58	39	39

their American-born counterparts indicated that, on the whole, the refugees' traits were similar to those of American-born high achievers—or perhaps even more generally, to the traits of high achievers regardless of where they come from. Certain attributes may be simply predictors or correlates of success. For instance, it is hardly surprising that the listees—whether American-born or former refugees—name "interested in learning," "hardworking," "achievement-oriented" among their most pronounced traits. That is typically how one gets into these elite compilations.

So much the more remarkable are the differences we did find between the refugee high achievers and the American-born high achievers. These were concentrated in three areas. The first was the refugees' affinity to that specific brand of high culture (e.g., "listen to classical music," "interested in the arts"). Second was a certain distance from traits associated with American general culture (e.g., "follow sports events,"[27] "easygoing," "religious"); third, certain remnants of their early refugee experience (e.g., "active in politics," "shy with strangers").

In terms of the refugees' affinity to high culture, we should note that this was the type of culture also revered by large sections of the indigenous educated elite. Historically, the American educated classes looked to Europe for inspiration and ideas about high culture. The refugees thus could garner respect and understanding for their cultural pursuits to a larger extent than could typical immigrants holding on to their ethnic roots. In many cases, the young refugees arrived with a perfect cultural match with the cultural sensibilities already adopted by wide segments of the American upper middle class. As will be discussed below in greater detail, the young refugees found that their cultural capital was convertible into American cultural currency.

Composite Traits

The questionnaire contained no fewer than 39 traits, and it appeared advisable, for further data analysis, to reduce the number of trait variables. We did so by constructing a smaller number of composite indicators that pooled the information of several individual variables that both correlated with each other statistically and were related in some substantive way, that is, "made sense together." Such composite indicators are more robust, that is, they have the advantage of being more reliable and valid than any of the individual ratings.

To construct those composite indicators for our sample of former refugees, we used two statistical procedures, multidimensional scaling and factor analysis, in combination (details in note 28). On the resulting map, spatial distance between traits represents how closely these traits are related to each other, and the different shadings show different clusters (or "factors") of traits that we use to construct composite traits for our subsequent analyses (see figure 5.2).[29]

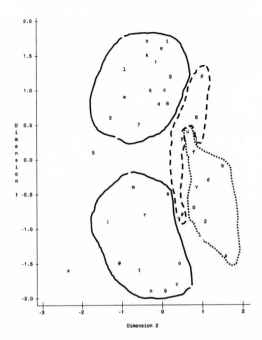

Figure 5.2   Multidimensional Scaling of Traits

Notes: a = outgoing, b = punctual, c = interested in socializing, d = organized, e = listen to popular music, f = ambitious, g = wear fashionable clothes, h = watch television, i = easygoing, j = involved in charities, k = interested in celebrities, l = lenient with children, m = like the outdoors, n = listen to classical music, o = interested in learning, p = religious, q = like to have a good time, r = active in politics, s = serious with close friends, t = interested in the arts, u = family-oriented, v = hardworking, w = interested in movies, x = shy with strangers, y = active in community, z = like to read, 0 = achievement-oriented, 1 = follow sports events, 2 = disciplined in work, 3 = interested in food, 4 = thrifty, 5 = emotional when frustrated, 6 = friendly with strangers, 7 = active in sports/athletics, 8 = do volunteer work, 9 = like to write, ! = like to paint, @ = like to play music, # = active in philanthropy.

At the top of the two-dimensional map, we find a cluster of traits comprising "watch television," "easygoing," "listen to popular music," "interested in celebrities," "lenient with children," "follow sports events," "wear fashionable clothes," "like to have a good time," "interested in socializing," "interested in movies," "outgoing," "friendly with strangers," "interested in food," and "active in sports/athletics." The underlying theme (or factor) of these traits reflects the traditionally easygoing and friendly American popular culture.

By contrast, if we look at the traits clustering at the bottom, we find "listen to classical music," "like to write," "like to read," "interested in the arts," "interested in learning," "like to play music," "like to paint," "active in politics," "like the outdoors," and "serious with close friends." The underlying theme here reflects what one might call high culture and a more serious and socially responsible approach to life.

The dotted cluster to the right consists of "thrifty," "disciplined in work," "achievement-oriented," "hardworking," "organized," "punctual," "ambitious," and "family-oriented." Most of these traits could be summarized under the heading of work ethic and achievement-orientation.

The hash-marked cluster wedged in the middle contains "religious," "do volunteer work," "involved in charities," "active in community," "active in philanthropy." One might characterize this cluster as social activism.

We also produced multidimensional scaling maps separately for men and women former refugees. Though they were not identical, they looked basically similar.[30]

We should also note that "shy with strangers" is very much uncorrelated with the other traits and is found by itself in the bottom left corner. This may indicate that shyness has relatively little to do with the processes that shape the other traits and is influenced by its own idiosyncratic causes. This finding appears to support Jerome Kagan's theory about the inborn factors determining shyness.[31]

After the components of the composite traits were determined, the scores for the composite traits were calculated by averaging the respective component traits. The "work ethic" composite had the highest average (5.30), followed by "high culture" (4.54), "social activism" (3.99), and "popular culture" (3.35). Women scored higher on the "popular culture" indicator and lower on "work ethic" that is consistent with the higher percentage of men being highly educated and having professional careers.

Having painted a broad picture of the attitudinal profile of the former refugees as a group, we shall, in the following sections, examine various internal differences among the former refugees in regard to that profile.

Collective Identities: Ethnic Option vs. Universalism

At least since the nineteenth century, a person's national identity has acquired central importance. Among the set of various potential collective identities an individual can adhere to, it is the one that often commands the highest loyalty from citizens of the modern nation states—sometimes to the exclusion of other identities. Obviously, the issue of national identity is more difficult for people with ties to multiple nations. Immigrants, for instance, have potential identity relationships with, at least, their native land and their new country. For refugee groups, the situation can be even more complex. As pointed out, some might see themselves as exiles, having been forced to abandon their homeland by an adverse political regime, but still hoping for a return. The national identity of these refugee groups typically focuses fervently on the old nation. Many Cubans who fled Castro, or Russians who fled the Bolsheviks, are in this category. They generally view their new home merely as a "waiting room," a temporary asylum before the eventual return. This mindset tends to become weaker, however, as time elapses, and as new generations grow up. But although the refugees from National Socialism, especially among the adults, also contained a small number of political exiles, the situation for the majority of the refugees was markedly different. Most felt doubly isolated from their old nation—by both a physical and symbolic rejection. Not only were they physically expelled under horrific circumstances, but also were they emphatically stripped of their national identity by the government. The former refugees' relationship with the old homeland is therefore an extremely challenging one, and it is worth exploring now in greater detail.

An immigrant from Central Europe himself, Erik Erikson did pioneering research on the concept of identity. From reading the pages of his "Autobiographic notes on the identity crisis" (1970), it quickly becomes clear that the issue of identity, and the challenges—and possibilities—that present themselves in this area to immigrants and refugees, had a deep personal relevance for Erikson. He wrote, "Migration means cruel survival in identity terms, too, for the very cataclysms in which millions perish open up new forms of identity to the survivors" (Erikson 1970:748). Erikson recognized that our group of refugees, as others, were faced with the task of somehow coming to terms with and organizing a jumble of identity fragments. Such a synthesis sometimes proves elusive and leads to certain identity elements being submerged in a negative identity. "Identity formation normatively has its negative side which throughout life can remain an unruly part of the total identity. The *negative identity* is the sum of all those identifications and identity fragments which the individual had to submerge in himself as undesirable or irreconcilable or by which atypical individuals and marked minorities are made to feel 'different' " (Erikson 1970:733). Sophie Freud (2001), one of the Second Wavers, also emphasized "many-sided selves" and spoke of the danger in building identity on only one or two categories. The complexities of identity formation that are inherent in the refugees' situation might well be paradigmatic of the challenges many people, be they refugees or not, face in their quest for an identity in modern, highly complex societies. In this sense, refugees might be considered exemplars in an age of identity proliferation.

Whereas academic scholarship as well as public sentiment traditionally focused on the processes by which immigrants are assimilated into American society—a process sometimes characterized by "melting pot" imagery—a more recent line of research, pioneered by Nathan Glazer and Daniel Moynihan's (1963) work titled *Beyond the Melting Pot*, emphasized that the ethnic dimension has provided fundamental and enduring features in the organization of American society. Far from being merely a temporary circumstance for newly arrived immigrants, the structures (such as ethnic enclaves and networks) and politics of ethnicity often play a role in the lives even of Americans of long standing.

Having identified plenty of Central European remnants among our group of former refugees, the crucial question is to what extent these remnants are integrated into the individuals' sense of identity. Mary Waters's (1999) evocative concept of "ethnic options" will guide our discussion. As Waters pointed out, white Americans have options about how they interpret and represent their ethnicity—from downplaying their ethnic roots (in favor of "generic" Americanness) to emphasizing them. In addition, the ancestral lines of many Americans comprise a variety of ethnicities, so that those individuals have choices as to which particular ethnicity to put in the foreground. The idea that, in contemporary America, ethnicity has become symbolic, that is, that people can invoke or downplay ethnicity, depending on their emotional needs and/or economic and political interests, was pioneered by Herbert Gans (1979)—a Second Waver himself.

What were the options for our group of refugees? One was thorough and complete Americanization. The second one was joining the ethnic landscape of American society by becoming Jewish American. (Those refugees from Central Europe who exercised the second option could not join an ethnic group that was an exact fit, but one that was an approximate fit, as is not unusual in America—the closest ethnic affiliation available was that with American Jewry.) These were the only two options taken by large proportions of our group. A third option, that of retaining a German or Austrian identification, was less widespread. But just looking at the participants' preferred broad identity labels, such as "American," or "Jewish-American" may be too superficial. More complex identity contours emerge upon closer inspection. We shall show that, owing to the particular history of our group, the first and third options sometimes entered a curious and unique symbiosis—neither complete Americanization nor ethnic option.

Diversity Among the Refugee Cohort

The group of refugees was internally diverse, and that diversity, to some degree, influenced which option individual refugees exercised. These differences among the refugees were, of course, most visible among the First Wavers, but, in our study, we investigate to what extent these differences found an echo in the Second Wave.

Two somewhat contrasting images exist of the refugees from Central Europe, as mentioned earlier. Much of the past research about them focused on the ample crop of first-rate scholars, artists, and intellectuals among them. These studies supported a generalized perception of the immigrants as sophisticated, cosmopolitan, and entirely removed from the traditional forms and expressions of Jewish customs and religion. The second, and less prominent, image emerges from in-depth studies such as Steven Lowenstein's (1989) portrayal of the German-speaking Jewish community in Washington Heights, New York City, and Rhonda Levine's (2001) work on German Jewish refugee cattle dealers in upstate New York. These social scientists have brought into view Central European immigrants who came from small-town or rural backgrounds, were conservative in their general world-view, and were strongly rooted in Jewish traditions, perhaps more strongly than their average American-born counterparts. The National Jewish Population Survey (NJPS) data make possible a quantitative look at these two images because, in addition to the basic variables of socioeconomic status, the NJPS contains a wealth of information about behaviors and attitudes in relation to Jewish religion and culture. (In the following, the "former Central Europeans" are those of the 1933–44 immigrant cohort, unless specified otherwise.)

Because the roots of most of the American-born Jews extended to Eastern Europe, it is not surprising that knowledge of Yiddish was more widespread among them (54 percent) than among the former Central Europeans (37 percent). However, whereas only one-third of the American-born Jews (35 percent) said they knew any Hebrew (other than just a few words and phrases), close to two-thirds (62 percent) of the Central European refugees who arrived in 1933–44 claimed to possess such knowledge. This probably is an aftereffect of the government-mandated religious instruction—in their respective faiths—for all school-age children in Central Europe. As one might expect, the Eastern European immigrants (both those who arrived during, and those who arrived after the war) were more likely than the Central Europeans to know Hebrew, and more likely than the American-born Jews to know Yiddish.

As to membership in temples or synagogues, similar percentages of the American-born and former Central European Jews belonged to one or more such congregations (62 percent vs. 64 percent).[32] Whereas 8 percent of the American-born individuals were members of an orthodox congregation, the corresponding percentage was twice as large (17 percent) among the Central European refugees (and the numbers for the Eastern immigrants were even substantially higher). While the American-born Jews reported an attendance of an average of 13.8 services during the 12 months preceding the survey, the former Central Europeans said they had attended 20.0 on average (and the former Eastern Europeans had considerably higher numbers). Clearly, these numbers attest to the strength of the "traditionalist" subgroup among the immigrants and help relativize the prevailing stereotype of the former refugees from Central Europe as secular cosmopolitans. They help highlight the usually somewhat obscured alternative reality of a more religious and observant subpopulation of Central European refugees. Ethnic stereotypes tend to neglect such internal complexities.[33]

The 1970 NJPS posed a large number of additional questions about the participants' attitudes and religious behaviors. We conducted a factor analysis (VARIMAX-rotated) to guide us in the construction of a few composite variables that made sense both in terms of the factor analysis and substantively. The composite variables were formed by standardizing the original variables and then averaging them, after reversing signs where appropriate (see note 34 for details).

In the following analysis of NJPS data, we again compare the American-born group with the 1933–44 immigrants from Central Europe. In terms of how strongly they affirmed a Jewish "identity" (see note 34 for variable definition), no difference was found between these two groups, on average, but education did matter here. Regardless of origin, the most highly educated (beyond college) scored lower on this composite variable than the others did. More "knowledge" about Judaism was claimed by the Central Europeans (vis-à-vis American-born Jews), and by the more highly educated (vis-à-vis the less highly educated), respectively. There was no difference in the "support for Israel," and none for the salience of "Jewish impact" on the participants' lives.

It may be worth mentioning that we detected several interactions between country of origin and education in influencing these composite variables. Although they were statistically significant, the effect sizes for these interactions were very small (r was in the .03 range[35]). The large N (number of subjects) in the statistical analyses yielded such high statistical power that even those small effects could be detected. These interactions are interesting because, taken together, they point to crucial differences in the role of ethnic communities in the societal fabric of Germany and Austria on one hand, and the United States on the other, and they thus provide an echo of a vanished sociocultural stratum.

When, in the following findings, we describe the means of the four groups formed to report these results, it should be noted that those means represent the main effects plus the interaction, but not simply the "pure" interaction (Rosenthal and Rosnow 1984:277–301). The highly educated former Central Europeans, as a group, had an unusually high "openness" (see note 34 for variable definition) score that far exceeded that of their American-born counterparts, whereas among the less highly educated, the country of birth made no difference (p < .05, for the "pure" interaction effect). Another interaction was found on the composite variable "religiousness." Again, describing the results of main effects plus interaction, the former Central Europeans of the highest educational level scored particularly low, whereas the rest of the Central Europeans had the highest religiousness score, on average. The drop in religiousness associated with higher educational level was much less pronounced within the American-born group (p < .05).[36]

We also constructed an index for the available NJPS variables for various religious observances connected with holidays (e.g., Passover, Chanukah), or with daily living (e.g., kosher). The index ranged from 0 (no observance reported) to 15.5 (maximum number of observances reported). The lowest average value was found among the American-born Jews (4.9), but the former Central Europeans of the 1933–44 immigration cohort scored only slightly higher (5.5). The highest level of observance was found among the postwar Eastern European immigrants (7.2). Here, too, an interaction was found between educational level and immigration status (p = .01). Whereas among the US-born participants, those with the highest level of education (beyond college) were more observant than those with lower levels (5.0 vs. 4.8), the opposite was true for all immigrant groups. Among the Central Europeans who arrived between 1933 and 1944, those with the highest educational level scored only 4.7 on the index, whereas the others scored 6.2.

These findings tie in with a major theme of this study. The core question here is to what extent cultural values and norms that were acquired early in life persisted across the discontinuities of migration. Among those who eventually attained postcollege education, the former Central European Jews differed from the American-born Jews in several attitudes and behaviors in ways that are reminiscent of how highly educated Jews in Central Europe—many of whom became "First Wave" refugees—fit into the social fabric of those countries. This observation is made more meaningful by the fact, which we shall discuss later, that the young refugees' socioeconomic achievement tended to be associated with the family's socioeconomic status back in Europe. The professionals among the Second Wavers thus disproportionately came from the "good families" and could be assumed to have picked up some of the characteristic values and attitudes of this stratum. Evidently, undergoing the later stages of advanced education in America did not entirely override certain elements of their previous socialization.

Although melting pot ideas were pervasive in America when the refugees from Central Europe entered, Central Europe had, for the Jewish population, been a much more intense de facto melting pot—until, of course, that pot shattered under the National Socialist regime. The orientation of the Jewish elite toward the national and cultural projects of Germany and Austria was much more complete and unequivocal. The Zionists naturally upheld an ethnic definition of Jewishness, and the Orthodox stayed at arm's length from the surrounding community; but the larger mainstream, while entering elevated socioeconomic positions, either entirely withdrew from anything Jewish or treated Judaism as a religious denomination (analogous and equivalent to Protestantism or Catholicism). "Making it" in society was typically associated with complete assimilation into a national and even cosmopolitan elite, where the zest for cultural and intellectual excellence took the place of religious fervor or ethnic attachment.

There existed no close counterpart to that particular kind of elite in America. Under the different conditions of a multiethnic society of immigrants, and despite the melting pot rhetoric, as Glazer and Moynihan (1963) and others have shown, ethnicity in general provided a more potent focus of identity and activity in America than in Central Europe. Instead of abandoning ethnicity, a larger proportion of the highly educated Jews was active within the Jewish community and provided leadership. Putting it simplistically (and with admitted hyperbole), a strong emphasis on Jewishness was associated with low status in Central Europe, but much less so in the United States. The NJPS data about the attitudes and behaviors of highly educated former Central European Jews and their American-born counterparts are consistent with that larger picture and demonstrate a certain persistence of this pattern, albeit in a much diluted form.

In sum, within the generation of young refugees, our analyses identified traces, faint as they may be, of that vanished highly assimilated and secularized Jewish elite of Central Europe—and thus give empirical support to the first image, that of a highly modern, sophisticated, and secular refugee group. At the other end of the spectrum, we found that considerable numbers of refugees were in some respects even more "traditionalist" than the American-born Jews, on average. Our data suggest great variability among the Central European refugees. Thus both of the above-mentioned images of the immigrants are true *partial* descriptions of an internally diverse group.

Additional data from our survey will allow us to substantiate these indications from the NJPS. We first turn to that second group for which the entry into American Jewry was a common option, although this, by itself, required some adjustment and assimilation.

Newcomers and American Jewry

In the American "nation of immigrants," immigration from the same region or ethnic group has usually been a long-lasting process, often with cyclical ups and downs. Because most of the refugees of the 1930s and 1940s were Jewish, their relationship with the Jewish-American community is of particular interest.

This community consisted of different layers of immigration. The earliest Jewish immigrants from the seventeenth century on were mostly Sephardic Jews; in the early nineteenth century, however, Germany became the area of origin of most Jewish immigrants (Cohen 1984, Soyer 1997:46). In a sweeping process of emancipation and assimilation, a great number of German Jews, as noted, moved from the countryside to German cities; but for some of them, moving into modernity meant immigration to the United States.[37] Toward the end of the nineteenth and in the early twentieth centuries, Eastern Europeans and Russians constituted the main group among the Jewish immigrants. Most of these Yiddish-speaking "shtetl Jews" (Cohen 1984:42) fleeing the oppression and pogroms of Czarist Russia came directly from traditionalist Jewish communities. The complicated and ambivalent relations (partly cooperative and partly antagonistic) between the more modern-minded and secularized Jews of German origin and the more tradition-observant Eastern European Jews in New York City (Lowenstein 1989:255–6, Soyer 1997) in some ways paralleled the relations in Berlin, Vienna, and elsewhere in Central Europe between German Jews and those who had arrived earlier on one hand, and the less assimilated *Ostjuden* on the other. The crucial difference was that (compared with New York City) the Central European cities proved to be much more of a melting pot of rapid assimilation for the Eastern European Jews. In other words, the ethnic principle for societal organization was much less dominant in Central Europe than it was in America. In New York, the Eastern European Jews established and maintained a thriving ethnic enclave that was much more typical for American Jewry than their counterparts (e.g., in the second district of Vienna) were for Central European Jewry.

Spanning decades and generations, an immigration tradition within an ethnic group typically created a mutually accepted (if sometimes grudgingly so) social hierarchy, in which the earlier immigrants served as the role models, guardians, and leaders of the later ones. But such a mutually accepted hierarchical relationship did not exist between the refugees from National Socialism and the previously arrived Eastern Jews. The two groups had differing models of social hierarchy in their minds, with neither group deferring to the other. This of course made for some friction.

For the new wave of German Jews, who in a considerable proportion came from cosmopolitan cities, the strong Yiddish element in the existing New York Jewish community seemed severely retrograde. "The Yiddish culture, which was of such great importance to the earlier Jewish immigrants from Eastern Europe, enabling them to create a cultural atmosphere of their own, is of no use to the Jewish refugees from Germany," commented Tartakower and Grossmann (1944:398).

Linguistically the distance between German and Yiddish is small.[38] Speakers of standard German might have less difficulty in understanding Yiddish than the Swiss-German dialects or the strong dialects of some other areas. Culturally and socially, however, a chasm separated German and Yiddish (each with its lively literature), and the German-speaking and Yiddish-speaking Jews (Lowenstein 1989:35). Most German-speaking Jews, who usually took great pride in the accomplishments of German *Kultur*, did not consider Yiddish their own language; and for those among them who had family roots in the East, it was often only an unwelcome reminder of an "unenlightened" past. One of our study participants, with slight amusement, made the point that he had to learn Yiddish in America.[39] Some American Jews of Eastern European extraction, by contrast, felt misgivings about the Central Europeans. "The age-old division between German and Eastern European Jews prevails to some extent in an intensified degree [in America], the former regarding themselves as a superior group and representing Western rather than Eastern culture. . . . On the other hand, some Polish and Russian Jews feel prejudice toward the German Jews because of their alleged mistreatment of Eastern Jews in the past and their unsympathetic attitude toward Palestine." (Davie 1947:389). Nonetheless, these initial frictions were usually relatively mild and could be overcome by those so inclined.

Discrimination

Becoming an American of Jewish descent—or simply being identified as a Jew by others—also carried potential problems for our group, especially that of being exposed to overt or covert anti-Semitism. Only about a third (31 percent) of the former refugees who replied to our questionnaire said they never experienced any discrimination, prejudice, or humiliation after arriving in the United States.[40] Nearly half (45 percent) said that instances of this kind had happened rarely to them, and 22 percent said they had experienced them from time to time. Two percent called them a frequent occurrence. Our group's reported experiences of anti-Semitism in the United States may of course have been colored by what they had gone through earlier on in Europe and during their migration. From those who said that they had experienced discrimination, we also inquired in what areas of life it had happened. Discrimination in social relations was mentioned most frequently (27 percent); other instances included discrimination in finding a job (18 percent), in school (18 percent), at work (17 percent), and in obtaining a place to live (7 percent).[41] A sizable group (22 percent) checked the "other" category, and one of the more typical explanations there referred to experiences in the United States military.

There were several potential sources of discrimination against the refugees. In addition to anti-Semitism, they might have been subject to antiforeigner or anti-immigrant sentiments. Moreover, the intricacies of Central European politics were lost on some Americans during war time, and it could happen that the status of being refugees was somehow mixed up with being Nazis, as in this example: "When in grade school, I was once called a 'dirty Nazi Jew' (a unique event—my brother and I were more amused than frightened)."[42] Or, "I was very much rejected by the children. . . . They called me Nazi because I'd come from Germany. . . . We were disdained by the community, too, sort of looked upon as 'those refugee children.' "

As to the most relevant origin of the experienced discrimination, anti-Semitism was named most frequently (69 percent). Anti-German sentiments (5 percent) and antiforeign feelings (5 percent) were mentioned much less often, and the other categories (racism, sexism) were checked by even smaller percentages. A sizeable group checked the "other" category that usually was explained as a mixture of the above-mentioned sources among which the respondents could not determine the most relevant one.

Progressive Arcadia

For obvious reasons, the Jewish ethnic option was typically not viable or attractive for the Christians among the refugees. But others, too, declined that option, and they often did so out of an allegiance to that old sociocultural formation, the Central European Jewish elite. This formation was exemplified by the famous refugees of the First Wave and has mostly vanished.[43] One of the Nobel Prize winners of our cohort, Jack Steinberger, recognized this fact without sentimentality, when he spoke of "this culture, which produced such men as Marx, Einstein, Freud, and Mahler and which is now extinct. Of course, there is nothing special about the extinction of cultures, this is their normal fate"(Steinberger 2005:4). Nonetheless, in our study of the Second Wave, we were still able to identify faint echoes and subtle traces. Thus, some members of the Second Wave could be considered the Last of the Mohicans, after an adventure story by James Fenimore Cooper mentioned several times as popular reading among our survey participants. They are the last of a disappearing culture.

Arcadia is the traditional name of a landlocked area in the middle of the Peloponnesian peninsula of Greece—a mountainous and rather bleak landscape where many of the population for millennia eked out a living as shepherds. In ancient Rome, spurred primarily by the pastoral poems of Virgil, Arcadia took on a symbolic meaning. It was transformed into a poetic dreamland, a mythical space, of peaceful and blissful living. When educated Romans spoke about Arcadia, this had nothing to do with the real Arcadia and the decidedly nonglamorous lifestyle of most of its real inhabitants; it was an utopian image of a rural paradise, channeling the dissatisfactions and angst of the turbulent times of the first century BC into an escapist fantasy world.

In their minds, many immigrants or refugees, arriving in America from all regions of the earth, transform the "old country" nostalgically into some kind of Arcadia. Though most early immigrants had come from poverty-stricken backward areas, after a while the memory of hardship receded and notions of beauty, simplicity, community, and morality prevailed. It was a vision of a backward and traditionalist state, but one cleansed of much of the unpleasantness realistically associated with it.

Yet, in most cases, that nostalgic Arcadia has a concrete reference point in space and in the present. Although it has also developed and changed to some extent, the "old country" usually of course still exists. There is a continual interchange of information and of people (e.g., of newly arriving immigrants), and this can enhance a feeling of belonging to, or being connected with a real counterpart of the nostalgically transfigured Arcadia of memory. But no such reference point existed for the refugees from Central Europe, young and old. Most of them were no exiles; for them, there simply was no "old country" one could to go home to.[44] Most felt that its sociocultural foundation had been irretrievably destroyed, and that the continuity had ruptured beyond repair. Their old social and political identity, as Germans or other Central Europeans, had also collapsed, under great trauma.

Yet some of them did not abandon Arcadia altogether for either complete Americanization or for becoming Jewish-American, but they clung to a special kind of it. From these refugees' viewpoint, their own Arcadia had no geographic coordinates; it was utopian in the literal sense. But it also was a "movable home," as one of our most distinguished interviewees put it. This "movable home" was made possible by a second, highly unusual feature: the radically modernist, or progressive, nature of those refugees' Arcadia. Because their ideals were universalistic, they could be easily transposed to a new environment. Along with a strong work ethic, this mind-set is certainly one of the causes for the relatively rapid socioeconomic integration of this refugee group (Strauss 1981:239). Still, this very Arcadia prevented them from becoming totally "Americanized" in their basic outlook. Within that outlook, one finds an "unstable equilibrium" (Strauss 1981:237) of German, Jewish, and American traits that will be interesting to explore among the younger generation.

The regular Arcadias typically satisfy refugees' emotional needs for tradition and connection to a simpler past.[45] But this did not apply to a sizable group among our refugees. Many immigrants from Central Europe came from a metropolitan setting; they did *not* come from a preindustrial community, nor did they idealize such a condition. For obvious reasons, they did not romanticize the Germanic premodern past, but they equally distanced themselves from any celebration of ancient Jewish roots and traditions. What is distinctive about their Arcadia is the deep commitment to a particular *Kultur*, paired with the expectation of high cultural achievement that had, for many of them, taken the place of religion. They did have another Arcadia, a radically modern Arcadia, an intellectual homeland defined by the landmarks of German *Kultur*—philosophy, music, poetry, science—in the grand synthetic tradition of the master intellectuals: a culture steeped in the ideals of Enlightenment, of universalism, cosmopolitanism, and emancipation. This Arcadia to which many of the refugees had their allegiance held the memories of a Golden Age that, in some regards, was more advanced than the present. It implied looking forward by looking back.

The Central European Jewish elite were assimilated to an extremely high degree, but assimilated to a particular kind of *Kultur*. They cleaved to the most fundamental and abstract core ideas of the Enlightenment version of *Kultur*—universalism and cosmopolitanism. They exhibited a fervent desire to attain *Bildung* (liberal arts education), a desire so strong that it laid the foundation of a *Bildungsreligion* for those secularists who had broken away from Judaism. This, rather than the more traditional layers of food, clothing, table manners, or folk festivals, was at the heart of German *Kultur* as most First Wave intellectuals understood it. The essence that remained for many First Wavers, as for the Second Wavers raised in that tradition, was a German *Kultur* without Germany, a reverence for ideas and ideals represented in the works of Bach, Goethe, Schiller, Schubert, and other cultural icons. This innermost of German *Kultur* contained nothing German (in the sense of the particularism of ethnic traditions) at all. That the very essence of German *Kultur*, as understood by them, was not German was a paradox appreciated by those intellectuals schooled in Hegelian figures of dialectical reason.

The relationship of the Central European Jewish intellectuals and the elite to actual *Kultur* was ambivalent, because, in addition to the elements that they loved, *Kultur* increasingly took on elements they abhorred (Mendes-Flohr 1999). By the mid-twentieth century, their ideal *Kultur* was as far removed from real-life German culture—with its growing emphasis on ethnicity, blood, and soil—as Virgil's Arcadia was from the actual region on the Peloponnese. In a sense, thus, the progressive Arcadia—as a counterimage to reality—had started to develop already before the cataclysm. That progressive Arcadia where many among the Jewish elite found a permanent homestead was impervious to the mutations in real German

Kultur. Despite, or because of, what they considered the barbaric degrada-
tion and mutilation of *Kultur* at the hands of the National Socialists and
their assorted intellectual allies, they unfalteringly clung to their Arcadian
Kultur, even after their forced exodus from Central Europe.

This also makes plausible the reason why those Second Wavers who had
adopted for themselves this Arcadia would blend so well into the universalist
strand of American culture, and why they would not revert to ethnic
options and ethnic politics of the regular kind. Even though they, as
individuals, would be recognized for their (sometimes extraordinary) contributions to society, they would be somewhat undetectable on the radar
screen of American ethnic politics. Thus, herein may lie a partial explanation
of their puzzling invisibility—that they would leave so little trace as an
ethnic group, but so much as an aggregation of individuals.

The immigrants of the First Wave who had an allegiance to the Arcadia
of *Kultur*, and some Second Wavers who followed in their footsteps, as we
shall see, were the very opposites of the "urban villagers" described by
Herbert Gans (1982). They can be called "rusticated urbanites," as if driven
from the metropolis to the provinces. To put it somewhat hyperbolically,
after the joy of arrival had worn off, New York City was barely tolerable;
everything else was absurdly backward. One of our participants who
together with his family had arrived in New York City recounted his
mother's despair at the prospect of leaving that city. "HIAS suggested that
life in the provinces might be a little bit easier. . . . So my mother cried
because we were going to this little dinky town, Baltimore. All her life
she had lived in Vienna, Prague, London, New York."

More than one-third (36 percent) of the survey respondents were born
in one of the two metropolises of Central Europe, in Vienna or in Berlin.
A higher percentage of these former refugees than of those with other birthplaces had fathers who had worked as professionals in Central Europe
(40 percent vs. 25 percent). This suggests, among the refugees, a substantial
representation of descendants of the metropolitan Jewish elite described
above, that is, those who were most likely to subscribe to the ideals of the
progressive Arcadia.

Identity Labels

In our study, we presented our participants with various collective identity
labels and asked them how strongly they identified with each of the listed
terms that applied to their situation.[46]

Of our participants, 71 percent said that they identified very strongly
with being American, and an additional 25 percent said they identified

strongly with that label. A Jewish identity was felt very strongly by 47 percent, and strongly by 26 percent, of our refugee group. About equal parts stated that they identified very strongly (34 percent) or strongly (35 percent) with their local community (e.g., Los Angeles). By contrast, few participants felt a strong or very strong identity with their former homelands. As to Germany, the largest part (60 percent) said they did not at all identify with it, and a third (35 percent) said they somewhat identified with it. As to Austria, a similar picture emerged: 69 percent did not at all identify themselves with it, and 24 percent reported that they somewhat identified with that label.

Interestingly, the European label was more popular. While only a third (34 percent) said they did not identify at all with it, half (49 percent) identified somewhat, and 16 percent identified strongly or very strongly with it. The European label, of course, is not tainted by the severe negative connotations that the former home countries doubtlessly carry for a huge fraction of the refugees. Choosing that label might be a way of acknowledging one's connection with some positive aspects of one's upbringing.

Many of the interviewees expressed feeling, to various degrees, an element of Europeanness in their identity. "Yes, I do feel different from other Americans, but I regard myself, I would say, 90% American and 10% Viennese and Austrian. And the Viennese and Austrian part is not a question of outlook; it's a question of culture." "Well, I think it's extremely important because I still see myself as a European who grew up in America. . . . I consider myself an American but my cultural heritage is definitely European." "I don't consider myself 100% American. I think . . . a large part of me in many ways is still European . . . tremendous respect for elderly people . . . good table manners. And I have cherished my background, my family, my ancestors, our life there." "Upbringing and values instilled in me from childhood have stayed with me in spite of living in the US for 65 years. In my heart, I have remained a European."[47]

There were some gender differences: Women, as a group, identified less strongly than men with the American label, but more strongly with the Jewish label and the local community label. Furthermore, the intensity of American and local identities correlated with each other ($r = .35$), and the American identity was similarly related to the Jewish identity ($r = .20$). The latter correlation may correspond to the cultural pattern of being an ethnic American, with high loyalty to both the United States and the ethnicity. In some cases, the circumstances of expulsion tended to create a vacuum in terms of nationality, and conversely to heighten the salience of ethnicity. Thus, for some refugees, Jewishness could replace the nationality vacuum, and those immigrants could fit themselves into the American structure of hyphenated immigrant communities with the familiar dual allegiance. On the other hand, the cosmopolitan orientation of those having allegiance to the progressive Arcadia described above may also be reflected in that correlation (slightly reducing both American and Jewish identifications). Christian identity correlated with German ($r = .42$) and Austrian ($r = .40$) identities; that is, those respondents who identified strongly as Christians were likely also to identify strongly as Germans or Austrians.

The strength of the American identification was negatively related to the culture index score (i.e., to the extent of European cultural remnants; $r = -.18$). As one might expect, German ($r = .21$), Austrian ($r = .21$), and European ($r = .39$) identities correlated positively with the culture index. The more extensive the cultural remnants were, the stronger did the participants identify with those labels.

We posed the identity question also in a different format, by asking the participants to choose the one term from an array of terms that they prefer for describing themselves.[48] The label American was picked by about half (49 percent), and Jewish-American was second (26 percent). Nine percent preferred a triple descriptor—German-Jewish-American or Austrian-Jewish-American. Other possible labels (e.g., Jewish [4 percent] or German/Austrian-American [2 percent]) were chosen infrequently.[49] Again, women were less likely than men to choose American and more likely to choose Jewish-American as their preferred identity label.

The interpretation of these results gains from comparing them with a more recent study of the ethnic self-identification of eighth and ninth graders in California and Florida who were either immigrants or children of immigrants (Rumbaut 1994).[50] Only 11 percent in this group identified as American, whereas 40 percent identified with a hyphenated-American identity, 21 percent chose a pan-ethnic identification, and 27 percent identified with their national or ethnic origin. Among the foreign-born participants of that study (i.e., a subgroup that more precisely matches our cohort of young refugees), only 3 percent identified as American, 32 percent preferred a hyphenated-American identity, 22 percent chose a pan-ethnic identification, and 43 percent identified with their national or ethnic origin. In light of these results for a group of current immigrants, the so much higher—though not complete—degree of assimilation, in terms of identity, among our group of immigrants appears remarkable indeed.

Let us now briefly summarize some defining features of the former refugees' American identity: The underlying constitutional and political structure of American society was universally lauded. The participants said they dearly cherished the democracy, rule of law, freedom, and opportunity available in the United States, especially in view of what they had been through before they arrived. Despite this overwhelmingly positive notion, we also found two critical themes, one concerning specific U.S. administrations and their actions, the other being more general criticism of American culture. (Here again the Central European cultural remnants asserted themselves.)

Culture Remnants, Attitudes, and Identity

We now asked how the former refugees' self-rated traits were related to the extent of the cultural remnants and to the intensity of the European identity they reported. For an answer, we looked at the correlation of the traits with our two composite indicators for cultural remnants and for European identity. As one might expect, the reported extent of cultural remnants correlated extensively with the traits, with 26 of the 39 traits to be precise. The strongest correlations were on traits that most directly reflected a certain elite view of European culture, as described by our participants in that survey section: interested in the arts ($r = .19$), listen to classical music ($r = .14$), as well as like to write ($r = .13$). Fewer significant correlations were found between our indicator of European identity and the traits (13 of 39 traits). The strongest correlations here were again with being interested in the arts ($r = .18$) as well as with being serious with close friends ($r = .16$), like to play music ($r = .16$) and like to write ($r = .15$).

In addition, we correlated our composite traits with culture retention and the identity variables. Not surprisingly, the traits summarized under "high culture" correlated positively with the extent of cultural remnants from Europe that our participants reported ($r = .21$), whereas the "popular culture" traits correlated negatively ($r = -.13$). The composite trait "popular culture" also correlated with the strength of American identity ($r = .22$), local identity ($r = .26$), Jewish identity ($r = .22$), and German identity ($r = .14$). "High culture" had a slight negative correlation with Jewish identity ($r = -.10$), as well as slight positive correlations with German ($r = .11$) and Austrian ($r = .12$) identities, and a stronger positive correlation with European identity ($r = .23$).

Culture retention and identity themselves were also connected in obvious ways. The reported strength of European identity ($r = .39$), German identity ($r = .21$), and Austrian identity ($r = .21$) all correlated with the extent of reported cultural retention, whereas the strength of American identity correlated negatively ($r = -.18$). The frequency of returns to the homeland also had the expected association with the extent of cultural retention ($r = .21$).

The stronger a contact the participants maintained with fellow refugees, the stronger was their Jewish identity ($r = .18$), and the weaker was their

Christian identity (r = −.19). The same pattern was found for the relationship between membership in refugee organizations and religious identities (r = .15 for Jewish identity; r = −.15 for Christian identity). This, in a sense, illustrates that the refugee organizations are part of the ethnic option. They foster their members' Jewishness and are an environment in which those former refugees with a strong Jewish identification congregate, whereas others with a strong self-reported Christian identification—who, of course, were in the minority among the refugees we studied (7 percent)—might feel marginalized.

Both gender and socioeconomic position were found to influence the participants' propensities to identify with their culture of origin and with certain collective identities.[51] Turning first to gender, the women, as noted, were more likely than the men to self-identify as "Jewish-American" and less likely to self-identify as "American." The following results support the emerging picture of our female former refugees, as a group, tending toward the ethnic option (in comparison with the males) and also retaining more of the culture of their origin. The women reported that they retained more European culture (3.2 vs. 2.8), had a slightly weaker American identity (2.6 vs. 2.7), a stronger local identity (2.1 vs. 1.9), a stronger Jewish identity (2.3 vs. 2.0), and a stronger European identity (1.0 vs. 0.8).

As to socioeconomic position, we formed a dichotomous distinction between professionals and everybody else and found that the professionals retained a larger amount of European cultural elements (3.1 vs. 2.8). More specifically, this difference is concentrated in the areas of tastes and preferences (54 percent vs. 47 percent) and cultural interests (63 percent vs. 52 percent). The professionals among the former refugees showed a lower interest in popular culture (3.2 vs. 3.6, on a scale from 1 to 7) and a stronger interest in high culture (4.7 vs. 4.3), but they also showed a lower interest in social activism (3.8 vs. 4.2). They further reported lower levels of work ethics, social activism, and religiousness, and a higher level of life satisfaction.

We also found that the professionals had a higher composite identity (7.5 vs. 7.1).[52] That higher composite score was due to elevated levels on the peripheral identities, whereas they actually identified slightly less with America than did the nonprofessionals (2.6 vs. 2.7), less with their local community (1.9 vs. 2.1), and less with their Jewishness (2.0 vs. 2.3). By contrast, they identified slightly more strongly with Austria (0.4 vs. 0.3) and with Europe (0.9 vs. 0.7). This pattern is borne out by their stronger identification with a European composite (1.3 vs. 1.0).[53]

It is necessary to look at gender here, because the professional category contains predominantly men, and some of the observed differences might go away once controlling for gender. We therefore estimated ANOVA models for each of the variables on which the above differences were found under the inclusion of the gender variable and an interaction term between gender and professional status. The previously observed differences were confirmed concerning culture retention, the strength of collective identity, European identity, life satisfaction, popular culture, high culture, and religiousness. As to work ethic, an interaction of professional status with gender was evident. Among the nonprofessionals, the work ethic was stronger among the men than among the women, whereas among the professionals, the means for men and women were about even.[54] An interaction was also found on social activism: Among the nonprofessionals, the men had a higher level than did the women, whereas the reverse was the case among the professionals.

A key result in terms of identity was that, when asked about the preferred identity label, 55 percent of the professionals, 48 percent of the managers, but only 30 percent of the participants working in the "other" category chose "American." By contrast, only 21 percent of the professionals, 25 percent of the managers, but 42 percent of the "others" chose "Jewish-American." Apparently, the professionals, as a group, preferred a national outlook to that of their ethnic group, whereas the opposite was the case for the participants in the "other" occupational category. At the same time, the professionals' actual attachment to the American identity was slightly weaker (as shown above) than that of the "others," but their attachment was considerably weaker for the Jewish identification—again signaling their tendency to espouse the "progressive Arcadia."

In a somewhat different context, J. W. Berry (1990) distinguished four types of acculturation that fit in a two-by-two table: integration, assimilation, separation, and marginalization. It seems useful to adapt this typology for our purposes, defining one dimension of the table as the strength of American identity (high/low), and defining the second dimension analogously as the strength of Jewish identity (high/low) (table 5.5).[55]

Table 5.5 Two-By-Two Table of American and Jewish Identities

Jewish Identity	American Identity	
	High	Low
High	Integration 70%	Separation 2.5%
Low	Assimilation 25%	Marginalization 2.4%
N = 1407		

Glancing at the table, it becomes immediately apparent that a low American identity is very rare among our group of former refugees. Virtually all identify as Americans, and neither "separation" nor "marginalization" occurred to any considerable extent. The majority also has a strong Jewish identity (70 percent) and thus appears in the "integration" category, but there was a sizeable minority (25 percent) in the "assimilation" category, characterized by high American and low Jewish identity.

These categories were found to be related to occupational status, underscoring our previous findings. Among the nonprofessionals with high American identity, 81 percent were in the "integration" category, but only 67 percent of the professionals with high American identity were in that category.

All these results combine to present a fairly consistent picture: In terms of their outlook, the professionals among the Second Wavers tend to be more aligned with the old Jewish Central European elite and with the progressive Arcadia. As we shall discuss below in greater detail, the professionals among the Second Wavers were particularly likely to have had a father who had also been a professional in Europe. Moreover, even statistically controlling for the Second Waver's own professional status, the father's professional status in Europe was found to an additional effect on the Second Waver's outlook.

The picture thus gains sharper contours when one looks at the *father's* occupational status. Those Second Wavers with a father who, in Europe, had worked in one of the professions—in other words, a member of the *Bildungsbürgertum*—reported a higher level of cultural retention, on average (3.3 vs. 2.9) than did the Second Wavers whose fathers had worked outside the professions. Interestingly, six out of the seven individual aspects of European culture showed a significantly elevated level for the refugees with a father who had been a professional in Central Europe.

In terms of composite traits, the Second Wavers whose father had been a professional, showed less interest in popular culture (3.1 vs. 3.4), more interest in high culture (4.7 vs. 4.5), and lower levels of work ethic (5.2 vs. 5.4) and social activism (3.8 vs. 4.1), compared with Second Wavers who did not have a professional as a father. The direction of the difference in work ethic is certainly intriguing. One might speculate that the work focus—that was still very high, of course (5.2)—was somewhat tempered by another inheritance from the *Bildungsbürgertum*, by broader interests in *Kultur* and Bildung and by what one might perhaps call a lifestyle oriented toward the good and valuable things in life. This lifestyle may also have tended to keep them aloof from certain forms of community activism.

In terms of collective identities, the Second Wavers whose fathers had been professionals, on average, had a somewhat weaker American identification (2.6 vs. 2.7) and a considerably weaker Jewish identification (1.8 vs. 2.2). However, their European identity, on average, was stronger (1.0 vs. 0.8), as was, at a generally very low level, their German identity (0.6 vs. 0.5) and their Christian identity (0.5 vs. 0.3).

Finally, returning to the two-by-two identity types discussed above, among the Second Wavers with high American identity who had a professional as a father, 61 percent were in the "integration" category. This percentage was considerable lower than the corresponding percentage (78%) for the Second Wavers with high American identity whose father had not been a professional.

Now, in this last series of statistics, we finally touch, through the characteristics of those Second Wavers, the cultural soil—the "father lode"—of the Jewish *Bildungsbürgertum*, and the melody of that old sociocultural formation comes through louder and clearer. Their cultural sensitivities have been shown to resonate in the attitudes and traits of a certain group of Second Wavers. Here we have identified traces of some deep-seated characteristics that were imparted to many Second Wavers in their youth by a father (and, by extension, by a family) committed to certain ideals of *Kultur* and that endured, in some diminished form and not for everybody of course, but still in a statistically measurable way.

Chapter 6

Ingredients of Success

Having provided ample documentation for the socioeconomic success of the young refugees, as a group, we now turn to examining some of its possible causes. In particular, we are going to explore the idea that their cultural heritage (as well as their austere experiences during their youth) might have actually helped the former refugees thrive in the United States, in short, that they might have enjoyed a distinctiveness advantage.

We should emphasize again that, at the most basic level, we conceptualize the young refugees' outcomes as the interplay of their early socialization and experiences with the opportunity structure they encountered in the United States.

General Conditions

We start with broad factors that benefited the U.S. population of that age group generally. These factors need to be mentioned because they contributed to the former refugees' socioeconomic outcomes and, in some cases, may have been their necessary preconditions; but, by their very nature, they are not sufficient explanations for the unusually high level of the former refugees' career success.

After the Great Depression, the American economy slowly recovered and moved into an expansive phase. Starting with World War II and in the years following, the economy had been booming, and so the former refugees who were looking for jobs or seeking advancement had at that time great prospects for successful careers, just as the other Americans of a comparable age. Some of the fields to which many former refugees were attracted experienced a particularly strong expansion, for instance, science and higher education in general. Our group thus benefited from a generally favorable climate in the economy and in the labor market, as well as from the expansion in specific sectors.

A functioning system of public education made it possible for children and young people of financially disadvantaged backgrounds to attain high levels of education as a stepping-stone for successful careers. The following reported memory stood out because it was so atypical. "And the school experience was awful. It was a real slum high school, and so I didn't want to go there anymore. I wasn't learning anything, and it was just a nightmare, and there were bullies around, and I was always getting in fights with bullies in my school years. I was always defending the underdog." But in most cases, the young refugees received decent schooling. As many of them spent their youth in New York City, that city's educational system was pivotal for the educational careers of the young refugees, as a cohort. Some were able to go to prestigious public schools, such as the Bronx High School of Science and Stuyvesant High School. Many went to Washington High School in Washington Heights, where they usually did well. New York City also had excellent public institutions of higher education, such as the City University and Hunter College that were popular choices for former refugees to attend after high school. Others were able to go to first-rate private institutions, often on scholarships.

In this context, several of our participants mentioned the G.I. Bill, providing a college education to all who had served on war duty from December 1941. Military service and its consequences were of significance for many men of our cohort. As noted earlier, of the men who responded to our survey, 52 percent reported they served in the U.S. armed forces in World War II (2 percent of the women did). Military service could be considered one of the factors eventually contributing to the socioeconomic success of this group of young refugees (especially, of course, for the men among them), as it probably could be for initially deprived native-born Americans The cornerstone of such an argument is likely to be that military service allowed the veterans to take advantage of the G.I. Bill, which opened the door to the higher-level occupations that require a college education. Additional arguments might be that military service provided speedy access to citizenship; that the veteran status furthered one's career as it conveyed a positive image and conferred prestige that helped to counteract potential prejudices against immigrants or Jews; that the military provided a thorough socialization into American culture[1]; that the military enabled the soldiers to make contacts and form networks that later on might have proved valuable for their careers; and that it may have helped some to mature faster.

Surprisingly, however—even though the G.I. Bill was frequently acknowledged as a crucial advantage that made higher education possible for individual participants—we found no straightforward "G.I. Bill effect." The situation turned out to be more complex than it seemed first. Both veterans and non-veterans in our cohort of former refugees certainly had very high educational achievements, on average, but looking at a contingency table of education versus military service among our male participants, we found that *fewer* of the veterans than of the nonveterans eventually went to college[2]: Among the veterans, 26 percent had only high school or less, whereas, among those who did not serve, that percentage was only 18. As one might expect, birth year was a strong predictor of military service. Among those born between 1918 and 1924, slightly more than two-thirds, 68 percent fought in the military during World War II, whereas those at the younger end of our cohort were not old enough to participate. But even looking at the relationship between educational achievement and military service separately by age cohorts, no educational advantage was visible for our veterans.

One might consider here that some of those who did not serve in the military did not join *because* they were already pursuing their higher education and/or other advanced training (in some cases, especially among scientists, in support of the war effort). To a small part, the absence of a straightforward GI Bill effect might also be explained by a slight difference in socioeconomic background between veterans and nonveterans[3]: The veterans were more likely to have a father who had been neither a professional nor a manager (in Europe) (34 percent vs. 28 percent), and they were less likely to have a father who was a professional (29 percent vs. 37 percent). Here two common patterns combine: Traditionally, the troops in wars are predominantly from the lower classes, and individuals of a lower class background are typically less prone to attain higher education. Even controlling for the father's socioeconomic status, the educational achievements were higher, on average, for nonveterans than for veterans. (This is especially astonishing for young refugees from a nonprofessional and nonmanagerial background, where one would expect the G.I. Bill to be a particularly valuable opportunity that would be reflected in a higher percentage of veterans than of nonveterans from that group to go to college.)

Although there was no close link between veteran status and higher education, we did find that, controlling for other factors (such as, first of all, gender, but also father's occupation, the ancestors' socioeconomic background, and own age at arrival), the odds for ending up in an occupation within the professional or managerial classifications were 1.9 times as great for those who had served in the military during World War II as for those who had not served.[4] As one might expect from the preceding discussion, this advantage was more specifically attributable to the managerial, and not to the professional careers. The veterans' odds of becoming managers, as opposed to having a nonprofessional and nonmanagerial occupation, were 2.8 times as great as the nonveterans' odds. To sum up, the benefits of serving in the military in World War II, at the aggregate level lay less in receiving a higher education through the G.I. Bill, but in reaping the benefits of other advantages (such as those described above) for one's occupational career, especially in terms of obtaining managerial positions.

Distinctiveness Advantage and Cultural Capital

We have documented that the former refugees were very socioeconomically successful, as a group, and we have also seen that they retained elements of their Central European background. Apparently, full cultural assimilation was not a necessary precondition of our group's socioeconomic success. Yet there is a stronger case now to be made—that the refugees, on average, benefited from their distinctiveness, that they garnered, what we call a "distinctiveness advantage."

In this discussion, the theoretical concept of "cultural capital" will be central and will prove useful in understanding the young refugees' life trajectories. In everyday language, as well in the language of the economists, capital is virtually synonymous with financial or economic capital, or money. Having a lot of money is obviously valuable for one's position in life and society, that is, one's social status. Social scientists, however, have also considered additional types of capital that similarly exert an influence on a person's life chances and circumstances. As described by Pierre Bourdieu (1983), cultural capital is one form of capital next to social capital and economic capital. Social capital describes the resources that are tied to a relationship network of mutual acquaintance and recognition.[5] Cultural capital, which we examine in the following section in greater detail, is subdivided into three types: the embodied state, the objectified state, and the institutionalized state.

Typology of Cultural Capital

The *embodied state* of cultural capital consists of long-lasting dispositions of the mind and body. Here we can count the deportment, values, and expected behaviors that the young refugees imbibed in their early years from their families and the surrounding environment. Within a society, the most salient aspect of cultural capital is that of supporting a social hierarchy—separating the "haves" from the "have-nots." In an immigration situation, however, cultural capital that permeates the whole society from which the immigrants come also takes on an important role. Embodied cultural capital is something nobody could take away from the refugees (unlike economic capital), and that they took with them to wherever they went. For instance, certain educational strategies of the family, placing extraordinarily strong value in education, were likely to convey the disposition of *libido sciendi*—the yearning for learning. A disposition of this kind is much more general than the acquisition of specific job-related skills and knowledge, and thus wider than the notion of human capital that one occasionally hears. Nonetheless, concrete advantages in knowledge and skills were, of course, also part of the embodied variety of cultural capital. Several participants used the word "ridiculous"—in the sense of ridiculously easy—when describing their high school experience in the United States.

The *objectified state* of cultural capital takes the form of cultural goods, such as books, instruments, machines, and so on. Typically, the young refugees, many limited to one suitcase, could take some choice items of it with them—some favorite books, their stamp collection, and so on—but most of it was left behind.

The *institutionalized state* of cultural capital provides legal credentials and qualifications. These are degrees, licenses, and so forth. On the bearer, they convey the halo of officially recognized cultural capital that does not have to prove itself, but is generally acknowledged. Our group of refugees was typically too young to have accumulated any institutionalized cultural capital of importance. Their cultural capital was almost exclusively of the embodied type.

By contrast, the institutionalized cultural capital was where many in the *parent* generation of the refugees (if they had the luck to escape from Europe) took a painful hit in the United States, a hit that to some was perhaps more demoralizing than the loss of economic capital. Not only was the loss of cultural capital an obstacle on their path toward regaining economic capital (e.g., by practicing their old profession in the new country), but it also devastated their social status directly. Respected professionals and pillars of the community from Berlin, Frankfurt, or Vienna, for instance, found their diplomas and skills obsolete, and they were forced by the necessities of refugee life to work in jobs that many of them considered demeaning. As pointed out, this fate was particularly prevalent among the lawyers, whose expertise was worthless in a country with a legal system very different from the one they were trained in. We have heard stories of groups of adult immigrants who carefully kept addressing each other with the titles that meant so much to them because they symbolized a central source of their self-worth: "Herr Doktor, Herr Direktor, Herr Rechtsanwalt," and so forth. In their immigrant circles, they tried to keep alive the universe of social distinction that had little validity in their new environment. The academics had the most advantageous position, because their institutionalized cultural capital (e.g., doctoral degrees) most easily converted into that of the new country and could, in principle, be harnessed into teaching positions at universities or research positions in industry.

Social Capital

It is an old story of immigration into the United States (as well as elsewhere) that new arrivals often try to take advantage of social capital manifested in ethnic networks. New arrivals may be able to mobilize assistance, advice, and also economic capital from more established people to whom they are tied by ethnic origin. Recent work on immigration has emphasized the major role that such networks play in helping immigrants settle in the new country, find a way to make a living, and even thrive.

Sociologists of immigration have long focused on the ethnic niches in which newly arrived immigrants cluster that make available crucial social capital for their settling into the new country. The prevailing opinion among those scholars ascribed two characteristic features to the ethnic niches: First, their existence was considered to be a temporary phenomenon that would fade away as immigrants became more established; and second they were thought to be populated predominantly by immigrants with no or few skills. Newer research, in direct contradiction to this opinion, has found that those niches are more permanent in nature and that relatively high-skilled immigrants also use them (Waldinger and Der-Martirosian 2001). This suggests that social capital, as produced by ethnic networks, has an even more important role in the process of immigration than previously thought. Our group of young refugees provides a case example by which to study the existence and impact of ethnic social networks among high-skilled immigrants. We will particularly focus on how some of our Second Wave young refugees profited from the First Wave of adult refugees.

Ecology of Capital

Often, different types of capital go together, and they can be converted from one to the other. Those with a lot of financial capital also tend to have a lot of cultural and social capital. Also important is the fact that all forms of capital can be passed down to one's offspring, although the modalities differ for the respective forms. Money and economic capital, in general, can be most easily transferred by gift or by inheritance (although, in many cases, the government might appropriate some portion in the form of gift or estate taxes). The transfer of other forms of capital requires a more active cooperation and some effort on the recipient's part. Nonetheless, rich people can mightily facilitate that process, for instance by sending their children to the best private schools and by making beneficial connections for them as well.

Our group of refugees is sociologically interesting because here the various types of capital became disentangled to an unusually high degree. In Central Europe, the adults who later were to be persecuted had accumulated high amounts of all three types of capital, on average. As a rule, however, those adults who came as refugees with their families could not pass down their financial capital to their children; they were lucky to have escaped the National Socialists with their lives. And, of course, those who perished in the Holocaust were also unable to transmit their wealth to children who had escaped. For researchers, this dire situation provides a strategic research site for studying *the "pure" transfer of cultural capital in the absence of economic capital*, and for examining to what extent cultural capital helped the refugee children to succeed socioeconomically—in a sense, to regain the position that their parents had lost in a singular catastrophe or a traumatic spiral of downward mobility.

Gender Roles—Class Roles

In Marxist and allied theories, class is often conceived as a purely economic position that is defined, formally speaking, by one's relationship to the means of production; or, more informally, by the amount of one's money (economic capital). According to such a scheme, the young refugees typically experienced a drastic decline, because their families' money was in most cases lost (or, if they arrived alone, as a substantial fraction of youngsters did, they brought little, if anything, of monetary value). What then enabled them to be so successful, as a group, in reclaiming, or even exceeding, their families' former elevated socioeconomic statuses? An economic explanation is clearly insufficient here.

Sociologists of gender commonly speak of *gender roles* that embody deeply engrained cultural values and norms about what it means to be a man and how a man is supposed to act, and what it means to be a woman and how a woman is supposed to act. It may be useful for our understanding of the young refugees' collective career trajectories to use an analogous, but much less common concept, that of *class roles*, with the purpose of moving from an economic toward a cultural conceptualization of class.[6] The class role consists of an individual's generalized outlook and dispositions—or "habitus" (Bourdieu 1990)—as well as his or her goals, aspirations, deportment, and expected behaviors that have been shaped by the person's social position and environment. That class role is closely connected to cultural capital. On one hand, the acquisition, preservation, and transmission of specific forms of embodied cultural capital was an essential element—a core normative requirement—of the class role prevalent in the Central European middle and upper-middle classes where most of our participants grew up. On the other hand, one might even consider the class role itself, as transmitted through early socialization, a key piece of cultural capital.

Pseudoaristocratic Impulse

As Peter Hall (2001) pointed out, being from a "good family" was a vital part of the class role prevalent among the Jewish professional class in Vienna, and this was doubtlessly true also for the other regions of Central Europe (and, of course, for upper-middle and upper class non-Jewish families).[7] The embodied cultural capital that was transmitted to many members of the cohort under study thus contained what might be termed a pseudoaristocratic impulse concerning the multigenerational standing of the family. Many of those young refugees tried to live up to a central aspect of their class role: to make up for the setback suffered by the parents, and to reclaim the family's rightful status so that eventually economic capital and outside recognition could again be brought in line with their class roles. There was often enormous pressure—subliminal or even explicit—from the parental generation that sent their children on a mission of vindication. As one of our participants put it, "There were well-defined family pressures that left me with the responsibility to recover the 'standing' of our family." The aristocratic flavor of this attitude is directly captured in the following quote: "My father gave me a couple of books . . . and one was *The Prince and the Pauper*. And I knew about that story because I thought of myself as the Prince. Temporarily financially embarrassed, but someday I would get even."

Here are a few more quotes to illustrate this crucial point. "In Europe the family had a maid for the children and a cook for the household. In the US, we lived in a third-floor apartment and had no domestic help. . . . this created family pressure for me to succeed re: status, finances." Another one said, "I was determined—hell or high water—to obtain an education, equivalent or nearly so to what I would have obtained in Vienna." And,

"My European parents' expectations probably pushed me to higher goals." One may speculate that, for many of the children who arrived alone and lost their families, there was an equivalent "virtual" pressure to reassert the class standing of the family before its destruction.

This pseudoaristocratic impulse differs from the more individualistic generic American dream of success. It is not about an individual's "rags to riches" improvement and accomplishment; it is about preserving a family status, or about reclaiming it after a setback.

Cultural Capital of the Same Currency

The Central European lawyers who arrived in the United States were the classical case for the nonconvertibility of cultural capital: their skills and certificates were simply worthless in the new country. In a more generalized sense, however, the Central European currency of cultural capital was recognized also in America. The academic, intellectual, artistic, and scientific fields were to some extent modeled after the Central European core concept of *Bildung*. Whereas, in many cases, the culture of immigrants tends to be devalued in America as premodern, irrelevant, or even inferior, there were varying degrees of respect for the Central European *Kultur* in America. At that very basic level, the cultural capital possessed by the refugees was recognized (although, as we shall see, there were differences between Central European and American cultural styles).

In the following sections, we will describe some of the different ways in which many refugees made use of their cultural capital, and we then will explore more specifically to what extent that cultural capital was passed down across the chasm of flight and immigration.

Career Choice and Career Success

The notion of the distinctiveness advantage of the former refugees as a group was overwhelmingly supported by the material we collected. As mentioned, the majority of our survey participants thought that their early upbringing in Europe influenced their later life "decisively" (9 percent), "strongly" (22 percent), or "considerably" (37 percent), whereas only 3 percent responded with "not at all."[8] A similar picture emerged in answer to the question as to how strongly the experience leading up to and during the migration influenced their later life. Here, 63 percent of the participants said "decisively," "strongly," or "considerably."[9] A large majority (87 percent) agreed with the statement that their immigrant group *in general* blended European and American characteristics in a way that was conducive to great success. A slightly smaller, but still sizable majority (81 percent) agreed that this statement was true *in their special case.*[10] Numerous comments offered by our interviewees, and presented in the following section, illustrate this important point and bolster the theoretical argument about cultural capital.

Central European Cultural Capital

To start with, here is a selection of quotes from different participants, drawn from our rich material of interview responses in our database, which indicates in their own reports the belief in the mainly positive role of the Central European cultural capital in the former refugees' career success:

A foreign service officer explained, "My European upbringing fostered a strong interest in the lifestyles and goals of individuals living outside the U.S. Hence the desire to enter the Foreign Service."

An art historian recalled, "Very early, I frequented museums. I think my family background predestined me to an interest in such things as literature, music, and the study of history without coercion or pressure—these things simply seemed to be interesting. . . . I was conditioned by my background" to choose art history. And another art historian made a very similar point. "Well, the choice of art history—interest in art—certainly is due to my mother, who was so interested in art, who'd take me . . . to exhibitions. And, you know, we had original works of art in the house . . . and she had lots of art books among this collection of many, many books, so that art was something that she introduced to my life and my interest and to which I responded. I mean, some of my favorite books in my teenage years were illustrated books of Renaissance Italy and things like that. . . . Then I think it did help greatly that I knew German, and that I knew French, and a little bit of Italian, and so forth . . . that helped a great deal."

A translator explained, "[My European background] helped me very much in my career. I had the language, and basically I'm interested in intercontinental philosophy, but mostly general philosophy—Kant to the present. And in that respect, of course, it was very helpful to me. Also the discipline, study discipline, and just the hard intellectual work that I learned in school very early taught me very much the ability to concentrate."

Further examples from our interviews and questionnaires allow us to illustrate and explain these influences further and in vivid detail (extensively drawing on the participants' own words). These responses again show that early cultural formations were, in many cases, used advantageously as cultural capital.

The following themes could be discerned. To begin with, many participants praised the values that were imparted to them by their family from early on in life, values such as "punctuality, respect for authority, reliability, intense hard work," as one participant put is, as well as discipline, perseverance, dedication, and responsibility. In short, these were values and traits that are commonly associated with socioeconomic success all over the world, but many participants felt that they were exposed to them to a particularly high extent.

Here are two more quotes—chosen from many of this sort—illustrating this theme. ". . . setting goals and being orderly and planning . . . you know the Germans are very orderly. . . . I think that's part of the genes, part of the heritage, part of the gene pool. And so I think setting goals has always been part of my makeup, and that has had, I think, an impact on my success."— "I think in my old age, I recognize some of the rigidities, that side of me, and I think that's where they come from. The thing is, you've got to be on time, you've got to do your duty. . . . You don't do things sloppily and get away with it. And I take that stuff seriously! I'm quite convinced that it has to do with this Germanic upbringing."

Nonetheless, a few critical voices about their early upbringing could also be heard, for instance about the authoritarian parenting and schooling styles prevalent in Central Europe at the time. For instance, "I became a parent educator because I didn't like the German authoritarian upbringing I had and didn't want to repeat it with my children." Or, "I think that my upbringing was something to kick against and therefore had an indirect and adverse influence on my success (Whatever I succeeded at then and succeeded at presently was and is in spite of my upbringing and experience.)"

Some participants felt that those cultural differences held them back in some ways. For instance, "I think I'm different in the sense that I am more demanding. I demand perfection of myself, and I demand near perfection of those that I'm associated with, which doesn't always go over too well in this country most of the time. But that's why I don't have very many collaborators."

Another type of negative influences of European values that some of our participants mentioned concerned what they considered a lower level of self-centeredness or aggression in Europe. "The European influence prevented me from having broad career choices. . . . It limited my success because I was not as self-centered or egotistical as most Americans. Also, I believed loyalty to my employers would be repaid with commensurate advancement."

A second and related theme was the influence of German culture that in addition to emphasizing the above-mentioned values to a particularly high extent put a premium on broad intellectual interests and the idea of

Bildung. In comparison with American pragmatism, the Central European tendency traditionally was to reason from principle, to look at the big picture, and to cultivate a comprehensive worldview (*Weltanschauung*).

"[Father] was much more educated than I am in terms of the classical sense, history, in terms of philosophy. . . . So my parents gave me that. And he [also gave me] an appreciation of classical music. And those were three incredible gifts." Or, "When I think back, I think about the landscape. . . . I think there was a certain amount of culture that became part of me and has not left me, you know, that might be in my taste in literature or in music or even in art. You know, even as a child I had relatives and I used to go to museums. . . . All of that was very important."

"From my earliest age, I was exposed to classical music. Instead of lulla-bies, my mother sang opera to me. I was also introduced at age 4 to litera-ture when I taught myself how to read. Art entered my life soon after. . . . There must be more [European influence on me] than I am aware of since, as I found out recently, our children called our home 'Vienna on the Connecticut.' "

The importance of taking a broad and principled view of life was emphasized time and again as a cultural heritage. Here are several represen-tative quotes: "It influenced my desire and attitude to understand basic principles, and be disciplined in pursuing my endeavors."—"It gave me a broader outlook, allowing me to consider more than one aspect of problems & tasks."—"Excellent broad education, exposure to arts, theatre, books, sci-ence and engineering."—"My horizons tended to be broader than those of others, and my knowledge of German, French and Scandinavian literature, drama and music, widened the field of my knowledge and competence."— "A general education and an enthusiastic interest in everything instead becoming over-specialized."

Even some natural scientists said that traces of Central European her-itage manifested themselves in their stronger interest in broad, fundamental questions and their greater reluctance to specialize, as compared with their American colleagues. A few participants said that this viewpoint might actually have disadvantaged them in the short run (e.g., "It may have hurt to some small extent since I was brought up to have broad interests."), although it paid off in the long run. An astronomer commented: "Initially, my European upbringing was a hindrance. I was always seeking to find insight into larger questions, while American colleagues emphasized spe-cialization on US institutions and ways of life. Sabbaticals abroad were seen as frivolous, and I regularly lost research grants because of such absences. Later, when big science became a necessity and international collaboration was the only way to success, my knowledge of languages, cultures, insight into foreign governmental institutions and priorities finally paid off."

Third, as already indicated, many participants mentioned the superior quality of the schooling they had received in Germany or Austria. Secondary education in those countries was much more hierarchical than the American system, and its top tier (the *Gymnasien*) to which students were admitted only after thorough examinations provided an education that was typically perceived as much more challenging than what the young refugees encountered in American high schools. (Graduates from the *Gymnasien* routinely received advancement at the college level in the United States.) One of the former refugees stated, "High school [in Europe] was very strong in mathematics, physics, chemistry." Another one, "I went to an elite high school in Vienna (I still have some friends from then). I always felt that I received an excellent education in those 3 years before I left."

Moreover, the former refugees enjoyed other, obvious advantages in terms of cultural capital in the most general sense, advantages stemming from the fact that they had grown up in Central Europe and thus had acquired a high cultural competency for that region. Here we talk about cultural capital that essentially was attached to a national population as a whole. Most young refugees were, as a matter of course, familiar with the German language, German culture, and customs. Some of the participants made direct use of this capital by becoming translators, language teachers, and military personnel in Central Europe during and after the war, business people dealing with the European markets, or scholars on European history or politics, or similar disciplines. In the United States, some of the most distinguished scholars of Central Europe are Second Wavers who have taken the cultural capital stemming from their origins and, through their interest, talent, and hard work, have multiplied it enormously. One might immediately think of Fritz Stern and Peter Gay, but the list is copious. Most of them drew major lessons about human nature and history from what happened in Central Europe in the 1930s and 1940s. In the words of one of our respondents, "The Nazi regime's horror showed me the danger inherent in fame/notoriety/power/charisma. The most important aspect of being a professor for me is the education of young people, not self-aggrandizement or fame. Although I certainly appreciate recognition, I also have a sense of providing service to students."

Here are some more quotes from our participants in various career fields: "I decided to teach history at the college level + taught introduction + advanced courses in European history, Western Civilization, World history, History of Science."—"I was able to communicate with professional colleagues who were foreign on a different cultural basis than my native-born associates [could]."—"Exposure to international cuisine created interest in food service."— "I was eventually offered a transfer to the international division of the company. A European background and language skills certainly helped."

We should also note here that for many social scientists of the Second Wave, their early experience provided a dual impetus for their work and career. On one hand, the change of culture and the status of being a stranger and having no easy or "normal" identity generally tend to sharpen an individual's perception of social phenomena and to encourage analysis from a theoretical and critical distance. On the other hand, the particular horrors of their childhood and youth often infused the Second Wavers' scholarship with a social activist and humanitarian impulse—to understand better the dark side of human nature, and to help prevent it from being unleashed again. One of our interviewees, who became a social scientist, said he chose psychology partly because of its social relevance. "[I was interested in] the relationship of personal identity to group identity and the relationship, the personal relationship to collectives. . . . Starting from the time I came to America, I juggled three identities." An economist said, "Never quite being part of the community, always having an outsider's view" was crucially important in being able to predict economic tendencies. "Because the work that I did, and in many ways do, really involves trying to anticipate how others as groups will react to changing circumstances. And if you're not part of any group, it's easier. . . . I've had, from my point of view, a more satisfying career as a result of having immigrated." Peter Suedfeld (2001) edited a most instructive volume by and about former refugees who became social scientists.

Even some of those whose careers did not directly use that cultural capital mentioned an unusually broad outlook on life—acquired through having seen and experienced different cultures early in life—as a beneficial influence later on. One participant, for instance, spoke of, "Taking a broader, cross-cultural view of most aspects of my life."

Social Capital

Recent research on immigrants to the United States, as mentioned, has emphasized the great importance of social capital, in terms of networks, for immigrants (Waldinger and Der-Martirosian 2001). These networks were found to be neither merely temporary (for the newest arrivals) nor only for immigrants at the lowest rungs of the socioeconomic hierarchy. There was also social capital embedded in the American system of higher education of which the Second Wavers could avail themselves.

We already noted that the particular advantage of bearers of Central European culture in the American environment—and one of the ingredients facilitating the successful blend of European and American features among the Second Wave—was that the American "liberal arts" education was modeled to some degree after the Central European style of culture that was generally held in high esteem among the educated Americans. Furthermore, many adult refugees, the members of the First Wave, strengthened that element by working on American faculties. The presence of First Wavers made American institutions of higher education more familiar and compatible to the earlier education many of the Second Wavers had gone through. Thus, the following two comments were not surprising. "[W]hen I finally went to college . . . they considered my European background an asset." And, "I think having a German accent and liking classical music gave the illusion I was much smarter than I really was." This reception symbolized the convertibility of cultural capital already mentioned. Yet an element of social capital was often added that concretely facilitated the conversion of cultural capital. We have several reports from Second Wavers who sought out and were mentored by First Wavers. Here we found evidence of ethnic networks—social capital—being used by the young refugees.

We now change perspective: Whereas, up to now, our primary focus was on cultural and social capital and other advantageous factors that applied to the refugee group in general and helped them succeed, owing to a distinctiveness advantage, we now look at factors that internally differentiated the refugee cohort, and we examine to what extent they determined socioeconomic outcomes. We start by looking at the refugees' social background.

Transmission of Social Status

One of the key questions of our study was: To what extent does an elevated socioeconomic status get passed down from parents to children, even across the hiatus and disruption of persecution, flight, and loss of wealth and status on part of the parents? In several cases, participants emphasized that a strong family tradition of a productive and intellectually demanding life instilled in the children a sense of both legacy and obligation. Here we see cultural capital in terms of values and a class role being passed down. One former refugee blithely wrote: "Success was expected in my family." According to another one, "Professional occupation was always expected by family and teachers." Two more examples of this crucial point: "Trying to meet our parent's expectations. At all times. Raising our children to honor Grandparents. Observe religious training, stress on continued education, family and community contacts. Be friends with relatives." Another spoke of, "Emulation of my father's professional dedication and hard-work." This is the pseudoaristocratic impulse of the "good family" described earlier. As one participant put it, it grew out of the "recognition of social classes and order in the structure of the society—motivated to reach for the best and highest." We, therefore, hypothesized that the occupational status of parents and other forebears had a substantial impact on the Second Wavers' eventual occupational status.

Our extensive questionnaire survey allowed us to examine the issue of the generational transmittal of social status also in a quantitative fashion and over four generations (the former refugees' grandparents, their parents, the former refugees themselves, as well as their children).

To start with, we should stress again that the young refugees, as a group, tended to come from well-to-do backgrounds. Of the former refugees responding to our survey, 30 percent had fathers who had been professionals in Central Europe,[11] 38 percent of the fathers had been managers, and only 32 percent had had one of the "other" occupations. It is even more informative, however, to look at a few basic conditional probabilities for the former refugees. Of the male professionals in our survey, 42 percent had a father who had been a professional in Central Europe. Of the male managers, only 20 percent had a father who had been a professional, and of those who worked in other occupations, only 9 percent had a father who had been a professional. Having a father who had worked in one of the professions thus substantially boosted the male former refugees' probability of becoming professionals themselves. A similar picture, although at generally lower probabilities and with less extreme differences, was found for the female former refugees. Of the female professionals, 35 percent had a professional father; of the female managers, 25 percent; and of the women in other professions, only 14 percent.

Another practical way of expressing findings such as these is through odds and odds ratios, and we will extensively use those odds and odds ratios in the following discussion of our results. Here is an example of the concept. The odds for male former refugees in our sample of having a professional occupation (vs. any other occupational type) were 232 : 53, or 4.4 : 1, if their father had a professional occupation in Central Europe. If their father had been neither a professional nor a manager, these odds were only 151 : 110, or 1.4 : 1. Forming the odds ratio (4.4/1.4), we find that the odds of the male former refugees working in a professional occupation were more than three times (3.1) as great for those with a father who was a professional as for those with a father who worked in one of the nonprofessional and nonmanagerial occupations.

Thus, whereas the group of former refugees as a whole gravitated toward professional occupations, the father's professional status made a big difference—which confirms our initial hypothesis of the transmittal of occupational status across the discontinuities of flight and immigration. This is one of the major findings of our study, and we shall explore it in more detail.

Our interest focuses on the former refugees' occupational status, which has been coded in three large categories (professional/managerial/other), and we ask to what extent this status is influenced by other variables, such as the father's occupational status, and so on. This suggests a log-linear analysis, in which we treat the refugee's occupational status as the dependent variable (although in a log-linear analysis there is technically no distinction between dependent and independent variables).[12] A key advantage of log-linear analysis over the simpler and more traditional statistical methods is that it facilitates the analysis of models with many variables (which are difficult to deal with by examining two-dimensional contingency tables). Log-linear analysis easily extracts net effects—which can be presented as odds ratios—controlling for other effects in the model.

In a first, basic model, we look at three variables: participant's occupation, the father's occupation in Central Europe, and gender (added as an important control variable). In this model, the estimated odds of being a professional rather than in the "other" occupational category were 6.4 times as high for men as for women among our cohort of former young refugees. Furthermore, we found that the estimated odds of being a professional rather than in the "other" occupational category were almost 5 (4.9) times as high for those who had a father who had been a professional in Central Europe as for those who had a father who had worked in the "other" occupational category before the flight.

We now consider more complex models that include several additional effects. But even in the most extensive model (shown in note 13), the odds ratios were still highly significant, though they were somewhat lower, just as one would expect (gender: 3.5; father's occupation: 3.3).[14]

Grandparents' Occupation

We also collected information from our participants about their grandparents' occupation. We should note that on almost half of the returned questionnaires, the space for this information was left blank (or, technically put, the data were "missing"). Almost half of the grandfathers for whom we had data were managers, and around 15 percent were professionals. Most grandmothers might not have participated in the labor force at all (for about 95 percent—of both paternal and maternal grandmothers—we had no recorded occupation). The occupational pictures emerging for the paternal and maternal grandfathers were very similar.

We formed dummy (dichotomous) variables for all four of the Second Waver's grandparents and for the Second Waver's mother that indicated whether the respective person was reported to have been in one of the top two occupational categories, or not. The only gender difference found on those summary variables was that the men's paternal grandfather was more likely than the women's paternal grandfather to have been in one of the top two professional categories (32 percent vs. 25 percent).

There was some evidence for occupational status congruence both among the parents' and among the grandparents' generations. The father's occupational status strongly correlated with the mother's (his wife's). The two grandfathers' statuses correlated very strongly with each other. This tendency toward status congruence between the paternal and maternal grandfathers appears to indicate an element of assortative mating in marriage choice not only among individuals (the former refugees' parents), but also among families. Of particular interest to us is the extent to which the status of other relatives (other than the father's) had an additional impact on the participants' status. A log-linear model that included the grandparents' and parents' occupational status in addition to gender showed that not only was the former refugee's occupation related to that of his or her father, but the father's occupational status in turn was also related to that of his own father. This is probably the most important connection in a patrilinearly organized society. *Occupational status was clearly passed down the generations.*

In a model including participant's occupation, gender, father's occupation, as well as the mother's and the two grandfathers' occupations, the estimated odds of being a professional rather than in the "other" occupational category were 2.4 times as high for those Second Wavers who had a maternal grandfather who was a professional or a manager in Central Europe as for those who had a maternal grandfather who worked in the "other" occupational category, even after controlling for the father's occupation.

Analogous effects were found for the paternal grandfather's occupation and the mother's occupation. Again controlling for father's occupation, the estimated odds of being a professional rather than in the "other" occupational category were 1.9 times as high for those Second Wavers who had a paternal grandfather who was a professional or a manager in Central Europe as for those who had a paternal grandfather who worked in the "other" occupational category. Similarly, when it came to the mother's occupation, the estimated odds of being a professional rather than in the "other" occupational category were twice as high for those Second Wavers who had a mother who was a professional or a manager in Central Europe as for those who had a mother who worked in the "other" occupational category.

We formed a composite variable to indicate the combined occupational status of the ancestors (other than the father). This variable had three levels (low, medium, high) depending on how many of the other ancestors were reported to have been either professionals or managers: none, one, or two and more. We entered this variable in the extensive model shown in the table in note 13. The effect was indeed significant, and the estimated odds of being a professional rather than in the "other" occupational category were 1.7 times as high for those Second Wavers who had ancestors of collectively high occupational status as for those who had ancestors of collectively low occupational status. What makes this odds ratio astounding is that it applies *even after controlling for the father's occupational status*, as well as other variables.

Our results suggest the potency of long-term familial factors that span the generations and reproduce social class. They point to the importance of cultural capital being passed down through the early socialization of class roles.[15] The American opportunity structure that the former young refugees encountered (exemplified earlier in the ecology of aid organizations) enables people to thrive who, even without financial means, have this kind of cultural capital. It is an opportunity structure that is open and flexible, contains multiple chances and options, and puts a premium on "getting out there" and taking advantage of opportunities, even if they are not formally presented. People with a sense of agency, initiative, entitlement, and expectation of success—all components of the cultural capital of the upper middle classes—will tend to be successful under these conditions. Lower class people, in Central Europe as probably elsewhere, were more likely to be socialized to take rules seriously, not to make too many demands, and to take No for an answer.[16] In some structural sense, this lower class role has an equivalent in the female gender role. Here is an extreme example of a female refugee's unsuccessful pattern, where the early experiences had led to a loss of the sense of agency: "I felt I had no choice. I felt like a sort of puppet, an actress whose role was determined by whatever situations she found herself in. Such choices were for other people."

A sociological aside: In a "normal" societal hierarchy, entitlement claims and deference tend to be complementary, that is, how people act and how they are treated usually go together. Individuals of an elevated socioeconomic background, for instance, may be more persistent in pursuing opportunities, and their social environment may be more willing to grant them those opportunities. The refugee situation disentangled these two components that usually reinforce each other. In this case, little deference was usually given to the newly arrived refugees, so that the observed consequences of an elevated socioeconomic background can be more precisely pinned down to the effect of socialized class roles.

Parents' Status Hazard and Fathers' Fate

Because a large proportion of the parents of our cohort belonged to the upper middle classes of Central Europe, flight and immigration created a huge potential for status loss and downward social mobility for them. This indeed occurred often, but not in all cases, and there were interesting differences between occupations, to which we already alluded. Here now is a more detailed quantitative picture of the fathers' changes in status. Changes of this type, endured by their parents, may have considerably affected many of the former young refugees.

If we compare the participants' fathers' occupational categories before and after the immigration, we see that 69 percent of the fathers who were professionals in Central Europe eventually were again professionals in the United States—at least nominally. But the percentage of those who were able immediately upon arrival to maintain their occupational status was, of course, smaller. Thus, even for many of those who ultimately settled in well, the initial years were full of socioeconomic deprivation. For instance, we were told of formerly well-established physicians studying extremely hard, but repeatedly failing the licensing board exams, before they were eventually able to practice again. Among the former managers, only 36 percent were able to establish themselves in that occupational category; sizable groups moved downward to the sales worker category (20 percent) and the clerical worker category (15 percent).

Different professions had markedly different outcomes. For instance, of the former medical professionals, 90 percent eventually ended up in the top two occupational categories; and, of those, 92 percent worked again in medicine. However, only 56 percent of the former lawyers succeeded in entering one of the top two occupational categories. And among those fortunate ones, only 36 percent worked as lawyers again; sizable groups went into the financial field (25 percent) and into industry (19 percent).

As already mentioned, we heard several stories of First Wave women refugees transforming themselves quickly and radically. Some of them once were glamorous socialites used to running large households with the help of several servants; they turned into hardworking menial laborers who provided crucial income and support for the refugee family to survive, especially right after their arrival. These are, of course, extreme examples of a reversal of fortune, but the general pattern was clearly reflected in our data. In Central Europe, only a minority of our survey respondents' mothers had participated in the labor market, and that proportion more than doubled upon arrival in the United States (from 24 percent to 50 percent). Here are some statistics about the mothers' employment trajectories. Among the young refugees' mothers whom our participants reported as working in the United States, only 31 percent had had any reported occupation in Central Europe. The other 69 percent (for whom no occupation in Central Europe was recorded) entered all types of occupations in the United States, the major categories, as defined by the Census, being operatives (28 percent), service workers (18 percent) clerical workers (16 percent), professionals (12 percent), and sales workers (11 percent). Of the women who had been professionals in Central Europe, 44 percent again worked as professionals in the United States, 36 percent had no recorded occupation, and the rest worked in various other occupational categories. Of the women who had been managers in Central Europe, only 19 percent had a comparable occupation in America. Thirty-four percent had no recorded occupation, and the next largest group (14 percent) worked as operatives. Of the women who had worked in "other" (that is, nonprofessional and nonmanagerial) occupations in Central Europe, 58 percent did the same type of work in the United States, and 32 percent had no recorded occupation.

We further wondered if, in addition to the effect of the father's socioeconomic status in Central Europe on the participant's socioeconomic status, the father's fate after the disruption had an impact on the child's career path. Did it make a difference if the father was absent or present when the young refugee was growing up in America; did it make a difference if the father worked in the same socioeconomic category as he had in Central Europe, or in a different one? We therefore added a three-level variable to our log-linear analysis: father absent, father present with status change, and father present without status change.

Controlling for the other effects included in an extensive model shown in note 13 (gender, father's occupation, ancestors' occupation, age at arrival), the father's fate indeed made a difference. The key difference here lay between the professionals and the managers. The estimated odds of becoming a professional rather than a manager were almost twice (1.9 times) as high for those Second Wavers with a father who worked in the same occupational category in America as he had in Central Europe as for those with a father who was absent. Or, put another way, the presence, after immigration, of a father who worked in his original occupational category, directed the young refugee toward the professions.

Science and Social Mobility

Because science is one of the areas into which disproportionately many Second Wavers went, we now particularly focus on status transmission across the generations in that field. To begin with, we should note that, of the scientists among the Second Wavers, 6.0 percent had a father who worked as a scientist, but that, among the nonscientists among the Second Wavers, this percentage was four times smaller (1.5 percent).[17] In the United States, science careers have been an important avenue of upward social mobility for talented individuals from lower social backgrounds for several reasons. The science sector has expanded for much of the twentieth century, creating many job opportunities. Training has been readily available through the educational system, and success in science careers depends to an unusually high degree on objective standards. It is, of course, true that the social system of science is not a perfect meritocracy, and shortcomings in this respect have been studied extensively (e.g., Sonnert and Holton 1995a, 1995b). Nonetheless, in science, compared with other career fields, talent and excellent performance go quite a long way to make success probable.

Upward social mobility was indeed prevalent among the American-born listees in *American Men and Women of Science* of the relevant age bracket (i.e., our control group). In this group, whereas 27 percent of the fathers were professionals, and 14 percent were managers, 59 percent of the fathers had an occupation that fell in neither the professional nor the managerial category. The social origins of the scientists of the refugee group were dramatically different, with much less upward social mobility in evidence. Almost half of them (48 percent) had a father who was a professional in Central Europe, and another third (35 percent), a father who was a manager. Only 17 percent had a father who worked in an occupation of the "other" category. The most obvious reason for this relative dearth of social mobility is that the higher occupational categories were already highly represented among the parent generation of our young refugees from Central Europe, as documented above. For the Second Wave scientists who had fled Central Europe in their youth, their science careers typically represented the preservation or resumption of a family's elevated status, rather than a pattern of upward social mobility.

The social origins of the scientists who were non-refugee immigrants from Central Europe resembled those of the refugees in terms of the large percentage (47 percent) with a father who was a professional. However, the fathers of a third of the non-refugee immigrants worked in the "other" category (32 percent), whereas the proportion of managers among the fathers was smaller (21 percent). The non-refugee immigrants, as a group, thus were found to be in the middle—evidencing less social mobility than the American-born, but having more room and cause to rise than the former refugees did.

Children of the Former Young Refugees

Our data allow us to extend the analysis of the transmittal of social status to the generation that followed the Second Wavers. Most of the Second Wavers (92 percent) reported on our questionnaire that they eventually had children. The most common number of children was two (46 percent), followed by three (30 percent) and one (10 percent).

The professionals (91 percent) and managers (92 percent) were slightly less likely to be parents than the others (95 percent), but whereas this difference did not reach statistical significance, the following did: Those professionals and managers who did have children tended to have more (professionals: 2.6 children on average; managers: 2.6; others 2.2).

The data gave us once more a surprise beyond intuitive prediction. The occupational achievements of the refugees' children, as a group, were spectacular. More than two-thirds of them were professionals, a fifth were managers, and only a small group worked in other occupations. The gender gap in its traditional form—women, on average, receiving a lower level of education and working in lower-level occupations—completely disappeared among the children. If anything, the women among the children of our cohort of Second Wavers were slightly more likely to be professionals than were the men (73 percent vs. 67 percent). Similar percentages of men (21 percent) and women (18 percent) were managers.

Furthermore, among the children of the Second Wavers, both men and women had similarly high educational achievements, in aggregate. Of the men, only 10 percent had less than a Bachelor's degree, and of the women, that number was 9 percent. Among men 56 percent and among women 51 percent had an education beyond the Bachelor's level. On the whole, this children's generation thus upheld and carried on the tradition of high educational achievement established by their parents (and even earlier generations).

When comparing the children's educational achievements with their parents', it appeared more appropriate to look only at the nonelite portion of the sample (because the elite were, to some extent, selected for high educational achievement). The educational breakdown for the children in the nonelite portion was very similar to that of the whole sample. Again, only about 1 in 10 had less than a Bachelor's degree (men: 11 percent; women: 10 percent), and 53 percent of the men and 47 percent of the women had an education beyond the Bachelor's degree. When comparing these results with those for their parents' education, it becomes obvious that they, as a group, substantially surpassed their Second Wave parents in their level of education (even though the parents' level was already very high).

The results found for the children of the Second Wavers may, of course, be typical for the American upper-middle class. In other words, the high educational and occupational achievements of these children, as well as the absence of a substantial gender division in these respects might have very little to do with the parents' origin in Central Europe or their refugee and immigration experience. We therefore compared the children of the former refugees who were in three elite samples (those mentioned in *American Men and Women of Science, Who's Who,* and *Who's Who in American Jewry*) with the children of their American-born counterparts (i.e., those also mentioned in those compilations).

In that control group, gender also made little difference in educational attainment. Thus, for the younger generation of elite children, whether they were of refugee descent or not, the gender gap in terms of educational achievement broadly defined virtually disappeared. However, in the overall level of achievement, the children of the former young refugees who were listed in one of those elite compilations did better than the children of the American-born counterparts. Whereas only 7 percent of the children of these elite refugees had *less* than a Bachelor's degree, that number was double (14 percent) for the children of the comparison group. Of the elite refugees' children, 63 percent went beyond college, of the other children, only 46 percent.

A similar picture was found for occupational category. Of the elite refugees' children, 76 percent became professionals (of the others, 63 percent), 17 percent became managers (others: 23 percent), and 7 percent had an occupation that fell in the "other" category (others: 15 percent).

Among the Second Wavers' families, parental (i.e., the Second Wavers') occupation was found to be correlated with children's occupation, and the "family tradition" (of the transmission of cultural capital along the chain of generations) went remarkably farther than that. We estimated a log-linear model in which we entered the child's occupational category (treated as dependent variable) as well as the Second Waver's (i.e., the parent's) occupation, the Second Waver's father's occupation, as well as the socioeconomic indicator for other ancestors. *In addition* to the influence of the Second Waver's occupation, there was another statistically significant influence of the child's grandfather's (i.e., the Second Waver's father's) occupation (although that influence was not as strong). The estimated odds of being a professional rather than working in the "other" occupational category were 3.8 times as high for those children with a parent who was a professional as for those with a parent who worked in the "other" occupational category. And, on top of this, the estimated odds of being a professional rather than working in the "other" occupational category were 1.7 times as high for those children with a grandfather who had been a professional as for those with a grandfather who had worked in the "other" occupational category. The other ancestors' socioeconomic status failed to make an additional statistically significant difference, though even that variable approached significance ($p = .11$). As already expected from the simple gender comparison of occupational categories reported earlier, gender made no difference at all in this log-linear model.

We also can look at the transmission of socioeconomic status across the generations by comparing the children of the Second Wavers with the children of the control group. In a log-linear model, controlling for the parent's (i.e., the Second Waver's or control group member's) occupation and the grandfather's occupation, being the child of a Second Waver was associated with higher socioeconomic achievement.[18] Thus, the tendency toward high achievement in terms of occupational status was passed down even to the next generation—the children of the Second Wave.

Other Effects: Family and Community Circumstances, Age at Arrival, and Gender

Arriving as an immigrant in a new and strange culture is in itself challenging, but the problems are amplified for refugees. Raymond Buriel and Terri de Ment (1997:173) summarized the typical research findings on refugees: "Refugees also usually suffer increased psychological problems and have a more difficult time adjusting to American life than other immigrants." The same pattern has also been found specifically for young refugees (Coll and Magnuson 1997:101–4, Rumbaut 1991).

We were specifically interested in the family and community circumstances upon arrival for our young refugees, and how these affected their later career outcomes. Another factor of potential importance for the refugees' later life course is the age at which they arrived in the United State, which we will examine later in this chapter in a section titled "Age at Arrival."

The largest proportion (42 percent) of the former refugees who participated in the survey lived with immigrating family members after their arrival in the United States, 26 percent lived with family members who were already in the United States, 11 percent lived with foster parents or in a foster home, 8 percent lived alone (and small numbers in other living arrangements). As mentioned, most of those who, during or after their migration, had to spend time outside their immediate family (e.g., with distant relatives, or in a foster home) rated their overall experience in that environment as very positive or positive (54 percent), 17 percent said "somewhat positive," and the others reported various degrees of negative experiences. If other children were present in those environments, the participants rated their relationship with them as very positive or positive in 66 percent of the cases; 17 percent gave negative ratings.

Family Situation

A functional family has been found to be a positive factor in the stress management and the social and psychological adjustment of immigrant children as well as refugee children (Coll and Magnuson 1997:96–7, 102). Conversely, separation from the family in the course of migration has been identified as a source of additional problems for the children (see Ashworth 1982:79, Coll and Magnuson 1997: 98–101). As stated earlier, 46 percent of the former refugees reported in our questionnaire survey that they migrated without father or mother. Of those who were separated from both parents when fleeing from Central Europe, 49 percent were reunited with both, 38 percent were reunited with neither, and the rest with one parent.

How did the separation from, and in many cases loss of, their parents affect the young refugees who came to the United States? In most cases, one must expect, being separated from one's parents and sent to live in a new country indelibly burned itself into many a child's mind. In our interviews, while we found evidence of positive adjustments, in terms of increased resilience in some, others told us about life-long psychological scars (and we will discuss this in more detail in a subsequent section). In general, children who came with their parents were, of course, exposed longer and more intensely to the parental influence. Hence, one would expect their socialization to contain more remnants and elements of the Central European culture, or *Kultur*, as the parents might have called it. Those who came with parents were likelier, upon arrival, to live in a neighborhood that, to their knowledge, also included fellow refugees (67 percent vs. 53 percent), whereas unaccompanied children tended to be placed with foster parents (who were less likely to live in refugee communities). Those who came alone reported a higher current level of religiousness (1.02 vs. 0.86, on a scale of 0 to 3). This might at least partly be attributable to their fathers' (1.37 vs. 1.09) and their mothers' (1.44 vs. 1.16) higher religiousness levels. That, in turn, might indicate that parents who were at least somewhat religious were better able to avail themselves of the institutional infrastructure in their home country (such as a *Kultusgemeinde*) that supported the children's escape.

Those who came with parents were indeed found to differ from those who arrived without parents in additional respects also, though the average differences were generally small. One problem in looking at the effects of the family situation at arrival is that it is closely linked to another variable, age at arrival: The older the children were at arrival, the more likely they were to arrive alone.[19] For that reason, we used statistical models that looked at those two variables in conjunction.[20] For each of the two variables, we shall, in the following section, mention only those differences that showed up in combined models. Thus, the reported differences on one variable take into account the effect of the other as well as their potential interaction.[21] For these analyses, we distinguished between participants who arrived in the United States without parents and those who came with at least one parent. We now present only differences in cultural outlook and collective identities and will turn to differences in emotional reactions later.

Compared to the refugees who arrived with one or both parents, the refugees arriving without parents reported that their experiences leading up to and during the migration influenced their later life more strongly. Thus, our participants who were separated from their families perceived especially potent and enduring effects of those early life events. Being ripped from one's family at a young age remained, as one might expect, in the minds of many a major turning point in their lives (and even more so than did the refugee experience for those who went through it with their families).

The presence of parents also strengthened the link to the European background. Coming with one or two parents increased the likelihood of maintaining a special interest in the country of their childhood and of returning later on a visit to that country. Those who came with parents also reported stronger remnants of European culture. The presence of parents weakened the participants' tendency to associate with the American popular culture (as measured by that composite trait). Here, the refugee parents' enduring socialization influence on their children became apparent, instilling in many children the parental reverence for *Kultur* and immunizing them to some degree against the surrounding American popular culture. Whether or not parents were present did not make a statistically significant difference on the composite traits called high culture, work ethic, and social activism.

In terms of collective identity, the family situation of arrival made little difference. Whether the young refugee arrived with or without parents had no statistically significant main effects on either American, local, Jewish, Christian, German, Austrian, European, or other claimed identities. Neither did our composite for European identity and our composite indicating the general strength of the participants' identification with collective labels.

As to the relationship of familial disruption with socioeconomic status, in the nonelite sample, if they arrived without parents, participants were less likely to become professionals (41 percent vs. 54 percent) and more likely to become managers (33 percent vs. 24 percent) or work in other occupations (26 percent vs. 22 percent). However, once we controlled for other influences, such as gender, father's occupation, ancestors' occupation, and age at arrival, the effect of the presence or absence of parents slipped below statistical significance. Thus, whether the young refugees arrived with or without parents did not make a significant difference on occupational type, controlling for other factors. Although prima facie one might have assumed that such serious familial disruptions would heavily influence later career trajectories, this interestingly appeared not to be the case (at least at the aggregate level of statistical correlation). Here we begin to see a divergence that is worth exploring further. Early familial disruption did affect the outlook and attitudes of the young refugees in various ways (and we will hear more about this later), but it seems to have played less of a role in determining the former refugees' eventual socioeconomic status, for which we found their parents' original socioeconomic status to be important. In this case, we might have a prepotency of broad sociological factors over individual life experiences in explaining basic socioeconomic outcomes.[22]

We also examined whether eventual reunification with a parent after separation made a difference. (As mentioned, of those separated from both parents, 49 percent were reunited with both, 38 percent were reunited with neither, and the rest with one parent.) Compared with those who never saw their father again, those who were reunited with their father had less religious parents, believed that their early European experiences had less of an influence on their later life, tended to live more frequently in neighborhoods with fellow refugees, retained more European culture (probably a direct effect of resumed socialization), and had a stronger European identity.[23] The occupational status was not affected. A similar picture emerged if one compares those who never saw their mother again with those who did (there was of course a large overlap, as mentioned).

Age at Arrival

One might speculate that the age at which the young refugees arrived in the United States would have had some effect on their later careers. For instance, though school-age children may have benefited from the superior quality (as many of them reported) of their Central European schooling, they would have necessarily experienced some disruption in the transition to the American educational system. By contrast, very young children at arrival would have been able to move through their whole schooling and training period in the United States, but might have missed the "better" education in Central Europe. From a psychological perspective, one could perhaps hypothesize that very young children, owing to their limited understanding, might have been less traumatized than older ones by the events of persecution and escape. To examine the effects of age at arrival, we introduced a four-level variable into our analyses, indicating whether, upon entry to the United States, the participant was 6 years or younger, 7–12, 13–18, or older than 1.8.

Educational achievement was strongly related to the age at which the young refugee arrived in America, but maybe not in the way one might expect. Among those who had arrived at age 6 or younger, a small minority (7 percent) had received only a high school education or less. The percentage of individuals at this educational level increased to 23 percent among those who had arrived between the ages of 7 and 12, to 35 percent among those who had arrived between the ages of 13 and 18, and to 51 percent for the older ones. Conversely, at the other end of educational achievement, 65 percent of the youngest arrival cohort eventually received more than four years of higher education, and that figure dropped to 38 percent in the oldest arrival cohort (which, we should not forget, is still an extraordinarily high percentage when compared with the educational levels of the general population). We also found a statistically significant relation of age at arrival with occupational category. In terms of becoming a professional, the odds were particularly strongly stacked in favor of the youngest arrivals and against the oldest arrivals. Controlling for all other effects, the estimated odds for professionals to have arrived at age six or younger (rather than older than 18) were more than three times as large as the estimated odds for participants working in an "other" occupation.[24] The crucial difference, thus, was between those arriving before the start of primary schooling and those arriving after the end of secondary schooling, with the advantage (in terms of occupational achievement) going to the former group.

Here, again, the statistical analysis, at first sight, diverges somewhat from the participants' reports (many of the former refugees who had attended the *Gymnasium* were full of praise for its rigorous educational standards and counted it among their major advantages). This may certainly be true, but our multipronged methodological approach allows us to see a more complex picture and to point out that the younger refugees, who went through the American educational system from the beginning, had other advantages that were even stronger, on average, to ensure positive outcomes.

One might also think that the older these former refugees were before they came to the United States, the more they would hold different traits and attitudes from what they consider average American. However, we will find that things are much more complex with our group of former refugees. As a first step, we examined the correlations between the trait ratings and the age at arrival. Even the significant (at $p < .05$) correlations we found were rather small, indicating that the age at arrival was not an overriding factor in determining the traits. The older the participants were when they entered the United States, the less ambitious ($r = -.06$), the more easygoing ($r = .09$), the less interested in learning ($r = -.14$), the less hardworking ($r = -.10$), and the less achievement-oriented ($r = -.13$) they tended to be, on average. They also tended to like the outdoors more ($r = .05$), to like reading less (r = −.08) to like writing less (r = −.07), to be less interested in movies (r = −.06) and in food (r = −.11), and to be less emotional when frustrated (r = −.08).[25] Overall, thus, the picture that emerges reveals that those who arrived at a younger age, on average, were generally somewhat more driven to work and succeed, but that they were also more distant from some typically American leisure pursuits (movies, food). This may seem somewhat counterintuitive, but it also directs our attention to the efficacy of familial or subcultural influences on those younger children (about which more will come below).

We now summarize some results in the areas of cultural outlook and identity, in which age at arrival might have made a difference (we turn to the area of emotional reactions later). We again look at the effects of the age at arrival in conjunction with those of the family situation at arrival, because, as mentioned earlier, these variables were strongly related to each other. The following results are from models including both variables and their interaction.

The influence of migration on their later lives was considered more powerful by the older arrival cohorts. In addition, an interaction effect was found: The youngest and oldest arrival cohorts considered that influence more powerful if they had come without parents, the opposite was the case for the two middle cohorts.

The older cohorts reported thinking more frequently about their time in Europe; they also said they felt more strongly influenced by it. On the last item, there was also an interesting interaction. The arrival cohort of the 7–12 years olds, as a group, felt more influenced by their European background if they arrived with their parents, but the oldest arrival cohort felt more influenced by it in the absence of their parents. The latter result may be somewhat surprising. One might speculate that, among those older individuals who arrived unaccompanied, their life in Europe might have become enshrined in their outlook and in this process might have become more salient. Some of our interviewees, for instance, told us that they had resolved to lead their lives in a way that their absent parents would approve and be proud of them. Moreover, those oldest arrivals who came with their parents may have tended to distance themselves from the parental influence to assert their independence.

In terms of allegiance to American popular culture, an interaction was found between the two variables. Among the younger arrival cohorts, the presence of parents suppressed the level of popular culture identification, but not so among the older arrival cohorts, apparently reflecting the ubiquitous trend of parents' waning influence over their children as they grow older. Now our earlier results (showing younger arrivals more distant from American popular culture) become more plausible: Younger arrivals were more likely to be in the company of their parents whose influence helped distance them somewhat from the ambient culture. The other trait composites were not affected by age at arrival in a statistically significant way.

The oldest arrival cohort reported retaining the most culture remnants from Europe followed by the youngest cohort who had the second highest level on that composite variable. The 7–12 year old arrivals made the least frequent trips back to the country of their childhood. Among the youngest arrival cohort, having arrived with parents increased the frequency of return trips, whereas the opposite was the case among the oldest arrival cohort (for the latter group—the older ones who arrived without parents—one might hypothesize a heightened interest in exploring their past).

On the identity rating scales, the level of American identity was stronger for the younger arrival cohorts, on average. In addition, when asked to choose an identity label, the percentage of those preferring the identity label "American" was highest in the youngest arrival cohort (54 percent) and lowest in the oldest arrival cohort (42 percent). By contrast, only 18 percent of the youngest arrival cohort chose the second-most popular label, "Jewish-American," whereas about a quarter of each of the other arrival cohorts preferred that label. Thus, spending a longer part of one's childhood in America was associated with a greater propensity of identifying oneself as "American," as might have been expected. There was also an interaction on the rating scale of American identity. Among the younger cohorts, those arriving without their parents had a stronger American identity than those arriving with their parents, whereas the opposite was the case for the oldest cohort. No statistically significant differences in the ratings for local, Jewish, Christian, German, Austrian, European,[26] and other identities were found. The composite for European identity also showed no difference, but the measure for the strength of collective identification in general showed somewhat lower levels among the older cohorts.

If we compare the results for the family situation at arrival and the age at arrival, we see that age at arrival had more numerous effects on the various outcomes in terms of cultural outlook and identity than did the family situation at arrival. This may suggest that the timing of a major life event, such as becoming a refugee, within the sequence of age-dependent socialization and maturation processes is consequential, and perhaps even more consequential in determining cultural outlook and identity than are the special circumstances of that event, such as migration with or without family. This certainly dovetails with similar results in the realm of educational and socioeconomic outcomes where we found age at arrival to have played a more important role than has the family situation at arrival.

We also wondered if the *time period* of arrival in the United States made an additional difference. It seemed plausible that individuals who arrived early, that is, during the height of the Depression, might have occupational outcomes that would differ from those of the later arrivals, and one might even think of an interaction between time period of arrival and age at arrival in predicting occupational outcome. However, neither of these two effects rose to statistical significance.[27]

Another variable that might be of importance and that is somewhat connected to age of arrival is the *duration of the migration*. We distinguished those who migrated from Central Europe to the United States in one month or less time from those who had longer migration paths. We found that those with relatively short migration patterns were more likely than those with the longer patterns to have become professionals (60 percent vs. 50 percent), equally likely to have become managers (both 26 percent) and less likely to have worked in other occupations (15 percent vs. 24 percent). However, once, in a multivariate log-linear model, we controlled for the effects of father's occupation, gender, father's fate, and age of arrival, the duration of migration was no longer a statistically significant effect on the young refugees' eventual occupational status.

Immigrant Community

Here we explore whether the location of resettlement, be it amidst one of the refugee communities, such as Washington Heights in northern Manhattan, or a neighborhood in which they were isolated from other refugees, made a difference to the young refugees. As already mentioned, a major concern of the agencies helping the refugees resettle in the United States was to prevent the refugees' geographical concentration in a few refugee neighborhoods and to spread them out over the country.[28] The survey participants' initial geographical distribution reflected that concern to some extent. Whereas 40 percent of our participants settled in a neighborhood where there were no other refugees they knew about, 33 percent reported that at first they lived in a neighborhood with relatively few fellow refugees and 27 percent said fellow refugees were relatively numerous.

Statistically speaking, compared with the impact of the presence or absence of their parents, living in a community of fellow refugees or living isolated from other refugees had less of an impact on the former refugees' traits and outlook. Still, some differences emerged from our data. Those living in a refugee community thought that their early upbringing in Europe had influenced their later life more strongly than did those who did not live near other refugees (2.99 vs. 2.84, on a scale of 0 to 5), and a similar difference appeared on the question about the influence of the participants' experiences leading up to and during the migration on their later lives (2.85 vs. 2.67). Those initially living near fellow refugees also agreed more strongly with the statement that the group of immigrants blended European and American characteristics in a way that was conducive to great success (3.21 vs. 3.11 on a scale from 1 to 4). Apparently, they had seen more examples of this. The people living in the refugee communities considered themselves also somewhat more religious (0.97 vs. 0.88, on a scale from 0 to 3). In addition, they had returned to their homeland more frequently (2.39 vs. 2.23, on a scale of 0 to 4). They also retained more elements of Central European culture (3.12 vs. 2.65, on an index ranging from 0 to 7).

In terms of the emotions the participants reported about their migration experience—those they held shortly after arrival as well as those they held currently—not a single variable was significantly influenced by the type of community into which they settled. There was no effect of the three-level community variable[29] on occupational type, neither when it was the sole predictor nor after controlling for other influences, such as gender, father's occupation, ancestors' occupation, and age at arrival.

Gender

Gender powerfully influenced outcomes. In the cohort of young refugees, there were, of course, also examples of unfortunate outcomes and thwarted ambitions that resulted from the young refugees' early fate. Not always, but predominantly, it was women who had stories of this kind to tell. Here are some quotes:

"I arrived here in my second month of pregnancy, I worked until my 9th month as a worker in a handbag factory. Since I had no chance in Germany to learn a proper trade, I always earned my wages as a worker."—"My father! [He] was against my going to college. Wanted me to learn a 'trade.' And I married early and had no career."—"Wanted to go into a helping profession, i.e., medicine, but because I was (a) a woman, (b) non-veteran, and (c) Jewish, I had little chance to get into Med Schools after World War II. (There were quotas for Jews in many schools.)"—"Did not have success in career!! Did not find the right choices of career. My brother became a professor. I rejected European upbringing in many areas."

As our analysis of the U.S. Census data already indicated, we again found among our participants that, frequently owing to economic exigency, women faced disproportionately high obstacles in their career paths. The barriers were so much the more perceptible and excruciating as these women often came from backgrounds that had high expectations for their occupational achievement. Especially immigrants from big cities, such as

Vienna with its tradition of leftist politics and socialist municipal govern-ment, were more likely than their American-born counterparts to hold what might be considered "progressive" attitudes about women's education and work. As one woman recounted, "Teachers [in Vienna] did not differ-entiate between boys and girls . . . from that I got a lot of my feeling of independence and of being equal to men in many respects, you know, because I had never been treated unequally in school." Another one got sup-port from her mother: "My mother was a very intelligent woman—ahead of her time. She had a career and always felt like a women's-libber. (Term unknown, then, of course.) She wanted me to be able to make a living. She encouraged me to write. She was an excellent writer herself." Another woman told us, "I had an aunt who was a lawyer, a woman lawyer in Vienna. And so we knew that women—our pediatrician was a woman—so we knew that women could have careers also."

Some women were tenacious in their ambitions, even if initially denied. "I was highly motivated and returned to college at age 46 to get a B.A. I was mar-ried, had two children at home and was teaching at pre-school. At that time, that was more unusual than now. I went to [college] at night and Saturdays."

In the collective experience of this group of immigrant women, as already mentioned, might lay one of the seeds that would germinate into the feminist movement in the 1960s and 1970s. Hanna Papanek (1973), a Second Waver, did seminal work on the two-person career (in which women make crucial, but informal and undervalued contributions to their husbands' careers) and one of the most distinguished American scholars on women's issues, Gerda Lerner (1971, 1986–93, 2002), is also part of our refugee cohort.

Looking back on our analyses of what influenced the socioeconomic outcomes of the young refugees from Central Europe, a major theme that emerged was the great power of family socialization of values and behaviors (e.g., of *Bildung* and "class roles") early in development. Even though the continuities of material wealth and social status were severed, the opportu-nity structure that the young refugees encountered in the United States allowed especially the young refugees of elevated socioeconomic back-grounds to capitalize heavily on their early socialization and thus to become highly successful. In addition, of course, there were many other factors of importance, not the least the psychological effects of early persecution and flight to which we turn now.

Success out of Adversity

So far, we have explored the factors that helped the young refugees succeed in spite of the adversity they encountered early in their lives. Now, we look at how these refugees, as a group, succeeded *because* of this adversity. In other words, we examine the psychological dynamics, set in motion by the events of flight and immigration that contributed to the documented great success. The basic concept here is resilience, the amazing ability of the human spirit to rise from disaster.[30] In our group of former refugees, we found plenty of evidence that striving for success was a powerful coping mechanism for many. One of our participants said, "[A]ll the defeats and all of the impediments, all of the difficulties I had as a child and a young man, instead of breaking me, did the opposite. And I consider myself a very strong person today. A lot of people rely on me, and I've become a leader instead of a follower." Another had this to say, "I got several punches from life in Germany . . . and in Chicago, and what ended up was a tremendous determination to succeed and to be somebody." And a third, "I suppose that it instilled me with a desire to emulate the resilience of my parents, whose adaptive strengths greatly impressed me. I often wonder whether I would have been as successful if I had grown up in a Nazi-less Europe. I think not."

Life Satisfaction, Feelings and Attitudes about the Migration

While 56 percent of the men on the questionnaire indicated they were very satisfied with their life in general, 43 percent of the women expressed a similar level of satisfaction.[31] The "satisfied" category was chosen by 34 percent of the men and 44 percent of the women, so that, among both genders, overwhelming majorities of the participants gave one of the top two responses. This may be an indication that our group of Second Wavers, on average, thinks that they had coped with their challenges and that things, on the whole, had turned out well.

Before describing the psychological factors that helped bring about the former refugees' resilience in greater detail, let us look at a quantitative picture of the refugees' reported basic emotions shortly after arrival and now. Of our participants, 55 percent responded that, shortly after they arrived in the United States, they felt various degrees of anger about their migration and the events that led to it; 45 percent said they felt no anger.[32] 79 percent said they experienced intense or considerable feelings of gratitude. The reported feeling of sadness was especially pronounced among the women. While 57 percent of the women said they felt intense or considerable sadness, only 40 percent of the men did so. The same gender pattern appeared in the area of guilt (i.e., "survivor's guilt," see Hirsch 2003): 16 percent of the women, but only 7 percent of the men reported considerable or intense feelings of guilt.

When asked about the *current* level of these emotions, the anger levels remained essentially unchanged, on aggregate.[33] Sadness subsided substantially for both men and women, with the original gender pattern being preserved. The guilt level remained stable for the whole group, and gratitude grew somewhat stronger (now 89 percent of the participants reported intense or considerable feelings of gratitude).

In addition to looking at the development of these emotions at a collective level, it might be interesting to see how the intensity of these feelings changed for individuals. Considering only those who reported a change in intensity, we found that, in terms of anger, those who got angrier (47 percent) and those who got less angry (53 percent) were about evenly balanced. Guilt was somewhat more likely to decrease (in 58 percent of those reporting changed levels) than to increase over time. Two-thirds (67 percent) of those who reported a change in their level of sadness indicated a lessening. Gratitude typically grew stronger (in 77 percent).

Both for the early emotions and the current emotions, we formed a composite index of the net strength of negative emotions by adding the scores for anger, guilt, and sadness together and subtracting the gratitude score (resulting in a scale from −3 to 9). The average level of this index was higher for the early emotions than for the current emotions (.50 vs. −.06), indicating, as might be expected, a general subsiding of negative emotions. For the early feelings, the women's average score (1.00) was higher than the men's (.24), signifying a higher collective level of negative emotions in that initial phase.

We also wondered if age at arrival had any impact on the emotional state of our participants.[34] Here lay probably the most interesting result in the comparison between the "early" emotions, that is, the emotions the former refugees reported to have had shortly upon their arrival in the United States, and the emotions they said they held currently.

The level of early anger was lowest among the youngest arrivals, as a group (0.6), and higher among the other cohorts, with the 13–18-year-old refugees having the highest average level (1.2). Similar patterns were found for early sadness and early gratitude. No arrival cohort effect was detected for early guilt. The current anger level was actually highest among the youngest arrival cohort and lowest among the oldest arrival cohort (1.2 vs. 0.8, on a scale of 0 to 3).[35] Current sadness was highest among those who had arrived between the ages of 7 and 12 and lowest among the oldest arrival cohort. Current guilt was also highest among those who had arrived between the ages of 7 and 12, but lowest among the youngest arrival cohort. The youngest arrival cohorts had the highest levels of current gratitude. On the composite for earlier negative emotions, the older arrival cohorts showed higher levels, whereas, on the composite for current negative emotions, we found the opposite, that is, the older arrival cohorts had lower levels.

The pattern reversal on anger (and to a lesser extent on gratitude and on the composite) may suggest interesting psychological dynamics in how people cope with early potentially traumatizing events, such as National Socialist persecution and the often- narrow escape from it, over time. Young age and hence a limited understanding of the unfolding events, as well as (in many cases) the presence of their parents, may have shielded the very young refugees from a deeply traumatizing impact at the time. Over the following decades, as they matured, some of them perhaps developed deeper insights into the magnitude of what had happened to them, which may have led to a cognitive reevaluation of those early events and thus to an increase in anger levels. The older arrival cohorts, by contrast, had a better understanding of what happened when it happened and may have been initially more traumatized by it. Subsequently, many of them perhaps learned to come to terms with that trauma so that anger levels dropped. These are just speculations, of course, but the topic may be an interesting one for further psychological research.

Reactions to Flight and Immigration: Determination, Resourcefulness, Toughness, and Self-Reliance

Disruption and dislocation made many refugees more driven and ambitious. Several of the former refugees said that those experiences created in them an attitude that is popularly described as "hungry." Having lived through severe deprivations, they became determined to improve their situation, and thus they turned into overachievers. One participant explained, "I think I have this hungry-man hypothesis view of life. . . . It's almost like in a computer, you have programs running in the background all the time." Another one said, "I wanted to be a lawyer. And I started developing an enormous sense of determination. It was sort of, 'I'll show all those kids who are beating me up and ignoring me' . . . and that has really been the theme of my life." To give another example, "As a refugee, I was expected to succeed independently and to make a great effort to do so. This led me to be ambitious and to use all my powers to succeed in research."[36]

A related pattern was that the early experiences called forth, in the former refugees, traits, such as resourcefulness, toughness, and self-reliance that then helped them throughout their lives. For example, "[the refugee experience] probably contributed to my ability to adapt to new circumstances." Or, "It has toughened my character, made me a self-reliant person." And, "These experiences made you want to overcome [them] and this strength prepared you for future struggles." Here we found a variation on a common sociological theme, that of newcomers trying harder.[37]

Instant Adults

These traits and features of resilience could perhaps be subsumed under the general heading of the former refugees having often become, as already described, "instant adults," handling adult problems and responsibilities at an early age.

It was one of our most consistent findings that the events and experiences surrounding their oppression in, and flight from, National Socialist Germany or Austria, made many of the young refugees "grow up" quickly and take on adult responsibilities at an early age. "The discipline to survive the horrors of the '30s never leaves you," said one participant. This forced instant adulthood, as one might call it, is likely to have contributed to their later success in the United States; but some also frankly mourned the loss of their childhood this entailed. "I am and always was more careful to preserve and save whatever I had. Also, when you become fully aware at the age of five and a half that you are no longer a child, those children who survived the Nazi persecution were never really children again." Another person wrote, "I think I grew up more serious than a normal teenager. I had to stand on my own feet at age 15 and even as a child [during National Socialism]. The constant pressure being Jewish did not allow for a carefree youth."

Here are a few additional quotes from different participants to illustrate this central point: "This feeling of insecurity, which came already with me from Germany, continued in the United States. And there was a very great sacrifice I made as a child and even later on. That is, I never had a childhood. I never played. I cannot remember once playing ball on the street or anywhere else. I was deprived of a childhood."—"It made me grow up. It took away my childhood. I think I've always been an adult."—"The truth of the matter is that after the 'Anschluss' I really was never a kid again. I didn't think the way kids think. I didn't play the way kids play. And for quite a spell . . . I was pretty much on my own. My mother was in no position to do anything. . . . My dad was totally out of the picture, and I had to become self-sufficient."

This theme of instant adulthood had two variations, for those who arrived with and those who arrived without their family, but the overarching structure—having to shoulder adult responsibilities at a young age—was the same. Here are some examples of young refugees who, in the common role reversal, became parents to their parents.[38] "I was the only breadwinner of the family . . . and I was very proud of the fact that I was the only one who was earning money and all that." The instinct of protecting the parents and shielding them from any additional worries and disappointment was a powerful incentive to do well. "My sister and I always, and even to this day, always tried very hard to do our best. . . . I think partly it was because we didn't want to impose additional worries on our parents. . . . We felt that would be one way of perhaps making life a bit easier for them." Those who had been separated from their families carried a different burden, but they, too, felt they had to act mature beyond their years.

Finally, one might speculate that some individuals who had been robbed of their childhood might still have retained some of it at a subconscious level, which, especially for innovative work, might constitute an "up side."

Revenge, Responsibility, and Giving Back

"Success is the best revenge," said one of our participants poignantly—a sentiment echoed by a few others. The refugees' success in their new life, in this sense, would be the ultimate refutation of, and revenge for, the National Socialist persecution.[39] Turning it positively, several participants said that they felt a great responsibility to make the most of their lives because their survival was such a rare and unlikely gift.[40] "I think my origins in life gave me a lot of drive. I don't think my parents ever said we have a special responsibility, but I think I've always felt like I have a special responsibility, because we were able to leave, because we were able to emigrate here, and given all these opportunities. So I think that has been quite influential in my approach to life." Having been through so much, some remarked that they were more grateful for the things they can enjoy in this country. "I appreciate this country more than friends who were born here, take nothing for granted." Or, "Made me more aware of appreciating my blessings and having responsibilities toward my community and the USA."[41]

A widespread theme, as already mentioned, was that of giving back to the country and community—trying to make them better places—both through the choice of occupation and through political and volunteer activities. Many of our participants said that they volunteered to speak at school and on other occasions so as to help prevent the reoccurrence of the kind of atrocities they went through.[42] Several of those with a strong Jewish identity also said they felt a responsibility toward the Jewish people.[43]

The following quotes illustrate that frequent theme of promoting social justice and humaneness: "I've been sensitive to 'discrimination,' or unfairness. I recall going to bat for my first USA friend, a Catholic, who left school early every Wednesday (3rd–4th grade) to attend catechism class.

She didn't do well on tests covering work done when she wasn't present. My intervention helped. That experience stayed with me all my life. It ultimately contributed to my interest in a second career as an attorney." And, another example, "I am very conscious of discrimination against groups of people. I think it's very important to speak out against oppression."[44] Furthermore, "Exposure and life during the Nazi era matured me early. My father's death in the concentration camp did so as well. Problems of adjustment during migration have given me openness and understanding towards others in similar circumstances."

Several former refugees remarked that, in a cruelly ironic way, Hitler actually did them a favor by expelling them. For instance, "Thinking back about this whole business I think that inadvertently Hitler did us (at least me) a favor. What would my life have been like if World War II had never happened? In discussing this with a friend of mine from [German city], we conclude that: I would never have gone on to high school, let alone college or university. I would have had to continue living with my parents who would have expected me to support them or at least 'help out.' "[45]

Chapter 7

Anguish—Privatized Costs, Socialized Benefits

Some of the former refugees told us that they were keeping their pantries stocked with several months' worth of supplies, always carrying their passports and important papers with them, and generally were living in preparation for a major emergency. They appeared to have never been able to regain the basic trust and confidence, prevalent among most people, that things will, by and large, turn out all right and that disasters will never occur, or at least very infrequently.

The refugees' early experiences, in many cases, exacted a heavy psychological cost to which we now turn. In the previous chapter, we focused on resilience, on the positive psychological adjustment to these experiences that contributed to the refugees' success in this country, as a group. For a subgroup of our cohort of former young refugees, even though their adjustment was often connected to outward success, it had also a dark side that needs to be explored.

Enduring Trauma

For the First Wave, Saenger (1941:40–2) listed some common psychological reactions the refugees evidenced as a result of being oppressed and persecuted by the National Socialists, all of which could be considered detrimental in some way. Arranged in an approximate order of severity, these are

1. putting on a "mask of outwardly cool and reserved behavior";
2. retreat into books or work;

3. escapism and denial of reality;
4. increased irritability and petty aggressiveness;
5. becoming utterly apathetic to life while being outwardly normal;
6. mental disorders (e.g., depression, nervous breakdown) and insanity; and
7. suicide.

Many of our group of Second Wave refugees reported signs of enduring psychological trauma that one nowadays would probably classify as Posttraumatic Stress Disorder (PTSD). From our participants, we heard, among other symptoms, stories of continual nightmares, sleeplessness, and depression. As one wrote, "To this day I occasionally dream of being persecuted, imprisoned by Nazis." And another, "Feelings of lack of stability and lack of serenity . . . have become part of my personality." In the course of our research, we have also learned of suicides and other tragedies that might be attributed to early psychological traumatization.

Even the resilient drive toward overachievement was, in some instances, motivated by the desire to overcome some basic insecurities generated by the immigrant and refugee experience. "I think being different, having a different experience, not expecting to be treated in the same way . . . taking fewer things for granted, I suppose in some ways it's a hard thing to come to grips with." Here are a few quotes to illustrate this pervasive theme. "I probably work harder than most people. I am a workaholic. Maybe that's another reflection of insecurity. And, undoubtedly, I also was very eager to succeed, having been kicked out of Germany."—"The insecurity of being a foreigner and making one work hard and striving for excellence, at least for approval of the Americans."—"What defines me as being very ambitious, driven, was clearly established by the time I was 7 or 8 years old, and actually was not modified. . . . I felt different. I think that I didn't feel accepted. I've always felt different. I still do. . . . I feel like an outsider. . . . I've always felt like a stranger looking in. It's like I'm wearing somebody else's clothes." Sometimes, however, these insecurities were debilitating. "I am less competitive, less sure of myself—therefore not very successful."

Here are some other typical psychological reactions that emerged from our participants' reports.

Aloneness and Alienation

"I was excommunicated by law, the police, the Army, the general population [under the National Socialists]. They were out to kill me. All of a sudden, I had to leave my beautiful, comfortable, charming, prosperous home. They were out to destroy our home. I was five-and-a-half when it started. I didn't want to leave. In all the eight-and-a-half years [following] I couldn't go back home. Finally after 18 months hiding in Holland (the Gestapo immediately searched for Germans who arrived after 1933) we escaped to the US. I didn't want to go. I would never go home again. I felt like a freak for years." Like this participant, many others talked of feeling like outcasts, and often this feeling became a permanent sense of being an outsider, of not belonging, and made it difficult, even later on, to connect and attach to other people.[1] Here the general phenomenon of being an immigrant in a strange environment and of going through the refugee experience overlaid and reinforced each other.

The impact of culture on the lives of the former refugees has been much more complex and wide-ranging than the notion of cultural capital accumulation can capture. One of the downsides was cultural alienation, "the 'outsider' feeling," as one of our participants called it. Another said to us, "I believe that my ideas about child care draw on my remembrances. Also my parents never really became Americanized, and so even here I was influenced by their European ideas. My manners in particular are more European than American, especially in how I use a knife and fork. My attitudes about religion and politics are like my parents': left-wing and atheistic that seems to me to be more unusual here than in Europe." In a similar vein, this participant highlighted cultural differences thus: "We grew up in a society (pre-Nazi) that functioned with co-operation, not individualism. I still believe it was more ethical. Through the socialist government (so-called 'Red Vienna'), and the numerous actions it took to improve the life of the citizenry, I absorbed the idea of cooperation and political action for the common good. And I am thoroughly fed up with selfishness as [an] idea here, since the Reagan years." A participant who had become a mathematics professor simply wrote: "I suspect I never quite became an American."

"I remember feeling left out and feeling isolated," another former refugee told us, "and not being able to be accepted in school. . . . I was sort of an outsider looking in. And I think that has in fact influenced a lot of what I've done and not done, and how I've done things that I have done. So it is an outsider feeling that is one that is still there." Another said, "After 60 years in the U.S., I still do not feel at home. I have been depressed for many years, starting in the '80s. I have marked memory loss; it began with depression." And a third person simultaneously saw the advantages and disadvantages of the outsider position. "Yes, the good is that . . . our minds perhaps were sharpened by events. We became more aware of what's going on in the world. At the same time, we were held back by the fact that we were outsiders. So, all in all, I would say it balances out." A positive effect of aloneness can be glimpsed from this response: "[My experiences leading up to and during the migration] made my relationship with myself the most important relationship. It has made me a very good friend of mine."

The residue of cultural capital was sometimes perceived not only as a boon, but also as a burden. One of our participants recalled the initial uneasiness of being different: " 'I'm more sensitive to being Jewish—more aware of being different because of where I was born—my parents were foreigners.' This is how I felt when we first came to America! I wanted to be like everyone else!"[2]

Fear, Insecurity, Survivor's Guilt, and Inferiority

Other emotions were also frequently mentioned. Some refugees, for example, told us that their early experience left them with an enduring and all-consuming sense of fear. One wrote, for instance, "My having to escape the Nazi regime without family was traumatic. . . . In one word, the greatest influence [that these experiences] had on my life is FEAR. I am now 79 years old, and have never been able to shake living in fear." Another of the former refugees wrote on the questionnaire, "Fear of anti-Semitism—sensitivity to it; some fear of the Christian world; separation anxiety—first years. Fear of and inability to travel and more."

Insecurity was another, connected, theme. "The displacements of my early life made me emotionally insecure." And, "They left me with a permanent underlying feeling of the impermanence of any stage of life." A few former refugees talked about survivor's guilt, for, instance, "Feel guilty for my good luck when so many others and more worthwhile people perished."

Some participants also reported persistent feelings of inferiority stemming from the early experience. "I have the most horrible inferiority complex because my life was so bad in England [that] I could never advance myself enough. So therefore, I have a horrible hang-up. I felt always like a failure."—"My fear of being Jewish has been difficult to overcome. Hitler made us feel so inferior and that has been the difficulty in my life, never feeling good enough."[3]

Separation from Family

In the survey, we found some evidence of the psychological scars left by the children's separation from their families. "Although I consider the USA my home, as I have spent most of my life here and own my own home, I am basically rootless and untrusting of my environment. . . . Having been torn from my nuclear family at age 13, I've had to learn to depend on myself . . . and never trusted another enough to marry. Changes in residence and positions, voluntary though they may be, are always very difficult for me to make."

Being ripped out of one's family and from one's familiar environment was, as one might imagine, a very heart-wrenching experience for many of the children. A participant in the *Kindertransport* said, "You know, you're away from your family; you're away from all your friends, with these people and I didn't know any of them. And it's scary, very scary."

Special circumstances of the migration sometimes heightened the children's feelings of abandonment, as in the following case. "The ship landed in New York. . . . A distant relative of mine was supposed to pick me up at the ship, and forgot about it. So there were two children on a totally empty ship. Sailors, everyone was gone. Just the two of us sitting there quietly crying because nobody picked us up. That was probably the worst day of my life. And then she finally came [after about nine hours] and picked us up."

Some of these lonely and isolated youngsters drastically reduced their time horizon, did not engage in long-range planning, and lived from day to day. One of our interviewees described this in the following words, "You see, as I left Germany and grew up by myself, it was sort of—I mean, people have said to me, 'Were you happy? Were you unhappy?' Who knows? Who cared? There wasn't anybody. Who did you complain to? Nobody cared. Nobody wanted to know. You lived a life of a youth from day to day. You didn't wonder. I don't remember ever thinking, 'What am I going to do in three years from now?' "

Here are some of the differences between those who did and those who did not arrive with their families. The children who came without parents in retrospect reported a slightly higher level of anger upon arrival than did the children who arrived with at least one parent (1.11 vs. 0.98, on a scale of 0 to 3).[4] They reported more sadness (1.51 vs. 1.17) and more (survivor's) guilt (0.50 vs. 0.19). The level of gratitude was not significantly higher (2.14 vs. 2.04). As to current feelings, sadness about their migration was still higher among the children who arrived without parents (1.17 vs. 1.01), as was guilt (0.39 vs. 0.22), but the differences had shrunk.[5] Both composites for earlier and current emotions showed higher levels of negativity for the children who had arrived without parents. In this series of results, we glimpse some quantitative evidence of the psychological ordeals the refugee children who were separated from their families endured. There was, however, no statistically significant difference in the level of life satisfaction between those having arrived without and those having arrived with their parents, it being high in both cases (5.11 vs. 5.21, on a scale of 1 to 6).[6]

Yet, from our interviews, a more complex and perhaps puzzling picture seemed to emerge. It appeared that at least some interviewees who had been unaccompanied refugees gave the impression of being relatively less troubled by their refugee experience. This leads to an interesting follow-up question about the difference between a swift break occurring in a single stroke and a wound that continued to fester—between being cut off from one's parents in one cataclysmic event and witnessing them wilting slowly, being unable to regain an earlier elevated status and resentfully yearning for the "good old days" (as many adult refugees did).[7] This would certainly be an interesting topic for further study. It may also be worth restating our—perhaps surprising—finding that, even though early familial disruption affected the outlook and attitudes of the young refugees in various ways (as we saw earlier) and their psychological make-up (as we just described), it had hardly any effect on their socioeconomic outcomes, whereas their family's original socioeconomic status made a considerable difference. This suggests powerful mechanisms of status transfer.

A final observation needs to be made: The former refugees typically do not broadcast or publicly emphasize their status. In one extreme case, we were told that two scientists in the same discipline had known each other professionally and had actually collaborated with each other on scientific projects, but only much later discovered that they both had been on the *Kindertransport*. To be sure, some of the participants do not wish to remind themselves of their childhood life in Europe at all. Some wrote, "I tried very hard to forget," or words to similar effect.[8] There might actually be some positive and functional aspects to such repression. Especially in the early days of arrival, several of our interviewees deliberately focused all their energies on the future—toward surviving and prospering in the new country. (Nowadays, however, as reported, the majority does think back. For them, the early period of their lives is still a part of their current thoughts, for better or worse.[9]) The former refugees had additional reasons for not touting their experiences, especially in the early postwar decades. First, the whole societal climate was relatively unsympathetic to victim stories. Furthermore, the former refugees realized, of course, that, among those who suffered under National Socialism, theirs was not the worst lot. How could they complain in comparison with those individuals who survived Hitler's rule in death camps, forced labor camps, or in hiding, or under similarly atrocious circumstances? In the past, occasional controversies flared up about who should be called a "Holocaust survivor" and whether the refugees who had left early would qualify for that label.

Anguish and Achievement

It would seem reasonable to assume that psychological anguish and socioeconomic achievement are, to some extent, inversely correlated, in the sense that those plagued by intense anguish might be too immobilized or at least hampered by it to pursue successful careers, or conversely, that those who enjoy socioeconomic success might have more easily got over initially perhaps troubled feelings. This may certainly be true in cases of extreme, debilitating trauma, but in our data, we did not see a particularly strong relationship of this kind. In enough cases to be noteworthy, even great outward achievements and socioeconomic success went hand in hand with psychological feelings of inferiority. An accomplished scientist wrote, "The persecution and propaganda we endured [in Central Europe] have given me a life-long inferiority complex." Another individual mentioned "feelings of inferiority in spite of my many achievements. I won the lifetime achievement award for my work. . . . I still work at 74 because of my fear of poverty and rejection."

Deep-seated fears were powerful motivators of the drive toward socioeconomic success. In some cases, one could even speak of a desperate striving for success. In the minds of those former refugees, the only chance to survive was to excel. A former *Kindertransport* participant said, "I know that I was scared as hell. That much I know. I was very, very scared. I got married and said, 'Oh, my God, now what? I have to have a place for us to live. I have to have a job. I've got to succeed; I've got to do something. I cannot afford to fail.' It's as simple as that."

In these cases, the pattern that we call "privatized costs, socialized benefits" is the most poignant. The former refugees did very well, as a group; and, as a nation, America has reaped tremendous benefits from this cohort (recall that the *Who's Who* contains 15 times as many names of former refugees as one would expect, based on the size of the refugee cohort). For many refugees, however, the refugee experience of their childhood and youth has left permanent scars, and for some, still festering wounds. This psychological anguish has been considered a matter to be dealt with privately. It is the refugees themselves who "pay" the price of their psychological problems; and, in the most extreme instances, they do so by making extraordinarily large contributions to society.

Syndromes

We now present four syndromes that emerged from our interviews with the former refugees. They demarcate the wide range of adjustments that the former refugees went through. In two of them, we find considerable amounts of psychological anguish and in the other two, anguish is largely absent; but, in each one of the four, the early experiences are dealt with in a different way.

The first syndrome is described by the "privatized costs, socialized benefits" theme. Fear and the feeling of not belonging were often at the root of socioeconomic success, and, importantly, they did not abate or get extinguished as success materialized. As noted, a recurrent theme among our interviewees was that they felt "like an outsider." In a typical case, one of our participants reported that, as a reaction, he always felt he had to prove himself and ended up as an academic and one of the worldwide acknowledged leaders of his academic discipline. Yet even though he achieved a position of recognized excellence in his field, this psychological mechanism is still in force. Here, in a sense, extraordinary achievement has always remained a basic necessity of survival.

A second syndrome is that of survivor's guilt—for instance, "The guilt factor . . . is very prevalent in me. . . . Why was I spared?" At the root of this anguish is sometimes the belief that each person has an account with a certain, finite amount of good luck. Through their lucky escapes during the National Socialist era, some former refugees appear to feel they had already overdrawn this account and so eventually they would have to balance the account out. "So when I will pay for it, is . . . still very much there. When will there be some cataclysmic event that will bring me to the same situation that so many of my relatives had to endure? And if it's not exactly concentration camp, who knows what it will be? I do not anticipate dying quietly in my bed. . . . I might be killed on the street corner by a drunken driver. But I have a feeling that it will be a more universally cataclysmic event, you know, maybe something like the towers, the New York World Trade Center. I don't know. So that's always there."

The third syndrome is characterized by the absence of psychological torment, and its main theme is revenge and getting even. There one might find an unequivocal condemnation of the former home country, as in the following instance. "I don't forgive. I don't forget—for sure not, but I don't forgive either. I think Germany is warlike and I think they don't deserve to exist." At the core of this syndrome is an abiding interest in projecting strength, so as never again to be in that position of weakness that precipitated the persecution. For instance, "[The gentiles] should know Jewish blood is not cheap, and we know how to fight. You touch a Jew, you're going to pay the price."

The fourth syndrome can be described as devoting one's life to making the world a better place and finding personal peace in the process. The early experiences are interpreted as a responsibility and motivation to help others. One interviewee described "the feeling that there must be more to life than suffering . . . there must be more to life than enduring and putting up with everything that's wrong. I mean, there must be ways to deal with that." In the place of condemnation or resentment vis-à-vis the events of the 1930s, one finds the quest for understanding and the hope that humankind might learn. "I don't blame—I'm not in the hate game or the blame game. I think a number of factors came together to produce [National Socialism], and it's our business to try to find out why they did [what they did] and why what happened and learn from it."

Chapter 8

Epilogue: Lessons for Current Refugees

One of our interviewees pointed out that extreme situations polarize. They bring "into stark relief the positive and negative features of humankind. It's like . . . our normal lives are in sepia. And . . . there is lots of evil in people which we don't see mostly in this environment. It sometimes bursts out. And there's also a great goodness in people, which we tend not to see. And then an extreme period, like the period . . . leading up to the Second World War, and the Second World War, brings out the bad . . . the evil and the good and accentuates those things."

An analogous assumption could be made about the life courses of refugees who went through such extreme situations in their youth. Their life trajectories might be more volatile and less likely to cluster around a "normal" or average life course. For them, one would expect a greater degree of polarization, or bifurcation, and a larger proportion of extreme outcomes—higher probabilities of either brilliant success or abject failure. The slogan "Yale or jail" might apply here. Or, to put it metaphorically, if an extraneous object intrudes into an oyster, it might, on one hand, become sickly or even die from it, or on the other, it might produce a beautiful pearl!

In the case of our Second Wave refugee group, the general bias of these deviations was to the positive socioeconomic extreme. The refugee children, as well as the adults, were not accepted with open arms by the American public at large when they started arriving during the Depression era in the 1930s. Had it not been for the vigorous humanitarian efforts by a multitude of nongovernmental organizations and private citizens, even fewer would have been taken in, and they would have had an even rockier start. In the end, we now see, America did well by doing good. The nation reaped great benefits from giving refuge to these youngsters, as these children surpassed all expectations by becoming highly productive members of American society. Very many of them have led successful lives and in some cases have had extraordinary achievements. They have turned the challenges they faced to their advantage, even while, in some cases, paying in personal terms a heavy psychological price. In this work, we have presented, for the first time, a quantitative picture of their socioeconomic achievements as a group.

Early observers of our refugee children assumed their rapid and total Americanization as well as their rapid and total psychological recovery. Both assumptions were too simplistic. As our study showed, there were some lasting influences from the young refugees' childhood experiences, both in terms of cultural traits and psychological characteristics.

Most importantly, contrary to older theories of assimilation, the obliteration of early-life experiences was not the precondition for success in the new country. Many former child refugees were able to use their Central European background in positive ways by converting it into useful cultural capital. They enjoyed what we called a distinctiveness advantage, for instance, through an energetic and creative blending of American and Central European traditions in their lives and careers.

At the psychological level, we did find ample evidence of the negative legacy predominantly discussed in the psychological literature—childhood trauma and the person's lifelong struggle with it. Yet, more often we encountered resilience and positive psychological reactions that coped with challenging childhood experiences in very productive ways. What seems to have happened to many of these at-risk children in their new milieu— excepting a relatively small number of tragedies—is that they rapidly became effective adults (often the effective head of the family) and in many cases replaced their childhood, even in their early teens, with the rapid acquisition of success-driven adult characteristics.

While America has benefited greatly from this influx of refugees, the balance sheet for the former refugees is somewhat more mixed (and it varies widely from person to person). On one hand, most can be justifiably proud of their achievements. Not only did these achievements mean positive contributions to the national welfare, but they were also a source of socioeconomic gratification for the individuals themselves. As noted, many told us that they were convinced that they had achieved more in the United States than they would have achieved in Central Europe if the National Socialists had never come to power. On the other hand, in numerous cases, we found psychological costs to be paid by the former refugees and perhaps by their families in the form of lasting anxieties and other aftereffects of the trauma they received as children or youths. It is thus not an entirely positive story, but it shows how, under the right conditions, human beings can rise above horrendous tragedies.

We now have keen insights into the effects on the former young refugees' career outcomes of family background, of the role of accompanying families, of networks, of languages, and other cultural capital, among many. In short, we know numerous major factors determining the whole trajectory, from the arrival of poor refugee children to eventual career success in America.

We are of course fully aware that the situation of the Central European young refugees was very different from that of many young refugees and immigrants currently coming to the United States. There are also similarities and continuities, however; and we even think that the differences between then and now do not necessarily make our results less relevant for the current situation. On the contrary, we would argue that comparing a largely successful refugee group with less successful groups and contrasting their respective framework conditions might help tease out the circumstances that facilitate integration. These circumstances then would fall into two categories—those that are unique, that is, cannot be reproduced or re-created, and those that can. Information about the latter would be extremely helpful for agencies involved in supporting current refugees, while a deeper understanding of both sets of circumstances would advance the scholarly understanding of the immigration and integration process.

Contemporary theorizing and research about young refugees and young immigrants currently arriving and living in the United States have moved beyond the older, relatively linear and uncomplicated assimilation theories.[1] A highly influential concept is that of segmented assimilation, as pioneered by Alejandro Portes and Min Zhou (1993, see Portes and Rumbaut 2001, Rumbaut 1994, Zhou and Bankston 1998), according to which newly arrived young immigrants face a situation that is substantially different from the one encountered by earlier immigrant streams. Those new immigrants, it is posited, may follow different paths, not just the path of assimilation into mainstream America; some of these paths may lead to permanent marginalization. Other scholars (e.g., Alba and Nee 2003), by contrast, have argued that the assimilation concept is not quite obsolete yet. We wish that our historical-sociological case study of the complex, yet, on average, highly successful integration of a group of young refugees would be of value not only for its own sake, but also for the sociological discourse about contemporary young immigrants.

Thus, our research findings and hypotheses we presented about this particular cohort of young refugees could well be found useful not only by general readers, historians, sociologists, and those who belong to, or are related to, the Second Wave, but also by scholars and aid organizations who deal with current waves of immigrants. We hope that the story of the Second Wave will lead to positive lessons for current young refugees or immigrants. If the experience of this group of refugees served in some way to improve outcomes for other young newcomers, that would be, for the authors, the greatest reward of all.

Appendix: Samples and Methods

We defined our target population as individuals born between 1918 and 1935 in Germany or Austria[1] who immigrated to the United States as refugees from National Socialism primarily in the years 1933 through 1945, but we also included a few individuals of that birth cohort who immigrated after the war up to 1949. Our study used three main methods: secondary data analysis of existing representative samples, our own mail survey, and semi-structured interviews.

Target Population

The refugee and immigration streams leading to the United States during and after National Socialist rule are rather complex. They include the refugees who escaped to the United States before the Holocaust reached its peak, but also those who first found refuge in other countries (for instance, through a *Kindertransport* to Britain) and then came to the United States. After the war, individuals who survived in the death camps, in hiding, or by some other means, started arriving in the United States. The postwar immigration movement included many "displaced persons," as they were called.[2] These postwar arrivals—who are not the targeted population of this study—in any case tended to have birthplaces in Eastern, rather than in Central Europe, and thus fell outside of the purview of this study.

For our own survey, we decided to set the cutoff date of arrival at 1949 so that we could include, in addition to the young refugees who arrived before or during the war, also those young refugees who arrived after the war, often on circuitous routes. For our secondary analysis of existing data sets, however, 1945 is the cutoff date (or the date closest to it in time brackets used by the respective data set).

As figure A1 indicates, the bulk of refugees who participated in our survey arrived in the United States between 1937 and 1941 (72 percent). In this respect, the participants in our survey mirror the general pattern of

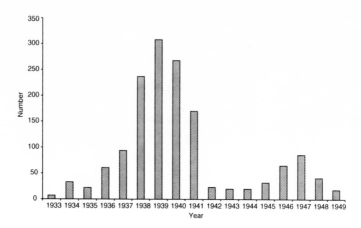

Figure A1 Refugees' Year of Arrival in the United States (among Survey Participants)

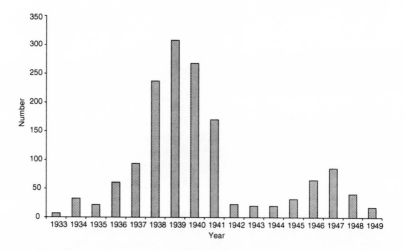

Figure A2 Refugees' Year of Departure from Central Europe (among Survey Participants)

refugee arrival in the United States (Davie 1947:29). A smaller group (16 percent) arrived in the immediate postwar period of 1945 through 1949. Those were typically young refugees who had left Central Europe and gone elsewhere before coming to the United States. This becomes apparent when comparing figure A1 (showing year of arrival) with figure A2 showing the year of departure from Central Europe. A total of 94 percent of our participants had left Central Europe by 1944.

In addition to the targeted refugee population, we used various comparison groups—typically, American-born individuals of the same age cohort, but also various other groups of immigrants—for our secondary data analyses as well as for our survey.

Secondary Data Analysis

We examined data from the United States Census, the National Jewish Population Survey, and the electronic *Who's Who* database.

United States Census

The public-use Census data we have analyzed are contained in the Integrated Public Use Microdata Series (IPUMS-98) that was created at the University of Minnesota in October 1997, and was available over the Internet. The standard Census data are of no use for this project; but, fortunately, a particular subsample of the Census permits valuable insights into some basic demographic and socioeconomic parameters of our group. That is, one of the long forms ("Long Form 1") used in the 1970 Census asked about the period of immigration that is a crucial prerequisite for identifying our cohort of immigrants. This was also a fortuitous point in the cohort's life course. In 1970, our cohort born between 1918 and 1935 was between 35 and 52 years old. Having reached mid-adulthood, they had completed their formal education and, in the typical case, were well established and active in their careers so that an examination of their socioeconomic status at that time is meaningful. Moreover, mortality was not yet a major factor at that time.

Only a 5 percent subgroup of the total United States population received Long Form 1 of the 1970 Census and thus was asked when they immigrated. The data set from that Census form specifies the interval in which a person came to the United States. The 1935–44 cohort is the one that is of prime interest to us. It is not a perfect fit to our purposes because it does not include the earliest refugees who arrived in 1933 and 1934, nor those who arrived in 1945, but it still is a reasonably good approximation.

Three samples of this 5 percent subgroup (Long Form 1) were available, each of which contained 1 percent of the 1970 Census population. Because the three 1 percent samples were mutually exclusive, we combined all three to create a 3 percent sample of the Census population. This sample contained 798 persons (392 men, 406 women) who were born between 1918 and 1935 in Central Europe (Germany, Austria) and immigrated to the

United States between 1935 and 1944. The total number of individuals in this sample—people in the target age range, regardless of birthplace—was 1,251,851.

National Jewish Population Survey

Because the vast majority of the young refugees in our study were of Jewish ancestry, we thought it instructive to compare the immigrants from Central Europe with American-born Jews. The 1970 National Jewish Population Survey (NJPS) enabled us to make such a comparison, although the relatively small number of Central European immigrants in this survey limited the possibilities of statistical analysis, which had been less of a problem with the U.S. Census data. In our cohort's age range (birth years 1918 through 1935), the 1970 NJPS contained a total of 5,154 respondents, among whom 84 were born in Central Europe and immigrated to the United States between 1933 and 1944. The 1970 NJPS data were made available by the Mandell L. Berman Institute-North American Jewish Data Bank. (Neither the original source or collectors of the data nor the North American Jewish Data Bank bear any responsibility for the analyses or interpretations presented here.) In addition to the 1970 NJPS, we explored the data of the 1990 survey of New York City Jews, also made available by the Mandell L. Berman Institute-North American Jewish Data Bank. However, because the survey contained only 43 members of the cohort on which we focus primarily (immigrants from Central Europe who were born between 1918 and 1935, and entered the United States between 1993 and 1944), no results are reported from that 1990 survey.

Who's Who

Computer-aided searches were performed in *The Complete Who's Who on CD-ROM* (Winter 2002–2003) on three subdatabases: (1) *Who's Who in America* (current listees); (2) *Who Was Who in America* (deceased listees); and (3) *Who's Who in America* (previous listees, i.e., those who were included in an earlier edition, but not in the most recent edition, typically owing to retirement). The occupational distributions in these three subdatabases were overall similar. Hence, the three subdatabases were added together; and, in this book, only the results from that composite database were reported.[3]

Our purpose was to compare the overall group of all listees born between 1918 and 1935 with the listees belonging to our refugee cohort. We identified those immigrants who, according to their biographical listing, were born in

Germany or Austria. Not all of these immigrants provided the year of their immigration so that there was some uncertainty about the cohort of immigrants in which we were interested (those who immigrated between 1933 and 1945).

There were three obvious ways of dealing with the immigrants of unknown year of immigration. The first was to exclude all those with a blank year of immigration, and thus to consider only those with a known immigration year between 1933 and 1945. This would result in an under-count of our cohort, because surely some of those with an unknown year of immigration came to this country between 1933 and 1945. The second was to include all those with a blank year of immigration, resulting in an over-count. The third was to apportion the group of immigrants with an unknown year immigration according to the observed ratio, among people with a known year of immigration, of those within our target cohort to those outside our target cohort. We compiled results for all three methods, but, in this book, concentrated on the third method, because it avoids under- and overcounts, and appears to be the best estimate of the true cohort size, in the absence of any known biases. (All methods generated substantially similar results about the internal composition of the group.)

Survey

After we designed and tested an extensive questionnaire of 104 questions on 14 pages, we distributed it widely and eventually gathered 2,480 filled-out replies that were entered into our electronic database. All respondents were assured that their names would not be used in the book. Of the participants, 68 percent were men, and 32 percent were women. Within the survey data-base, one can distinguish six major categories of participants, to be described below. Table A1 shows the breakdown.

Table A1   Survey Participants

1. Organizations		
a Holocaust Memorial Museum		331
b Kindertransport Association		248
c One Thousand Children, Inc.		240
d Washington Heights (Rabbi Lehman)		86
e Safe Haven, Oswego, NY		30
f Goldschmidt Schule		12
	Total	947

Continued

Table A1 Continued

2. "Elite"	
g American Men and Women of Science	304
h Who's Who	163
i Who's Who in American Jewry	23
j International Biographical Dictionary	86
Total	576
3. Others	
k Incidentals	263
l Spouses (of g through j)	25
Refugees Total	1,811
4. American-Born Controls	
m American Men and Women of Science—Controls	236
n Who's Who—Controls	283
o Who's Who in American Jewry—Controls	29
Total	548
5. Other Controls	
p American Men and Women of Science/early	13
q American Men and Women of Science/late	27
r American Men and Women of Science/non-refugee	59
s International Biographical Dictionary/late	4
Total	103
6. Next Generation	
t Offspring of *Kindertransport* participants (KTA2)	18
Database total	2,480

Organizations

This category contains mainly former refugees who were found through organizations and associations connected to former refugees, in addition to a smaller number found in other ways.

A valuable source of addresses of former refugees—especially those who were not so "famous" as to be included in the compilations listed below—were refugee-related institutions or associations: the United States Holocaust Memorial Museum (a.), the Kindertransport Association (KTA) (b.), One Thousand Children, Inc. (OTC) (c.), Safe Haven, Oswego, NY (an association of refugees who had been detained at former Fort Ontario) (e.). To protect the confidentiality of those organizations' address lists, the typical arrangement was for us to send questionnaire envelopes to the respective organizations who would then attach their mailing labels to the envelopes. In this way, participants could remain entirely anonymous to us if they so chose. We thank these organizations and their officers and volunteers for their gracious help in making the survey possible. We also approached the alumni of the Jewish Goldschmidt Schule of Berlin (f.).

The one subpopulation whom we found most difficult to access was religiously active refugees associated with synagogues and other Jewish organizations. Because these groups chose to ignore our repeated requests for information and assistance, we had to devise a special approach. We persuaded Rabbi Dr. Robert Lehman—himself a former refugee, a resident of Washington Heights, New York City, and a rabbi in this community—to help as a consultant for community liaison and for interviewing in Washington Heights, where many members of this subpopulation still live. He was able to get 86 survey replies for us (d.) (and also conducted face-to-face interviews, see below).

"Elite"

These were former refugees who were listed in *American Men and Women of Science, Who's Who, Who's Who in American Jewry*, or the *International Biographical Dictionary*. We sometimes call these participants our "elite" sample, for short.

g. American Men and Women of Science

A complication with this database was that the date of immigration to the United States was not available. We therefore sent a total of 1,356 questionnaires to all those with U.S. addresses who had been born in Central Europe in the relevant time period (1918 through 1935). In addition to the responses from refugees in our cohort (304), we also received responses from several other groups: those who arrived before 1933, that is, non-refugees (13), those who were refugees but arrived in the United States only after 1949 (27), and those who arrived in the United States as non-refugees after the war (59). These groups, in our database description, appear as p., q., and r.; see under "Other controls." Of the mailed-out questionnaires, 141 were returned for reason of no valid address and, in 28 cases, we were informed that the addressee was deceased. This results in a response rate of 34 percent (403/1187). We surmise, however, that the response rate among refugees was considerably higher, because the survey was ostensibly geared to refugees, so that non-refugees among the scientists should have been less likely to fill out and return the questionnaire.

h. Who's Who

We mailed out 337 surveys to those who immigrated to the United States between 1933 and 1945 or at unknown time and had a complete American address (with ZIP code). (We excluded duplicates from *American Men and Women of Science*.) We received 163 replies. Seven *Who's Who* listees were reported to us as deceased, for another seven we did not have a valid address, and four did not belong to the cohort. The response rate thus was 51 percent (163/319).

i. Who's Who in American Jewry

We mailed 105 questionnaires to listees in this compilation (again excluding duplicates). Of those, 33 were returned because of an invalid address, 2 listees were reported deceased. We received 23 replies. This resulted in a response rate of 33 percent (23/70).

j. International Biographical Dictionary

We mailed 187 questionnaires to listees in the *International Biographical Dictionary*. Of those, 11 were returned because of an invalid address, 5 listees were reported deceased, and 5 did not belong to the cohort. We received 86 replies. Hence, the response rate was 52 percent (86/166).

Others

We also contacted all other groups of former refugees and all individual former refugees we could find. An important aid here were individual referrals by other participants ("snowball method"). Those other groups included participants of a Stuttgart reunion, and of *Bundesgymnasium* XIX of Vienna, individuals connected with the William Breman Jewish Heritage Museum of Atlanta, and those belonging to the group of former refugees from the *Nürnberg/Fürth* area. Collectively, we termed the participants (a total of 263) in this category "incidentals (k.)."

We furthermore sent questionnaires to the spouses (wives, in most cases) of the participants from the elite compilations (*American Men and Women of Science, Who's Who, Who's Who in American Jewry*, and *International Biographical Dictionary*) who were identified as former refugees from the listees' responses (l.).

American-Born Controls

We surveyed randomly selected comparison groups of American-born listees of *American Men and Women of Science, Who's Who, Who's Who in*

American Jewry who were in the same age range as the former refugees (birth years 1918–35).[4]

m. American Men and Women of Science—Controls

A total of 870 questionnaires were sent to American-born listees in *American Men and Women of Science*. We received 236 replies, 129 surveys were returned for invalid addresses, 11 individuals were deceased, 2 did not belong to this population. This resulted in a response rate of 32 percent (236/728).

n. Who's Who—Controls

In all, 636 questionnaires were sent to American-born listees in *Who's Who*. We received 286 replies, 22 surveys were returned for invalid addresses, 6 individuals were deceased. This resulted in a response rate of 47 percent (286/608).

o. Who's Who in American Jewry—Controls

Of the 214 questionnaires we sent to American-born listees in the *Who's Who in American Jewry*, we received 29 replies; 76 surveys were returned for invalid addresses, and 7 individuals were deceased. Hence, the response rate was 22 percent (29/131).

Other Controls

As mentioned, this category includes listees from *American Men and Women of Science* outside our defined target population—13 who arrived before 1933 (p.), 27 refugees who arrived after 1949 (q.), and 59 non-refugees who arrived after the war (r.). There are also a few listees from the *International Biographical Dictionary* who arrived "late" in this country (s.).

Next Generation

This is a small group of offspring of former refugees, drawn from the membership of the Kindertransport Association (t.). Within the association, that younger generation is known as "KTA2."

Interviews

To gather in-depth information that a mail questionnaire is unlikely to elicit, we included an interview component in our study. We developed and tested an interview guideline for semi-structured interviews and conducted a total of 100 interviews, each lasting between one and two hours, on average. The interviews were taped and later transcribed.

As in our previous project on the careers of scientists (Project Access), we were very aware that the selection of the interviewer was critical because his or her personal characteristics could greatly influence—positively or negatively—the quality of the information collected in the interviews. After a lengthy and thorough search, we hired Alexandra Gross, who comes from a refugee family herself, speaks German, and is familiar with the interviewees' "milieu." She also had experience in interviewing. After we supervised her first few interviews, she conducted the bulk of the interviews by herself.

For logistic and cost considerations, a large proportion of interviews was done with former refugees in the New England area, but Ms. Gross also traveled to the New Jersey/New York areas, to Florida, and to the San Francisco Bay area. She also conducted several telephone interviews with people who could not be visited for geographical reasons, but whose views we considered potentially important.

Because of the evident reluctance of religiously active refugees associated with synagogues and other Jewish organizations in Washington Heights to communicate with us, we asked our consultant Rabbi Lehman (who also had helped us with the survey) to conduct ten interviews with members of that group. Sadly, Rabbi Lehman died in June 2003. He had completed 9 of the 10 interviews by that time.

When transposing the spoken language of the interviews into written text, we lightly edited the original transcripts (for instance, by removing false starts, word repetitions, major grammatical inconsistencies, and most of the stalling words, such as *you know*, *well*, and *I mean* that creep into almost everyone's speech). We believe that this approach, while maintaining the flavor of the spoken word, will make the quotations more readable.

Field Work

In addition to the above formal methods of data gathering, we undertook a host of informal activities that could perhaps be summarized under the heading field work. This includes, for instance, participation in reunions, such as those of the Kindertransport Association, of the Nürnberg-Fürth group, and of OTC, and in a Jewish-German dialogue group in Newton, MA. On a trip to Washington Heights (that has, naturally, changed much since the refugees arrived there), one of the researchers specifically visited George Washington High School that many of the former refugees attended, and where yearbooks from that time were still being kept and could be read.

Notes

Introduction

1. Office of Immigration Statistics (2004), *2003 Yearbook of Immigration Statistics*, table 15.
2. For excellent accounts of the refugee cohort who left Central Europe, see Laqueur (2001) and Whiteman (1993).
3. Tec (1993:276). A higher survival rate of 11 percent was given by Deborah Dwork (1991:xxxiii, 274), referring to reports published under the auspices of OSE (Oeuvre de Secour aux Enfants) by Jacques Bloch in 1946 and by Z. H. Wachsman in 1947. The survival rate varied greatly between countries. Of the Jewish children from Poland, only 0.5 percent survived. Also see Nicholas 2005.
4. Young immigrants, such as those in our cohort, are sometimes classified as the 1.5 generation of immigrants. This nickname was coined by the sociologist Ruben Rumbaut (1994:759, 1997b:29) to designate children born abroad and brought to the new country at a young age. A more detailed distinction differentiated the 1.75, 1.5, and 1.25 generations (Rumbaut 1997b:29, also see Oropesa and Landale 1997:432, Rumbaut 1997a:336). The first of these generations was defined as children immigrating before age six, the second as children immigrating between ages six and twelve, and the third as children immigrating at a later age. Our study contains participants of all three of these generations. On a specific definition of the 1.5 generation in the context of Holocaust survivors, see Suleiman (2002).
5. On the topic of young immigrants and immigrant families, see, for instance, the contributions to Booth, Crouter, and Landale (1997) and Suárez-Orozco and Suárez-Orozco (2001). For a brief overview of the current situation, see Rumbaut (1997b).
6. For details on samples and methodology used, see Appendix. For reports on some selected results, see Holton and Sonnert (2004) and Sonnert and Holton (2004).
7. There now exists an ample and rich crop of publications of an autobiographical nature by former refugees. The following is just a small selection: Bader 1995, Bradley 2005, David 1996, Eckfeld 2002, Eliel 1990, Foster 1990, Gay 1998,

Gershon 1989, Grunwald 1997, Hahn 1982, Heims 1987, Kanner and Kugler 1997, Krist 2001, Laqueur 1992, Lerner 2002, Meyerhof 2002, Ottenheimer 2000, Segal 1964, 1985, Stanley 1957, Trahan 1998, Watts 2000, Weil 1991. For the next generation, see Epstein 1979, 1997, and Hoffman 2004. Almost of third of our survey respondents (31 percent) told us that they had written some kind of autobiography (published or unpublished).

8. That was "Project Access" on gender differences in science careers. The methods used and the results are given in Sonnert and Holton 1995a, 1995b.

9. Other laudable efforts to preserve materials that pertain to varied aspects of the Second Wave include collections at the United States Holocaust Memorial Museum, at the Leo Baeck Institute, New York City (such as the Austrian Heritage Collection), and at the Shoa Foundation Institute for Visual History and Education at the University of Southern California, which was initiated by Steven Spielberg.

10. We should stress that the correlational statistical methods employed in this study do not determine causal relationships, and that the reported results from statistical regressions, log-linear models, and similar techniques should be understood with this proviso. Following common usage among social scientists, we will occasionally use words such as "impact," "influence," and "effect" in describing the relationship between dependent and independent variables— without implying that the obtained relationships among the variables reflect established causal relationships.

1   Exodus

1. For a general survey of refugees between the world wars in Europe, Russia, and the Ottoman Empire, see Simpson (1939).

2. Before the exodus, according to Lowenstein (1989:73), approximately 75 percent of the Jews in Germany were "urban liberal," 20 percent were "rural," and 2–4 percent were "separatistorthodox."

3. Six million is the customary figure (cf. Tec 1993:276). Davie (1947:13) gave the total number of Jews annihilated on the Continent as 6,200,000. Malcolm Proudfoot (1957:323) estimated the total wartime loss of lives among European Jews at 5,153,000.

4. Moser 1991:68–9, also see Rosenkranz 1978, Österreicher im Exil 1992:7–8, Strauss 1983: xv.

5. A person's ascribed characteristics—or ascribed statuses—are those beyond that person's control, for example, gender, age, and race. Achieved characteristics— or achieved statuses—can, to some degree, be controlled or influenced by the individual, for example, wealth, marital status, and political viewpoint.

6. For example, by Ash and Söllner 1996, Bentwich 1953, Boyers 1972, Coser 1984, Fermi 1971, Fleming and Bailyn 1969, Heilbut 1983, Hughes 1975, Ingrisch 2004, Jackman and Borden 1983, Kent 1953, Kettler and Lauer 2005,

Möller 1984, Pfanner 1983, Sokal 1984, Spaulding 1968, Stadler 1987, 1988, Strauss, Fischer, Hoffmann and Söllner 1991, and Timms and Hughes 2003.

7. On exile literature, see, for instance, Cazden 1970, and Walter 1984.

8. On persecuted children under National Socialism, see Angress 1988, Benz and Benz 1992, Hertling 1998.

9. Valuable insights into what it meant to be a Jewish child under National Socialism, can be gained, for instance, from the autobiography of Eric Kandel, published in the book *Les Prix Nobel 2000*, and from a book about the Jewish students of the Viennese *Bundesgymnasium XIX* (BG 19) (Krist 2001).

10. The *Hitlerjugend* (Hitler Youth) was the National Socialist organization for boys. Here is the story of a boy who attended a German school in a Latin American country, illustrating the powerful pull of that organization that instrumentalized boys' desires to belong, in some respects not unlike the Boy Scouts, who, in this case, provided a functional equivalent. "My classmates began to join the Hitlerjugend. And they had all kinds of privileges and they would take these great weekend hikes. And they could use the pool, you know, anytime during late afternoon. And they wore these neat uniforms. So I went home and said, 'Dad, I want to join the Hitlerjugend.' And Dad, you know, being a very wise individual—he didn't say, 'No, I forbid you to do this.' He said, 'Let me think about this.' And then he got hold of his good friend [who] . . . was a Scoutmaster. So I was immediately inducted into the Scouts before I was old enough to have a uniform. "

11. An additional quote: "My father . . . was picked up by the S.S. and kept for three days, came home. I never did discover what had happened. They said they wanted some information. Well, at that time they had access to his office; they had his office, so all the information was right in the files. And . . . in three days, he turned gray. . . . My father, for practical purposes, died spiritually the day he came home after those three days."

12. One of them survived to become the U.S. Treasury secretary: W. Michael Blumenthal. Among the others who went on to prominent careers is the distinguished numerical taxonomist Robert R. Sokal.

2   Advent

1. This obligation had given rise to numerous humanitarian aid organizations, such as the HIAS (Hebrew Immigrant Aid Society), many of which will be discussed in the following.

2. See Davie 1947:12, Proudfoot 1957:64, Zuroff 2000:273.

3. In 1943, an international agreement set up the United Nations Relief and Rehabilitation Administration (UNRRA) (Proudfoot 1957:100) to assist the refugees and displaced persons who had been victims of the Axis powers, and to aid their repatriation. After the war, UNRRA was superseded by another international organization to address the refugee problem—the International

Refugee Organization (IRO), founded by the United Nations General Assembly in 1946. At that time, a split had already developed between the Soviet bloc, which favored a policy of forcible repatriation, and the Western bloc, which favored resettlement of the displaced persons and refugees according to their own wishes (frequently they did not want to go back to the Soviet-controlled Eastern Europe) (Proudfoot 1957:400–1). On July 1947, IRO took responsibility for the care of 713,000 refugees, most of whom UNRRA had previously cared for (Proudfoot 1957:406). One result was that in the nine months from April 1946 through December 1946, 6,141 displaced persons were brought from Germany to the United States (Proudfoot 1957:294). Under the auspices of IRO, 329,000 refugees and displaced persons were settled in the United States between July 1, 1947 and December 30, 1951 (Proudfoot 1957:425). The second largest number (182,000) went to Australia, the third largest to Israel (132,000). Many individuals in this postwar resettlement wave that in total encompassed 1,039,000 people, had originally resided in Poland (357,000) or the Ukraine (114,000) (Proudfoot 1957:427).

4. Whereas about one-fifth of our participants said they received financial support from those organizations, a larger proportion received other kinds of help from them (e.g., useful information about jobs or housing).

5. Among those that provided assistance to refugees abroad were the American Jewish Joint Distribution Committee (or Joint Distribution Committee, or even "Joint," for short), the World Jewish Congress, the American Friends Service Committee (Quakers), the Unitarian Service Committee, the War Relief Services of the National Catholic Welfare Conference, the Emergency Rescue Committee (later International Rescue and Relief Committee), the Hebrew Sheltering and Immigrant Aid Society (HIAS), Hadassah, the Jewish Labor Committee, the National Refugee Service, the National Council of Jewish Women, various Zionist organizations, as well as scores of other refugee service committees and a myriad local groups (e.g., see Davie 1947:13).

To avoid duplication of effort, three Jewish emigrant aid organizations—HIAS, the Jewish Colonization Association (ICA), and Emigdirect—had joined in 1926 to form HICEM (the acronym combining letters from each constituent organization). HICEM carried out the refugee aid in all countries except in the United States where HIAS stood alone (Tartakower and Grossmann 1944:456–7). In 1940, the JDC (Joint Distribution Committee) made an arrangement with HIAS-HICEM, delineating their respective tasks: HIAS-HICEM would service immigrants from all countries, while JDC would not engage in any service activities in migration matters, but would provide as much money as possible for the transportation of refugees from Central and Eastern Europe. These funds would be administered and the connected administrative expenses covered by HIAS-HICEM (Szajkowski 1971:121).

Foremost among the German associations aiding emigration was the Hilfsverein der deutschen Juden (after 1935 renamed Hilfsverein der Juden in Deutschland). The Hilfsverein facilitated emigration to all countries except Palestine, for which the Palestinaamt (Palestine Office) of the Jewish Agency for

Palestine in Berlin was in charge (Tartakower and Grossmann 1944:461). Furthermore there was the Hauptstelle für jüdische Wanderfürsorge. The work of these associations was coordinated by the Reichsvertretung der deutschen Juden (Erichsen 1998:66).

When the refugees heading to the United States arrived in the ports of entry—New York City in most cases—they were met at the dock by representatives of various aid organizations, such as the National Council of Jewish Women, HIAS, the American Committee for Christian Refugees, the American Red Cross, and others (Saenger 1941:63–4). Many of these aid organizations that assisted the refugees once they entered this country belonged to the National Co-ordinating Committee for Aid to German Refugees (later simply called National Co-ordinating Committee [NCC]), which was established, soon after the refugees began arriving, as a national umbrella organization for several refugee aid organizations as well as numerous local aid committees (Davie 1947:96). (The National Co-ordinating Committee comprised 19 Jewish and non-Jewish organizations: American Committee for Christian-German Refugees, American Friends Service Committee, American Jewish Committee, American Jewish Congress, American Jewish Joint Distribution Committee, Committee for Catholic Refugees from Germany, Emergency Committee in Aid of Displaced Foreign Physicians, Emergency Committee in Aid of Displaced German Scholars, Federal Council of Churches of Christ in America, German-Jewish Children's Aid, Hebrew Sheltering and Immigrant Aid Society, Hospites, Independent Order of B'nai B'rith, International Migration Service, International Student Service, Musicians Emergency Fund, National Council of Jewish Federations and Welfare Funds, National Council of Jewish Women, Zionist Organization of America [Szajkowski 1971:118–19].)

HIAS, which was an already established and experienced organization of immigrant aid, viewed the newly formed groups with suspicion, and only somewhat reluctantly joined with them in the NCC (Szajkowski 1971:119). HIAS also was then an East-European- dominated organization, where Yiddish was an official language and few employees knew German (Szajkowski 1971:120).

Although the NCC was officially a nonsectarian organization, its financing basically came from Jewish fund-raising organizations, and soon after its foundation, it turned into "essentially a purely Jewish organization." (Szajkowski 1971:128). Notable among the social service agencies that worked as part of the Greater New York Co-ordinating Committee of the National Co-ordinating Committee were the New York and Brooklyn sections of the National Council of Jewish Women, the Jewish Social Service Association of New York, and the Jewish Family Welfare Society of Brooklyn.

Thus there existed multiple organizations supporting refugees that in reality were only loosely coordinated by the Co-ordinating Committee and that at times duplicated each others' efforts and squabbled among themselves about turf. This arrangement proved unable to provide efficient aid to the large numbers of refugees arriving during the peak years in the late 1930s. In 1939, therefore, the National Refugee Service (not a Federal agency) was established as a single multiple-function agency to supplant the work previously carried out by the slightly haphazard federation of independent agencies. The National Refugee Service now provided aid in a more integrated and centralized manner (Davie 1947:97). It had various departments and divisions, but also included, within its overall structure, a number of independently organized agencies, such as the European-Jewish Children's Aid and the Emergency Committee in Aid of Displaced Foreign Physicians and additional committees for other special groups (e.g., rabbis, musicians). The National Refugee Service also brought more than 900 local community committees under its influence. From 1939 to 1945, the Service provided financial assistance to more than 35,000 individuals (Davie 1947:99).

The orthodox Jewish community of America also had organizations, such as the Vaad ha-Hatzala ("Rescue Committee" of the Orthodox Rabbis organization), established in November 1939, and the Emergency Committee to Save the Jewish People of Europe, a high-profile group that lobbied for the formation of a Jewish army to fight alongside the Allies, but then turned exclusively to the rescue issue (Zuroff 2000:256–7). The Vaad ha-Hatzala viewed the rescue of imperiled religious scholars from Eastern Europe as top priority, whereas the less orthodox Jewry under the leadership of Rabbi Stephen Wise opposed the large-scale immigration of orthodox Jewish scholars (Zuroff 2000:88–9). The leaders of the more acculturated Jewish American organizations, such as JDC, HIAS, and so on, were very concerned about the effect on American public opinion of the immigration of this orthodox group en masse, although the immigration of a smaller number was deemed feasible. The different sets of rescue priorities resulted in some strain within the Jewish-American community. Aided by the Vaad ha-Hatzala, a group of orthodox scholars from Poland that had fled to Lithuania, traveled on to Kobe, Japan, and Shanghai, as already mentioned.

On the Christian side, there was the American Committee for Christian German Refugees (later called American Christian Committee for Refugees), founded in 1934 by the Protestant denominations, which aided "Aryan" and "non-Aryan" Christians. This Committee was started with Jewish as well as Christian funds (Davie 1947:97). The Catholic Committee for Refugees was set up in 1936. The Refugee Division of the American Friends Service Committee, in addition to its overseas activities, provided both general services to refugees in America and special programs for teachers, scholars, and professionals (Davie 1947: 97–8). For instance, the Quakers organized a series of seminars for European intellectuals and scholars, in which American teachers and graduate students acquainted the newcomers with the techniques of American pedagogy (Davie 1947:106). Christian groups had much smaller budgets than the National Refugee Service. Whereas the latter's annual expenditures exceeded $2 million between 1939 and 1942, with a peak of $3.5 million in 1940, the three mentioned Christian organizations' combined annual expenditures ranged between $300,000 and $400,000 during that period (Davie 1947:98).

Other Christian agencies included the Unitarian Service Committee, which focused on aiding political refugees, the Episcopal Committee for European Refugees, the Congregational Christian Committee for War Victims and Services, the National Lutheran Council, the Federal Council of Churches of Christ in America, the Greater New York Federation of Churches, and the Board of Missions of the Presbyterian Church. On one of the Christian efforts, see Davis 1977.

6. In 2005, HIAS reported that it had helped more than 4.5 million people during its then 124-year history.

7. In the following, we briefly survey the situation of refugee scholars, doctors, and lawyers, and the respective organizations set up to help them. The small number of world-famous scholars and intellectuals among the immigrants faced relatively minor difficulties in securing suitable positions because many American institutions felt honored and were eager to have them in their midst. The problems were greater for the much larger group of refugee academics and intellectuals who had less than superstar reputations in America. Yet assistance was forthcoming from many sources.

A major haven for them was the University in Exile of the New School for Social Research in New York, which was led by the renowned economist Alvin Johnson (Davie 1947:109, Krohn 1993, Luckmann 1981). The entire faculty of the University in Exile consisted of Europeans. In addition, the so-called Frankfurt School of unorthodox Marxist intellectuals and social scientists moved its *Institut für Sozialforschung* to New York City and, thanks to its endowment, was relatively self-sufficient. The Emergency Committee in Aid of Displaced German Scholars (later called Emergency Committee in Aid of Displaced Foreign Scholars), which existed from 1933 to 1945, helped refugee scholars find academic positions in the United States and partly covered their salaries (Duggon and Drury 1948). During its lifetime, the Emergency Committee assisted a total of 335 scholars (and, as in all cases, indirectly their families if they had come with them). In similar ways, the Oberlaender Trust of Philadelphia supported about 330 scholars, and the American Friends Service Committee, approximately 200. The American Christian Committee for Refugees started the Refugee Scholar Fund in 1943. In 1945 it created the American Committee for Emigre Scholars, Writers and Artists, which, in a more limited way, carried on the work of the folding Emergency Committee in Aid of Displaced Foreign Scholars. The Rockefeller Foundation was also active in aiding refugee scholars (Raven and Krohn 2000:xxv).

Before being able to practice medicine in this country, a refugee doctor had to obtain American credentials by fulfilling certain requirements and passing the necessary examinations. The American Medical Association and many American physicians were not particularly welcoming toward their European colleagues because they viewed them, first of all, as competitors (although, ironically, many American physicians had, in earlier years, traveled to Vienna or Berlin to learn their trade at the famous hospitals there). In addition to economic concerns, anti-Semitism also played a role. "With notable exceptions,

the attitude of American physicians has been one of resentment and hostility, which in some instances has taken the form of deliberate propaganda and
the spreading of rumors." (Davie 1947:263). Over the years, a series of
restrictive and protectionist measures made it harder for refugee physicians
to obtain their licenses, among them, for instance, the requirement of full
citizenship before admission to the licensing exam in 28 states (Davie
1947:267).

Parts of the profession, however, did make an effort to integrate the newcomers. The Emergency Committee in Aid of Displaced Foreign Physicians
(renamed in 1939 as Emergency Committee in Aid of Displaced Medical
Scientists) was established by American physicians in 1933. The work of this
group focused on physicians in medical research. From 1934/35 through
1941/42, it made 215 grants to 125 medical scientists in the total sum of
$294,075 (Davie 1947:276). In 1939, American doctors set up the National
Committee for Resettlement of Foreign Physicians to help physicians in private
practice and hospital employment as well as those in research. The committee
placed over 1,700 physicians, making particular efforts to resettle the physicians
in rural and underserved areas. In 1940, the two organizations merged offices
and secretaryships (Davie 1947:276-7).

Compared with the physicians, the refugee lawyers' situation was considerably
worse because their skills were not at all transferable. They found that their training
in the Continental legal systems—not to speak of the high social regard they had
enjoyed as professionals—had no relevance in the United States, with its very different legal system, rooted in the Anglo-Saxon common law tradition. However, there
were limited possibilities for refugee lawyers to enter the American profession. A special organization, the American Committee for the Guidance of Professional
Personnel (which later turned into the Committee for the Re-education of Refugee
Lawyers), devoted itself to retraining a selected group of refugee lawyers in the
American law (Davie 1947:289-90). The founders included John W. Davis, C. J.
Friedrich of Harvard University, and David Riesman, then at the University of
Buffalo Law School. Yet the number of refugee lawyers who completed their retraining and passed the bar examination by the end of 1944 was estimated to be only
"some 70-odd" at the most (Davie 1947:294). Of the 311 respondents to Davie's
questionnaire who had been lawyers in Europe, only 19 were again lawyers in the
United States. The largest single group (about 40 percent) worked as " bookkeepers,
salespeople, or other white-collar workers." (Davie 1947:299). The psychological
and economic effects on them and their families can easily be imagined. For
instance, one of our participants whose father had been a lawyer in Europe told us,
"[my father] had no idea how to do anything. So that became difficult and then my
father got a job as a . . . bath attendant at a hotel. . . . And then my father also was
not well." Frank Mecklenburg (1995:289) reported that in time about ten percent
(or approximately 200–400) of the Central European lawyers practiced in their original profession in the United States. A late reversal of fortune for some lawyers came
after the passing of the German restitution laws in the 1950s. These laws created a
considerable demand for lawyers who, working with colleagues in Germany, could

represent refugees in their restitution claims before German courts (Lowenstein 1989:63).

The political refugees were supported by left-wing, anti-Fascist, or organized labor groups. For instance, the Jewish Labor Committee, established in 1933, brought more than 800 labor leaders and intellectuals out of Europe. An early focus of these activities was the victims of General Franco's ascendancy in Spain. The Joint Anti-Fascist Refugee Committee aided Spanish refugees, most of whom were brought to Mexico and other Latin American countries, and only few to the United States. The Exiled Writers Committee, which helped former members of the International Brigade of the Spanish civil war and rescued a dozen writers, and the American Committee to Save Refugees, which helped refugees escape from France, both merged with the Joint Anti-Fascist Refugee Committee in 1942. The International Relief Association, established in 1933, supported anti-Fascist activists, and the Emergency Rescue Committee, set up in 1940, helped democratic-minded intellectuals, artists, and labor leaders escape from Europe. The representative of the Emergency Rescue Committee in Europe was the now legendary Varian Fry (1992), who led the *Centre américain de secours* in Marseille. A young editor from New York City, Fry had initially no experience in covert operations; but, using the *Centre* as a front, he succeeded in establishing a rescue network that brought more than 1,500 individuals to safety, among them many notable intellectuals and artists, such as Marc Chagall, Max Ernst, Hannah Arendt, Heinrich Mann, Franz Werfel, and Alma Mahler Werfel. Fry's activities led to his ouster from France and, back home, to an investigation by the FBI. He died in relative obscurity in 1967, but is now recognized and honored as one of the great humanitarian heroes of the refugee movement. Lisa Fittko (1985) was one of the helpers in this rescue network and guided refugees on dangerous paths through the Pyrenees from France to Spain. The two groups (International Relief Association and Emergency Rescue Committee) merged in 1942 to form the International Rescue and Relief Committee. Altogether these organizations brought a total of nearly 1,000 intellectuals and political activists to the United States, and another 1,000 to other countries of the Western hemisphere.

8. On admission practices at some elite academic institutions in that era, see Synnott 1979. On Harvard University, also see Keller and Keller (2001) and Rosovsky (1986).

9. The New World Club was founded in 1931 as "Deutsch-Jüdischer Club" by German Jews who had immigrated before the National Socialist period (Lowenstein 1989:46).

10. The *Aufbau* was the most important newspaper of the refugee community, but not the only one. Other journals were the bi-weekly *Jüdisches Familienblatt für die Gesamtinteressen des Judentums* and the *Jewish Way* (written in German despite its name) (Lowenstein 1989:48, 125–8).

11. Because of the large number of diverse refugee associations, three so-called roof organizations came into existence to coordinate and unify the community activities and serve as the refugees' voice. These organizations were the American Federation of Jews from Central Europe, Inc., the Conference of Jewish

Immigrant Congregations, and the Immigrants' Victory Council (Davie 1947:180). Since the postwar government of West Germany started a compensation program for the victims of National Socialism, several organizations within the refugee community have been addressing this issue. The American Federation of Jews from Central Europe (which is the American branch of the Council of Jews from Germany) has become recognized as the representative of the refugees' interests vis-à-vis the Federal Republic of Germany and the United States. The United Restitution Organization, which was under the aegis of the American Federation, helped many refugees receive support from Germany, such as compensation payments, pensions, and social security payments. The New York office of the United Restitution Organization processed 300,000 applications by 75,000 individuals. The Jewish Restitution Successor Organization has received

	Estimate based on arrivals by selected European "races" or peoples	Estimate based on arrivals from Europe as place of last residence
Professional pursuits		
Actor	767	836
Architect	402	380
Chemist	507	432
Clergyman	2,489	2,273
Editor	457	440
Engineer (technical)	2,818	2,471
Lawyer	1,989	1,819
Musician	1,501	1,281
Nurse	707	609
Physician	5,516	4,684
Professor and teacher	3,569	3,415
Scientist and literary person	1,900	1,907
Sculptor, artist	702	717
Other professional	2,211	1,578
Total	25,535	22,842
Commercial pursuits		
Accountant	253	200
Agent	6,045	5,441
Banker	805	808
Manufacturer	2,115	1,792
Merchant and dealer	30,000	26,196
Total	39,218	34,437

Source: Davie (1947:41), cf. Hirsch and Hirsch (1961:55).

compensation payments for the property of Jewish institutions in Germany and the property of individuals who perished in the Holocaust. Parts of these funds have been used to provide welfare programs for refugees in need. These programs have been carried out by United Help, Inc., founded in 1954 (Strauss 1981:250).

12. If one had data for Central European refugees only, this pattern might be even more pronounced.

13. Estimated Number of Adult Refugee Immigrants, Fiscal Years Ended June 30, 1933–44, who had, in Europe, Worked in Certain Professional or Commercial Occupations

14. Another nickname for this area was "Frankfurt on the Hudson," stemming from the fact that Rabbi Joseph Breuer and his followers had relocated their community from Frankfurt am Main to Washington Heights (see Kranzler and Landesman 1998). Steven Lowenstein (1989) provided a fascinating account of the Washington Heights refugee community, which, for this immigration movement, is the closest approximation to an ethnic enclave of "urban villagers" (Gans 1982). For a collection of biographical interviews, see Kirchheimer and Kirchheimer (1997). On the local politics of Washington Heights, see Katznelson 1981.

15. This policy was in line with the high priority placed on "assimilating" immigrants into the American mainstream, and also perhaps with the intention of minimizing an anti-Semitic backlash against the refugees.

3 Settling In

1. In the following description of how our group of refugees settled in, we can and will take advantage of thorough studies that had been conducted in the early phases of the refugees' arrival (e.g., Davie 1947, Saenger 1941).

2. Also see the title of the pamphlet "The Refugees are now Americans" (Davie and Koenig 1945).

3. Also see Helmreich 1996.

4. See Davie 1947:144–5. Because much of the previously published research about this refugee group has focused on the individuals who when they arrived were already famous—almost all of whom were men—the experiences of the women refugees did not receive the attention they deserved. Recent studies of refugee women have begun to address this imbalance (e.g., Häntzschel 1998, Quack 1995a, 1995b).

5. Here is an interesting comment from Ise Gropius, wife of the famous Bauhaus architect and later dean of the Harvard Graduate School of Design, Walter Gropius: "What really amazes the foreigner, however, is the way American men have been domesticated. Much as they compete with each other in business, at home they seem to be more or less content to leave the management of their private lives to their wives" (Davie 1947:61).

6. For instance, "I didn't have a very good relationship with my father. Maybe that's why I worked so hard . . . and I always resented the fact that my mother had to work so hard, and he didn't."

7. For a general perspective on unaccompanied children, see Ressler, Boothby, and Steinbock 1988.

8. In the aftermath, the United States Committee for the Care of European Children was organized in June 1940, under the sponsorship of Eleanor Roosevelt. It brought 840 British child evacuees to the United States for the duration of the war, as well as 86 other European children, including 40 children of Spanish loyalists. It also collaborated with the European-Jewish Children's Aid in bringing 350 Jewish children from Europe to this country.

9. *Hansard* 342, HC. Deb., 5.8, Nov. 8 to 25, 1938, pp. 1428–84.

10. Publications about the *Kindertransport* include Drucker 1995, Göpfert 1997, Gottlieb 1998, Harris and Oppenheimer 2000 (and a companion documentary film, "Into the Arms of Strangers"), Leverton and Lowensohn 1990, Turner 1991, as well as the booklet of the sixtieth anniversary celebration in London, UK, on June 15–17, 1999, titled *Kindertransport 60th Anniversary*. See also Segal 1964. We should also note that, after the outbreak of the war, the British government grew suspicious of the refugees and instituted internment policies (Gillman and Gillman 1980).

11. Saving the lives of 10,000 children, the *Kindertransport* was an enormously successful humanitarian enterprise. Yet for the children, some difficulties persisted even after their rescue. To begin with a minor one, ancient regional rivalries between the Prussian North Germans and the Southerners continued in Dovercourt, one of the main *Kindertransport* camps, where many of the Berliner and Viennese boys divided into two somewhat hostile camps, between whom fisticuffs and even occasional knife fights occurred (Turner 1991:66–7). A more serious conflict—and one that had wider ramifications in the community— was that between the orthodox Jews and the nonreligious and non-Jewish children at Dovercourt. The orthodox children and the orthodox Rabbis insisted on strict observance of their religious precepts. For instance, the orthodox children refused to eat because the German rabbi supervising the kitchen was not kosher enough for them, and this led to conflicts involving even the Chief Rabbi of Britain, Dr. Joseph Herman Herz (Turner 1991:237, Gottlieb 1998:113). Herz was also very incensed about the fact that a *Kindertransport* train was scheduled to leave Berlin on a Saturday. Consequently, the departure was rescheduled for the following Monday.

The mostly nonorthodox workers of the Movement tried to accommodate the orthodox children in terms of food and travel, yet an even thornier problem was that of the children's religious identity. There were not enough Jewish families, let alone orthodox families, who volunteered to foster a refugee child. Under the circumstances, the Movement welcomed any non-Jewish volunteer families, whereas the orthodox faction preferred hostels where life could be structured according to the religious traditions. When, after the outbreak of war, the "Kinder" participated in the general evacuation of British children to the countryside, that problem intensified. The orthodox group was incensed by suspected large-scale conversion attempts in Christian homes. It frequently accused the Movement of abetting such attempts, although the Movement made efforts to provide religious instruction according to the custom in the child's family (for instance through the Joint Emergency Committee for Jewish Religious Teaching).

The Movement also felt that children from nonreligious Jewish families should not be turned into religious Jews, whereas the orthodox group tended to argue that the parents of these children had simply downplayed their Jewishness to avoid the attention of the National Socialists (Turner 1991:238). The orthodox attack on the Movement reached a high point with the publication in 1944 of a pamphlet with the provocative title *The Child-Estranging Movement*, which was circulated to all Jewish congregations (Gottlieb 1998:130–1, Turner 1991:256–8). Similar problems around religion also occurred in the much smaller program for unaccompanied children in the United States (Baumel 1990:105–7).

12. On the children who found refuge in Australia, see Gill 2005.

13. The latter group included children who had participated in the voyage of the *St. Louis*, and for that reason were nicknamed "Cubans" within the organization.

14. On nearly 100 refugee children living in La Hille in Southern France, see Friedländer (2004).

15. This participant was then sent to two different foster homes. "In three years I went to three different high schools, which wasn't easy, you know."

16. The questionnaire item was: If, during or after your migration, you spent time outside your immediate family (e.g., with distant relatives, family friends, in a foster family/home), how do you rate your overall experience in that environment?

very negative □	*negative* □	*somewhat negative* □
somewhat positive □	*positive* □	*very positive* □

17. It has generally been found that such a readjustment to one's family is fraught with difficulties (Coll and Magnuson 1997:99).

18. Different educators gave varying explanations of superior scholastic performances. Some hypothesized that the refugee group was selected for high intelligence because only the more intelligent families would have been able to accomplish a successful escape from Europe. Others emphasized the extraordinary value that refugee families placed on academic achievement. A third group saw a combination of superior intelligence and favorable attitudes and habits regarding scholarship at work. A fourth hypothesis was that many young immigrants compensated for difficulties in social adjustment by striving for recognition in the academic field (Davie 1947:226–7).

19. Having examined the *Kindertransport* children's personal files kept by the British Refugee Children's Movement, Barry Turner (1991:216–34) described a long series of cases in which the child exhibited some form of deviance ranging from petty crime to psychiatric disorders to suicide. Yet because all these types of social and psychological pathology occur in the general population also, only quantitative information about the relative frequency of these cases—which was not presented—would permit the comparisons necessary for concluding that the refugee children, as a group, were particularly troubled. Turner's account, nonetheless, creates the impression that deviance was widespread among the "Kinder," owing to the severely traumatizing experiences they had to

endure. Major psychological problems were "survivor's guilt," and the mental stress and breakdown caused by the murder of many relatives in the Holocaust. Moreover, there was a "tendency for psychiatric disorders to show up more dramatically as the victims emerged from childhood." (Turner 1991:228). On the psychological situation of refugee children, also see Newman (n.d.). Anna Freud ran nurseries for refugee children in Hampstead, a suburb of London (see Freud and Burlingham 1943, and Fuchs 1992).

20. One has to take into account here a probable difference, between immigrants and native-born Americans, in the social acceptability of seeking mental health care, as well as perhaps a difference in the availability of such services.

21. On resilience and posttraumatic growth, see, for instance, Garmezy and Rutter (1988), Janoff-Bulman (1992), Taylor (2005), Tedeschi, Park, and Calhoun (1998), and Werner and Smith (1989, 1992).

4   Socioeconomic Achievements

1. In addition to the advantages mentioned in the text, the *Who's Who* database also has two important advantages in terms of research efficiency. First, the entries include current addresses (which made it possible to send questionnaire surveys to the listees). Second, the *Who's Who* database is available on CD-ROM and on the Internet, thus enabling computer-aided searches. Electronic searches saved substantial amounts of time and money, in comparison with what "manual" searches would have required. We used the CD-ROM, because the web database is updated too frequently to keep statistics constant for analysis.

2. The bulk of the immigration occurred in the years 1939 and 1940, with the numbers declining steeply in both directions. Because there were only few immigrants at the beginning and at the end of our period, the Census category provided a relatively good fit. From a table in Davie (1947:29) that covered the annual immigration figures from 1933 through 1944, we could determine the proportion of the German and Austrian immigration that occurred in the years 1933 and 1934. Moreover, the subsequent wave of postwar immigration began only after 1945, and so we assumed the 1945 number of immigrants to be equal to the smallish 1944 number. We calculated that 5.3 percent of the Central European immigration between 1933 and 1945 took place in the years 1933, 1934, and 1945, and that 94.7 percent of that immigration happened within the U.S. Census bracket of 1935 through 1944. This led us to estimate the size of the whole cohort (1933–45) as 26,600/.947, that is, 28,090.

3. We should stress that 713 is a conservative number for former refugees who were listed in the *Who's Who*, because it counts only those who immigrated to the United States from Central Europe between 1933 and 1945. Of the additional 100 *Who's Who* listees of Central European origin who immigrated between 1946 and 1949, many can be assumed to be refugees who had spent some time in other countries before coming to America. But because the refugee/non-refugee mix among those later arrivals is essentially unclear, we did not include these listees.

4. One reason for forming these broad composite fields is that some of the original *Who's Who* categories contained only few former refugees.

5. *Who's Who* data and Statistical Analysis

(a) Percentages of Who's Who Listees Among Practitioners by Field

	Female		Male	
	Immigrant	**Nonimmigrant**	**Immigrant**	**Nonimmigrant**
Science	9.2	0.7	33.1	1.1
Humanities	17.1	1.6	78.6	9.4
Public sector	18.6	1.0	32.1	2.4
Arts	51.4	2.5	45.3	3.7
Health	9.4	0.3	42.7	2.8
Business	1.4	0.2	8.8	0.6
Education	0.4	0.2	9.3	0.7
Law	11.4	1.7	61.3	4.5

(b) Arcsin Transformation of Percentages

	Female		Male	
	Immigrant	**Nonimmigrant**	**Immigrant**	**Nonimmigrant**
Science	0.61	0.17	1.22	0.21
Humanities	0.85	0.25	2.18	0.62
Public sector	0.89	0.20	1.20	0.31
Arts	1.60	0.32	1.48	0.39
Health	0.62	0.11	1.42	0.34
Business	0.24	0.09	0.60	0.16
Education	0.13	0.09	0.62	0.17
Law	0.69	0.26	1.79	0.43
Sum	5.63	1.49	10.51	2.63
M	0.704	0.186	1.314	0.329
S^2	0.203	0.007	0.290	0.024

(c) ANOVA with Field as Random Factor

Source	SS	df	MS	$F_{(1,7)}$	p	r
Fixed Effects						
(Between)		(3)				
Immigration	4.5150	1	4.5150	40.24	0.00039	0.923
Sex	1.1325	1	1.1325	14.78	0.0063	0.824
Immigration × Sex	0.4372	1	0.4372	12.04	0.010	0.795
Random Effects						
(Within)		(28)				
Field	2.0918	7	0.2988			
Field × Immigration[a]	0.7854	7	0.1122			
Field × Sex[b]	0.5362	7	0.0766			
Field × Immigration × Sex[c]	0.2540	7	0.0363			

[a] Error term for immigration effect
[b] Error term for sex effect
[c] Error term for immigration × sex effect

6. A technical note: The proportions were converted to arcsin transformations (a transformation that makes equal differences equally detectable, see panel b in table in note 5 above); and an analysis of variance (ANOVA) of the $2 \times 2 \times 8$ table of Immigration (2 levels), Sex (2 levels), and Field (8 levels) was conducted, with Field thought of as a random factor (see panel c in table in note 5 above). The largest effect found was the immigrant status advantage ($r = .92$, $p = .0004$); next was the advantage of males over females ($r = .82$, $p = .006$). Finally, the interaction of Immigration $\times$ Sex showed that the immigrant status advantage was greater for males than for females ($r = .80$, $p = .01$). That interaction effect highlighted the "glass half-full or half-empty" quandary of the immigrant women, mentioned in the text. We thank our advisory committee member Robert Rosenthal for kindly providing this analysis. Finally, we should note that we also calculated the percentages of the former refugees who were listed in the *Who's Who* in the various fields under a very "conservative" assumption (calculation not shown): By using the upper limits of the confidence intervals (2 standard errors) for the respective numbers of refugees, we minimized the former refugees' percentage rates of representation. Even under these conditions, the representation was higher for our cohort of immigrants than for the nonimmigrants in all categories.

7. We could not include the German-speaking refugees from Czechoslovakia (even though, in terms of language and culture, they should be counted among the group of Central European refugees), because we only knew the birth place of the individuals and this selection criterion, in the case of Czechoslovakia, would have resulted in cohort of diverse and uncertain composition of Czech and German speakers.

8. The standard error was calculated to be 1,023 that sets the 95% confidence interval at $26,600 \pm 2,006$ ("margin of error"). The determination of the standard error is complex because of the nature of the Census sampling. Our calculations are based on the tables of standard errors and correction factors published on the IPUMS website.

   Using Table A for 1-in-100 samples (from the section "1970 Approximate Standard Errors" of the IPUMS website), we find

   s.e. $(26,600) = 1,570 + (26,600 - 25,000)(2,230 - 1,570)/(50,000 - 25,000)$
   $= 1,612$.

   Multiplying with an adjustment factor of 1.1 (from table 2 of chapter 3: Sampling Errors), we get 1,773. Because we have a 3-in-100, rather than a 1-in-100 sample, we further adjust by a factor of .577.

   The exact formula for that adjustment is, according to the website,

   $$\sqrt{\frac{(1 - f_2)f_1}{(1 - f_1)f_2}}$$

with f_1 and f_2 being the respective sample-to-population ratios. Because, in our case, f_1 and f_2 are small (.01 and .03), the formula may be simplified to

$$\sqrt{\frac{f_1}{f_2}}$$

The adjustment yields a standard error of 1,023. To calculate the 95% confidence interval, the standard error is multiplied by 1.96.

9. See note 2 for the method of arriving at the group size estimate.

10. At the technical level, an added limitation results from the fact that we are dealing here with a 3 percent sample of the Census, rather than with the full Census. The reported numbers are estimates that have standard errors attached to them. Whereas these standard errors are negligible for the American-born group, owing to its large size, they are larger for the much smaller groups of our immigrants. Our analysis thus will lack the power to declare small differences found in the sample as statistically significant.

11. Thereafter that proportion slowly declined, although women continued to outnumber men substantially (e.g., 59.3 percent in 1965–70). This pattern is in marked contrast to the Eastern European immigration that over the years never strayed much from gender parity.

12. *Marital status*

In 1970, a total of 89.3 percent of the men from our Central European cohort were married, 6.6 percent had never married, and 4.1 percent had been in a marriage that had ended. Of the women, 86.0 percent were married, 4.2 percent had never married, and 9.9 percent had had a terminated marriage. The American-born contemporaries had slightly lower proportions of married persons (84.4 percent of the men and 79.2 percent of the women).

Age at first marriage

Conforming to a pervasive pattern in this and many other societies, the men of our Central European cohort, on average, were older than the women when they first married. The former Central European men's mean age at first marriage was 26.1 years, whereas the women's was 22.8 years— an average age difference of more than three years. The American-born contemporaries, as a group, were somewhat younger when they entered married life, yet a similar gender difference also existed among them. The men got married at the age of 23.9, and the women were only 21.2 years old, on average.

Children

In the 1970 Census, only female respondents were asked about their children. There was a considerable gap in terms of motherhood between women immigrants from Central Europe and American-born women, with the former group, as a whole, having fewer children, on average

(2.0 vs. 2.8). There was little difference in the percentages of women who had children. Of the formerly Central European women, 83.5 percent had become mothers, and this percentage was only slightly lower than the corresponding number for American-born women (86.3 percent). Yet if we look only at women with children, we find that the average number of children was markedly lower for the Central European women than for the American-born women. As of 1970, the Central European women who became mothers had almost one child fewer, on average, than their American-born counterparts (2.4 vs. 3.3). Hence, we note that the difference we observed above in the average number of offspring was mainly due to a difference in the numbers of children to whom mothers gave birth, and less due to a difference in the proportions of women becoming mothers at all.

13. The largest standard error for the women was 10.4 percent (Eastern Europeans of the 1935–44 cohort); for the men it was 7.4 percent (Eastern Europeans of the 1935–44 cohort). Note that these standard errors were calculated in the usual manner; hence they are somewhat larger than the actual standard errors would be.

14. Here we have a paradoxical case: When viewed separately, both the men and the women of the 1945–49 Central European immigration cohort received a higher average income than their American-born contemporaries (men: 142.4 percent, women: 118.5 percent); when viewed together as a cohort, however, their overall average income was lower than that of the American-born individuals—owing, of course, to the shift in gender composition and the gender gap in income. This could be considered an example of what statisticians call Yule's paradox or Simpson's paradox.

15. The Census used a definition of poverty originally developed by the Social Security Administration in 1964. The poverty level was pegged to the cost of the "economy food plan" devised in 1961 by the United States Department of Agriculture. The Census variable labeled "poverty" expresses family income as a percentage of that poverty level. For our discussion, we define poverty as a percentage score of 100 or less on that variable.

16. Note that, when we speak of "managers" in the following, this includes not only managers in the narrow sense, but the term is used as shorthand for all individuals who come under that large second Census category.

17. A career in the arts appeared to be particularly attractive to women formerly from Central Europe, although this did not reach statistical significance.

18. The largest standard error on the OIS variable (for Eastern European men) was 0.85.

19. The largest standard error on the SEI variable (for Eastern European women) was 1.9.

20. Educational Attainment (in Percentage)

21. 1970 NJPS Occupational Groups (in Percentage)

		8th grade or less	9th to 12th grade	Some college	4 years college	Over 4 years higher ed.
American-born men		0.7	23.2	21.8	18.9	35.5
(n = 2,055)	s.e.	0.2	0.9	0.9	0.9	1.1
American-born women		0.5	38.8	29.0	15.7	16.1
(n = 2,292)	s.e.	0.1	1.0	0.9	0.8	0.8
1933–44 Immigration cohort						
Central European men		2.3	16.3	14.0	11.6	55.8
(n = 43)	s.e.	2.3	5.6	5.3	4.9	7.6
Central European women		2.7	35.1	27.0	5.4	29.7
(n = 37)	s.e.	2.7	7.8	7.3	3.7	7.5
Eastern European men		0.0	28.6	28.6	21.4	21.4
(n = 14)	s.e.	12.1	12.1	11.0	11.0	
Eastern European women		0.0	33.3	22.2	0.0	44.4
(n = 9)	s.e.	15.7	13.9	16.6		
1945–49 Immigration cohort						
Central European men		13.6	36.4	31.8	0.0	18.2
(n = 22)	s.e.	7.3	10.3	9.9	8.2	
Central European women		10.0	50.0	15.0	10.0	15.0
(n = 20)	s.e.	6.7	11.2	8.0	6.7	8.0
Eastern European men		29.8	36.8	21.1	5.3	7.0
(n = 57)	s.e.	6.1	6.4	5.4	3.0	3.4
Eastern European women		35.2	44.4	14.8	3.7	1.9
(n = 54)	s.e.	6.5	6.8	4.8	2.6	1.9

Note: Standard errors (s.e.) are in italics.

	American-born		Central European		Eastern European	
	Men	Women	Men	Women	Men	Women
Professionals	33.6	33.4	59.1	61.1	21.4	57.1
			7.4	11.5	11.0	18.7
Managers	42.5	16.4	31.8	5.6	42.9	0.0
			7.0	5.4	13.2	
Clerical workers	3.0	37.8	0.0	16.7	14.3	0.0
				8.8	9.4	
Sales workers	13.7	8.7	4.6	16.7	14.3	14.3
			3.2	8.8	9.4	13.2

Craftsmen	3.6	0.9	2.3	0.0	7.1	0.0
			2.3		6.9	
Operatives	2.4	0.4	0.0	0.0	0.0	14.3
						13.2
Service workers	1.0	2.0	0.0	0.0	0.0	14.3
						13.2
Laborers	0.2	0.4	2.3	0.0	0.0	0.0
			2.3			
N	2,052	1,077	44	18	14	7

Note: The immigrants are of the 1933–44 immigration cohort. Standard errors are given where appropriate (in italics).

22. On September 15, 1935, the party convention of the National Socialists at Nürnberg enacted the infamous "Nuremberg Laws," which demoted Jews from German citizens to a segregated minority with limited rights. The *Durchführungsverordnung* (Executive Order) of November 14, 1935 for one of these laws, the *Reichsbürgergesetz* (Law of Citizenship of the Reich), detailed who was to be considered a Jew. The term *Volljude* was applied to a person with at least three grandparents of the Jewish religion. A "*Mischling* of the first degree" (*Halbjude*) was considered an individual with two Jewish grandparents; a "*Mischling* of the second degree" (*Vierteljude*) was a person with one Jewish grandparent. In many cases, *Halbjuden* were considered Jewish by the National Socialist regime. (See www.shoa.de.)

23. The denominator for calculating these percentages was our survey sample of all former refugees minus those with missing values, that is, minus those who neither self-identified as being of the Jewish religion nor filled out any information about their grandparents' religion.

24. The group of survey participants is described in detail in the Appendix. Note that, in the data tables presented in the following, the Ns (numbers of subjects) vary slightly, owing to blank or unusable responses on the relevant survey questions.

25. Broad Occupational Categories of our Cohort of Former Refugees (in Percentage)

	Men	Women
Professionals	62.7	49.0
Managers	29.2	17.5
Sales workers	3.8	5.0
Clerical workers	1.3	23.2
Craftsmen	1.5	0.9
Operatives	1.0	2.2
Farm workers	0.1	0.0
Service workers	0.5	2.2
N	945	543

Note: Categories are based on those of the U.S. Census.

26. The survey participants were asked to give their whole employment history, and the occupation used in the following analysis was the participant's primary occupation, defined as the one in which the participant spent the longest time.

27. Detailed Occupational Fields of Professional and Managerial Former Refugees (in Percentage)

	Men	Women
Arts	1.5	7.6
Associations and organizations	0.2	4.8
Communications and media	1.4	2.1
Education	3.5	21.2
Engineering	3.4	0.9
Finance	2.2	2.7
Government	0.5	0.6
Health	0.5	11.2
Humanities	6.5	8.5
Industry	31.8	28.1
Law	4.2	1.5
Life science	3.5	1.2
Math and Computer science	9.8	2.1
Medicine	8.5	1.8
Physics	6.1	0.3
Religion	0.8	0.0
Nat. science (other)	9.9	3.3
Social science	5.7	2.1
N	858	331

28. Broad Occupational Fields of Professional and Managerial Former Refugees (in Percentage)

	Men	Women
Arts	1.5	7.6
Education	3.5	21.2
Engineering	3.4	0.9
Humanities	7.3	8.5
Industry and business	34.0	30.8
Professional	13.2	14.5
Public sector	2.1	7.6
Science	35.0	9.1
N	858	331

29. Broad Occupational Categories of Former Refugees, Excluding "Elite Samples" (in Percentage)

	Men	Women
Professionals	47.9	46.0
Managers	38.2	18.3
Sales workers	6.5	5.3
Clerical workers	2.2	24.8
Craftsmen	2.5	1.0
Operatives	1.6	2.4
Farm workers	0.2	0.0
Service workers	0.9	2.4
N	555	509

Broad Occupational Fields of Professional and Managerial Former Refugees, Excluding "Elite Samples" (in Percentage)

	Men	Women
Arts	1.5	7.7
Education	3.8	22.7
Engineering	1.1	1.0
Humanities	7.0	7.4
Industry and business	47.4	33.4
Professional	11.0	14.7
Public sector	3.0	8.0
Science	25.4	5.0
N	473	299

30. One can only speculate as to the cause. One explanation would be that relatively few of these women were in the organizations or on the mailing lists we used for contacting former refugees. Another explanation would be that they were more reluctant than the other participants to return a filled-out questionnaire.

31. Broad Occupational Fields of Professional and Managerial Former Refugees and American-born Listed in Elite Compilations (in Percentage)

	American-born	Refugees
Arts	2.1	1.9
Education	11.2	3.3
Engineering	4.1	6.0
Humanities	8.3	8.6
Industry and business	20.3	16.7
Professional	16.4	15.5
Public sector	2.3	1.2
Science	35.3	46.9
N	518	420

32. A plausible explanation for this might be that, by the period in question, the biological sciences were highly developed and numerically strongly represented in the United States, whereas the Central European primary and secondary educational and science systems had a greater affinity to other disciplines, particularly physics, chemistry, and mathematics.

33. Fields of the Listees in American Men and Women of Science, Refugees vs. American-born (in Percentage)

	Refugees	American-born
Education	2.4	8.3
Engineering	7.5	7.5
Industry	13.0	14.5
Life science	9.1	18.9
Math	13.0	11.4
Medicine	14.2	9.6
Physics	16.5	7.9
Other natual science	20.9	20.2
Social science	2.4	1.8
Other	1.2	0.0
N	254	228

34. Highest Educational Level of Former Refugees (in Percentage)

	Men	Women
High School or less	22.0	50.3
Some college	0.6	4.6
4 years college	16.0	14.0
Over 4 years higher education	61.4	31.2
N	973	587

Highest Educational Level of Former Refugees, Excluding "Elite Samples" (in Percentage)

	Men	Women
High School or less	32.9	53.0
Some college	0.9	4.9
4 years college	23.9	14.3
Over 4 years higher education	42.4	27.9
N	578	553

35. Annual Household Income of Former Refugees (in Percentage)

	Men	Women
Below $20,000	1.0	12.3
$20,000–$49,999	10.2	34.6
$50,000–$89,999	26.0	24.6
$90,000–$149,999	31.4	16.9
$150,000 +	31.5	11.7
N	788	350

Annual Household Income of Former Refugees, Excluding "Elite Samples" (in Percentage)

	Men	Women
Below $20,000	1.7	13.0
$20,000–$49,999	14.4	36.8
$50,000–$89,999	27.9	25.4
$90,000–$149,999	31.8	14.9
$150,000 +	24.2	9.9
N	459	323

5   Partial Assimilation—Complex Identities

1. In light of their own experience with rapid immersion into the English language at school, several of our participants voiced their strong opposition to bilingual education in schools.
2. The presented data are in answer to the following questionnaire item: What other languages, if any, did you know while in Europe?
3. How often do you now think about your life in Europe?

   never □   *rarely* □   *from time to time* □   *often* □   *very often* □   *constantly* □
4. How often do you now think about events related to your migration?

   never □   *rarely* □   *from time to time* □   *often* □   *very often* □   *constantly* □
5. To what extent have you talked with your children about your origins and early-life events?

   never □   *rarely* □   *from time to time* □   *frequently* □
6. In your opinion, how strongly has your early upbringing in Europe influenced your later life?

   not at all □   *mildly* □   *somewhat* □   *considerably* □   *strongly* □   *decisively* □

7. In your opinion, how strongly have your experiences leading up to and during the migration influenced your later life?

   not at all □   *mildly* □   *somewhat* □   *considerably* □   *strongly* □   *decisively* □

8. Have you maintained a special interest in your country of childhood? *Yes / No*

9. Have you returned to your country of childhood since the end of the war?

   never □   *once* □   *twice* □   *3–5 times* □   *more frequently* □

10. If you have made one or more such trips, have you, at least on one occasion, brought your children or grandchildren to your country of childhood?

    Yes □   *No* □   *Have no children* □

11. Do you intend to make a trip (or trips) to your country of childhood in the future? *Yes / No*

12. Who was the most important person in introducing you to American culture? Check one.

    teacher □   relative □   friend □   spouse □   colleague □
    other □   (please describe:_____)

13. In which areas have you retained European ways?

Tastes/preferences	Yes / No	If Yes, please describe.
Values	Yes / No	If Yes, please describe.
Outlook on life	Yes / No	If Yes, please describe.
Food	Yes / No	If Yes, please describe.
Customs	Yes / No	If Yes, please describe.
Other behaviors	Yes / No	If Yes, please describe.

14. Survivor's guilt was also expressed by some. "I have been very lucky . . . but the other side of that is a tremendous feeling of guilt. "

15. A technical note on probability values (p-values): When p-values are reported here and throughout the book, it is important to keep the total sample size (N) in mind because the effect size at which an effect becomes statistically significant (e.g., $p = .05$) depends on N. As the N for our refugees is usually about 1,500 (it is, at maximum, 1,571, or somewhat lower owing to missing values), the significance level at which $p = .05$ is reached at an effect size of about $r = .05$.

16. How religious are you?

    not at all religious □   *somewhat religious* □   *religious* □   *strongly religious* □

    If you are religious, what is your religion?_____

    Did the intensity of your religiousness change markedly over the course of your life so far? *Yes / No*

    If Yes, please give details about the nature and circumstances of the change.

    Did you at any point convert from one religion to another? *Yes / No*

    If Yes, please note the religions involved and describe the circumstances.
    How religious were your parents?

    Father: *not at all religious* □   *somewhat religious* □   *religious* □   *strongly religious* □
    Mother: *not at all religious* □   *somewhat religious* □   *religious* □   *strongly religious* □

17. What types of organizations do you participate in actively? Check all that apply.
    fraternal or mutual aid □ *trade or professional* □ *religious* □ *civic or community* □
    cultural □ *social or recreational* □ *other* □ (specify type:_____)

18. Are any of the organizations in which you actively participate especially connected to former refugees?

    Yes / No

19. To what extent do you maintain contact with fellow refugees?

    no contact at all □ *accidental contacts only* □ *regular contacts* □ *membership in refugee-related association(s)* □

20. On a survey question about acculturation, 10 percent of the women and 7 percent of the men listed their spouse as the most important person in introducing them to American culture.

21. Spouses born in Europe would, in most cases, be fellow refugees, and the question about religion is a good proxy for Jewish ethnicity.

22. For comparison, 20 percent of both the men and women respondents to Davie's (1947) survey had married since their arrival in the United States, and although their ages were not reported, one might reasonably assume that the vast majority of the marrying individuals belonged to the younger age group. Davie (1947:164) found that, among those who married, 62.4 percent of the males and 71.4 percent of the females married other refugees; 30.2 percent of the men and 17.0 percent of the women married American-born spouses; and the remainder married pre-1933 immigrants. In keeping with general American patterns, there was a strong tendency to marry within one's faith, although the percentages of those marrying American-born spouses of a different faith were unusually high (Davie 1947:164–6).

23. Gender differences were absent.

24. Here is a fictitious example to illustrate that fallacy: If the group of those who entered second marriages was mostly composed of those who had been in an exogamous marriage the first time (the elevated divorce rates in this group would point in that direction), results that prima facie look like an increase in the exogamous tendency might mask an actual decrease, that is, the true trend, in this case, might have been returning to the fold rather than venturing out.

25. The Spearman rank correlation coefficient for the men's and women's ratings was .97.

26. As a reminder, the choices offered to them were "much less," "less," "slightly less," "same," "slightly more," "more," and "much more."

27. We should note here that the popular American sports were virtually unknown to the Central European immigrants. Conversely, the popular Central European sports—first of all Fußball, which in America now goes under the title of soccer—were hardly known in the United States.

28. Our starting point was the correlation matrix of the Pearson product-moment correlation coefficients of the 39 traits. The correlation matrix was converted into a similarity matrix by adding 1 to the correlation coefficients to avoid negative numbers. The technique of multidimensional scaling then represented the strength with which two traits correlated by their closeness in a two-dimensional

approximation of a multidimensional proximity structure. The resulting map allowed us to gauge which of the traits tended to go together—the closer, the stronger the correlation. Rather than simply clustering traits together based on a visual inspection and interpretation of the map, we chose a more formalized approach and performed an exploratory factor analysis of the 39 traits. This analysis revealed four factors that made intuitive sense. The factor structure could then be superimposed on the map.

29. In addition to looking at the proximity of attitudes based on the results for our participants, we also looked at the proximity of participants based on their attitude ratings. The results showed no apparent anomaly. Most participants clustered in a circular cloud in the middle of the map, with a few outliers around the fringes. Hence, this line of analysis was not pursued further.

30. To obtain a more formal assessment of the extent of gender differences, we did factor analyses separately by gender and examined the differences. The factor structure was found to be similar for men and women, with two exceptions: First, the trait "emotional when frustrated" was most strongly associated with the "work ethic" factor for men, but with the "popular culture" factor for women. (In neither case, was there a particularly close connection.) Second, the trait "serious with close friends" went with the "high culture" factor for men, but with the "work ethic" factor for women. Consequently, we did not include these two variables in any composites, but left them as single variables.

31. See Kagan and Reznick 1986.

32. Between the American-born and former Central European Jews in NJPS, there was also no difference in organizational memberships. Slightly more than half of the individuals in all groups belonged to, or supported, Jewish clubs or organizations (such as the Anti-Defamation League, Hadassah, Hebrew Immigrant Aid Society, Jewish Unions, temple-/synagogue-related organizations, etc.). Moreover, similar proportions among the American-born and the former Central European Jews were members of "general" (that is, not specifically Jewish) clubs or organizations.

33. This situation is somewhat akin to the more recent labeling of Asian immigrants as "model minority" for their collective high achievement. As many observes have pointed out, this stereotype does not do justice to the situation of all Asian immigrants.

34. The NJPS contained numerous statements, or items, with which the participants were asked to indicate their level of agreement or disagreement, typically on a 5-point rating scale. Guided by our factor analysis, we constructed composite variables from those items in the following way. The composite variable "identity" consists of the average of seven (standardized) variables: the levels of agreement with the NJPS items "I am happy to be Jewish"; "Being Jewish means something definite to me"; "It is important that there should always be a Jewish people"; a rating of the importance the participants attach to being Jewish; and the levels of *dis*agreement with the statements "I have mixed feelings about being Jewish"; "I don't care one way or the other about being Jewish"; and "If I could easily switch from being Jewish to being something else, I would do so."

The composite variable "openness" consists of the average of seven (standardized) variables: the levels of agreement with the 1970 NJPS items "It is all right for Jews to date Negroes"; "It is all right for Jews to date non-Jews"; "It is all right for Jews to marry Negroes"; "It is all right for Jews to marry non-Jews"; a rating of the extent to which the participant has dated non-Jews; a rating of the strength of their parents' opposition to their dating non-Jews; and the level of *dis*agreement with the statement "If a Jew marries a non-Jew, their children must be brought up as Jews."

The composite variable "knowledge" consists of the average of four (standardized) variables: self-ratings of the degrees to which the participants know Jewish history, Jewish culture, Jewish ethics, and Jewish religious teachings.

The composite variable "religiousness" consists of the average of nine (standardized) variables: self-ratings of the degrees to which the participants believe in the Jewish religion; believe in one God; pray; whether they attend religious services on the High Holidays and on some other occasions; whether they fasted on Yom Kippur; whether they attended a Seder; the level of agreement with the NJPS item "I live in a very Jewish home"; a rating of the extent to which they personally keep kosher; and the number of Jewish ceremonial objects in their home.

The composite variable "upbringing" consists of the average of five (standardized) variables: the degree to which their mother was active in Jewish life when they were between the ages of 5 and 13; the degree to which their father was active in Jewish life during those years; a rating of how strongly Jewish their upbringing was; whether they had four or more years of Jewish education in the form of afternoon Hebrew school; and whether they had four or more years of Jewish education in the form of Saturday or Sunday school.

The composite variable "community activism" consists of the average of four (standardized) variables: whether the participants are elected officers of a Jewish club or organization; whether they are active in a Jewish club or organization; whether they are active in a temple or synagogue; and whether they are a member of B'nai B'rith.

The composite variable "support for Israel" consists of the average of four (standardized) variables: the degree to which the participants would support Israel's interests if official United States policy were opposed to it; the levels of agreement with the NJPS items "Jews in the United States must do all they can to help Israel survive"; and "The Six Day War raised the status of the Jewish people in the eyes of American non-Jews"; and the level of *dis*agreement with the statement "The Six Day War created more problems for Jewish people in the United States than it solved."

The composite variable "Jewish impact" consists of the average of five (standardized) variables: the levels of agreement with the NJPS items "Being Jewish affects my occupation or job activities"; "Being Jewish affects my choice of personal friends"; "Being Jewish affects my choice of a place to live"; "Anti-Semitism is a serious problem in this city"; and whether they had personally experienced any anti-Semitism in the prior 12 months.

Finally, the composite "political activism" consists of the average of two (standardized) variables: the self-rated degree of activeness in fighting anti-Semitism; and the degree of activeness in fighting for civil rights.

35. For effect size estimates, Pearson's r was used. The formula applied was

$$r = \sqrt{\frac{F}{F + df}},$$

which was derived from Rosenthal and Rosnow 1984 (inside cover).

36. The following interactions fell shy of statistical significance, but they may be worth mentioning, because they dovetail well with the results mentioned in the text. In the 1970 NJPS data set, advanced education appeared somewhat associated with increased "community activism" in the Jewish community for American-born Jews, but with decreased activism for Central European Jews (though this interaction fell short of statistical significance, $p = .19$). Moreover, the degree to which the participants' "upbringing" was described as Jewish was not at all associated with educational achievement among the American-born Jews. The former Central Europeans who had received an advanced education in the United States had less of a religious upbringing, whereas the former Central Europeans at lower levels of educational achievement had more of a religious upbringing, on average, than their respective American-born counterparts did ($p = .16$).

An analogous situation was found in the 1970 NJPS dataset concerning "political activism" against anti-Semitism and for civil rights. Here, the highly educated former Central Europeans again scored unusually high and outscored the highly educated American-born. Among the less educated, the Central Europeans were, if anything, slightly less active than their American-born counterparts ($p < .10$). This finding may shed some additional light on Herbert Strauss's (1981:254) observation that the refugees as a group had little to contribute to tackling the big political problems of postwar America. If one believes the self-ratings, political activism was particularly high among the highly educated young immigrants. These were precisely the ones who were less inclined to community activism, and also may have felt the least inclination to portray themselves in public as Jewish activists, let alone as Central European Jewish activists. Most of these activists, we expect, thought of themselves as acting as American citizens, members of a political movement, or perhaps of a professional association, and so on. Such a pattern might contribute to the perception of a politically relatively dormant group.

37. In 1825, German and Polish Ashkenazim broke away from the congregation Shearith Israel (founded by Sephardim) and started New York's second synagogue, Bnai Jeshurun, and soon thereafter multiple congregations sprung up along lines of origin.

38. The bulk of Yiddish is formed by a kind of medieval German, with some Hebrew and Slavic elements added.

39. Another example: A refugee upon taking his first job in New York as a salesman reportedly complained: "Most of my colleagues were Jewish and disliked me too, mainly because I could not speak Yiddish. They claimed that I only pretended not to know this language. They also disliked refugees in general as a different species of Jew" (Perloff 2004:133).

40. How often have you experienced discrimination, prejudice, or humiliation in the United States? *never* ☐ *rarely* ☐ *from time to time* ☐ *frequently* ☐ If you did experience discrimination, prejudice, or humiliation, was it (check all that apply):

    in obtaining a place to live ☐ *in getting a job* ☐ *while at work* ☐
    in social relations ☐ *in school or college* ☐
    in other ways ☐ (please specify: _____)

    If you did experience discrimination, prejudice, or humiliation, what was its most relevant origin?

    anti-Semitism ☐ *anti-German sentiments* ☐ *anti-foreign feelings* ☐
    racism ☐ *sexism* ☐ *other* ☐ (please specify: _____)

41. For instance, into the late 1940s at least, advertisements for the rental of houses or apartments usually said "Restricted" (i.e., not for Jews or African Americans).
42. On this, also see Max Perutz's report in Medawar and Pyke (2001).
43. This elite also prided itself on speaking a polished and erudite German that would be fit for printing—that nowadays has become something of a lost art. Some refugees from Vienna, in particular, noticed on return visits that this polished German had given way to an upsurge of Austrian dialects.
44. As noted earlier, there was a small but sizable group of *exiles*, primarily among the political and intellectual refugees (Luckmann 1981, Papanek 1998). They did not wish to Americanize themselves, but viewed the United States as a temporary safe haven during the reign of their enemies, and were intent on returning to Central Europe as soon as National Socialism was defeated. Most refugees, by contrast, were emigres who made America their permanent home.
45. The attractive force of ethnicity-based nationalism—or, to be more precise, of at least some of its incarnations—emanates from an inherent duality: it is a strange hybrid, neither entirely premodern, nor entirely modern (Sonnert 1986, 1988). It satisfies emotional needs to belong to a grown community rooted in the past, but at the same time unleashes modernizing forces and serves a rational interest calculus of protecting and increasing a group's economic and political power. In a somewhat different context, Tom Nairn (1975) evocatively spoke of the Janus face of nationalism.
46. As to your identity, how strongly do you identify with *each* of the listed terms? Please circle the corresponding numbers. If a term does not apply to your situation, please circle "n/a."

	Not at all	Somewhat	Strongly	Very strongly	
American	0	1	2	3	n/a
Part of local community (e.g., Los Angeles)	0	1	2	3	n/a
Jewish	0	1	2	3	n/a
Christian	0	1	2	3	n/a
German	0	1	2	3	n/a
Austrian	0	1	2	3	n/a
European	0	1	2	3	n/a
Other (specify: _____)	0	1	2	3	

These rating scales did not entirely capture the complexity of most participants' ideas about identity.

47. "There is a small part of me, however, that is not American, and certainly not Austrian—it's perhaps European. . . . I really consider myself a citizen of the world . . . but I certainly am a European."

48. Which of the following terms do you prefer for describing yourself (check only one)?

American □ Jewish □ German □ Austrian □ Jewish-American □ German-American □ Austrian-American □ German-Jewish □ Austrian-Jewish □ German-Jewish-American □ Austrian-Jewish-American □ Other □ (please specify: _____)

49. Here is a rare example of an interviewee placing such strong emphasis on his Jewishness that he rejected the "Jewish-American" label: "So I wouldn't say Jewish American; I would say American Jew. The key here—I repeat, the key word has to be Jew."—9 percent of the participants' responses fell in the "other" category.

50. One factor identified by Rumbaut (1994) was language, which appears to have playe an obvious role our cohort(because their language acquiaition was rapid and pervasive). On the ethnic identity development in adolescent in general, see Rosenthal (1987).

51. We also examined whether the refugees' age at arrival was correlated with their propensity of choosing certain identity labels. No statistically significant effect was found.

52. By adding together the responses for the seven identity labels listed ("not at all" = 0 to "very strongly" = 3), we formed a general index of collective identification, ranging from 0 to 21. As multiple identifications were possible for all these participants, this index gives us a general indication of how strongly the participants in general associated themselves with collective labels. (The average score was 7.3.)

53. This composite was formed by appropriately combining the responses on the items regarding German, Austrian, and European identities.

54. Note that this is a description of the combination of main and interaction effects.

55. For the category "high" in this typology, we combined the two original response categories "strongly" and "very strongly"; and for the category "low," we combined the original categories "not at all" and "somewhat."

6   Ingredients of Success

1. The following two quotes, from two different interviewees, illustrate this point.
". . . despite our material comfort, my brother and I never felt that we really belonged. . . . I went into the Army and my brother didn't. And I often feel that he really missed something—that in many ways he was less American, in a certain way, than I became very quickly, because I think being in the Army was a very powerful experience."—"The Army had a strong influence on my

life . . . maturing, learning how to do things differently, becoming somewhat ambitious about getting ahead."

2. Likelihood ratio chi-square [LRCS] = 18.2, p = .0004, N = 950.
3. Marginally statistically significant; LRCS = 5.96, p = .05.
4. For an explanation of odds and odds ratios, see section Transmission of Social Status of this chapter.
5. We should note here that Robert Putnam's (1995) well-known concept of social capital is somewhat different from Bourdieu's understanding. For Putnam, a society with a high level of social capital is one that is well-integrated, and whose members cooperate with each other and trust each other to a high degree.
6. Historians of the working class movement have long understood that "working class culture" is not coterminous with the socioeconomic status of being a wage-laborer (see, for instance, E. P. Thompson's monumental work on *The Making of the English Working Class* [1963]).
7. This occurred, one might presume, because essential elements of the feudal system of social stratification survived in Central Europe, even as other elements—especially the economy—were modernizing.
8. The survey question was: In your opinion, how strongly has your early upbringing in Europe influenced your later life and career?

    not at all ☐   *mildly* ☐   *somewhat* ☐   *considerably* ☐   *strongly* ☐
    decisively ☐

9. In your opinion, how strongly have your experiences during the migration influenced your later life and career?

    not at all ☐   *mildly* ☐   *somewhat* ☐   *considerably* ☐   *strongly* ☐
    decisively ☐

10. The reported percentages combine the responses "somewhat agree" and "strongly agree" to the following questions: Some people say that the group of immigrants to which you belonged, in their later lives and careers, blended European and American characteristics in a way that was conducive to great success, on average.

    Do you agree or disagree with this opinion *as a general statement?*

    strongly disagree ☐   *somewhat disagree* ☐   *somewhat agree* ☐   *strongly agree* ☐

    Do you agree or disagree with this opinion *in your special case?*

    strongly disagree ☐   *somewhat disagree* ☐   *somewhat agree* ☐   *strongly agree* ☐

11. For coding the father's occupational status, we used the same Census categories that we used for the Second Wavers' occupational status.
12. Log-linear analysis is a way to analyze contingency tables. This analysis examines whether the predicted counts (in log transformation) in a given cell depend on main effects (i.e., marginal effects) and on interactions of the categorical variables in the table. It is these interactions that are important for the analysis. Here is a simple example: The log-linear model of a table with two categorical variables that includes the main effects of each of the variables and their interaction could be written as:

$\log_e F_{ij} = \mu + G_i + H_j + GH_{ij},$

where F_{ij} is the log count of the cell in row i and column j, μ is the global mean log count, G_i is the main effect of G (on row i), H_j is the main effect of H (on column j), and GH_{ij} is the interaction effect of G and H (on cell ij). Taking the anti-logs, we obtain

$$F_{ij} = e^\mu \, e^{G_i} \, e^{H_j} \, e^{GH_{ij}}.$$

This equation allows us to estimate odds ratios between predicted cell frequencies. The table in note 13 below, for instance, provides the anti-logs of the estimates given by the SAS procedure PROC CATMOD (with "loglin" option), from which the estimated odds and odds ratios (and compound odds ratios) can be calculated.

In selecting between different models, we considered the change of the likelihood-ratio-chi-square (LRCS) between models and the concomitant change in degrees of freedom. Increment(or decrement)-to-LRCS tests revealed if adding (or dropping) a certain variable made a statistically significant difference.

13. Log-linear Model—Determinants of Occupational Status

(a) Variables

Source	DF	Chi-Square	Pr > Chi-Sq
Occupation	2	43.53	<.0001
Gender	1	9.76	0.0018
Father's occupation	2	10.42	0.0055
Father's fate	2	14.32	0.0008
Ancestors' occupation	2	17.77	0.0001
Age at arrival	3	43.12	<.0001
Occupation × Gender	2	40.93	<.0001
Occupation × Father's occupation	4	27.9	<.0001
Occupation × Father's fate	4	13.98	0.0074
Occupation × Ancestors' occupation	4	11.3	0.0234
Occupation × Age at arrival	6	21.99	0.0012
Likelihood ratio	320	375.91	0.017

N = 1071

(b) Parameter estimates and odds estimates

Parameter		Estimate	Anti-log
Occupation × Gender	Professionals: Male	0.2303	1.26
	Managers: Male	0.1642	1.18
	Others: Male	−0.3945	0.67
	Professionals: Female	−0.2303	0.79
	Managers: Female	−0.1642	0.85
	Others: Female	0.3945	1.48
Occupation × Father's occupation	Professionals: Professionals	0.3554	1.43
	Professionals: Managers	−0.1035	0.90

	Professionals: Others	−0.2519	0.78
	Managers: Professionals	−0.0303	0.97
	Managers: Managers	0.0479	1.05
	Managers: Others	−0.0176	0.98
	Others: Professionals	−0.3251	0.72
	Others: Managers	0.0556	1.06
	Others	0.2695	1.31
Occupation × Father's fate	Professionals: Absent father	−0.1587	0.85
	Professionals: Changed father	−0.044	0.96
	Professional: Unchanged father	0.2027	1.22
	Managers: Absent father	0.1096	1.12
	Managers: Changed father	0.0439	1.04
	Managers: Unchanged father	−0.1535	0.86
	Others: Absent father	0.0491	1.05
	Others: Changed father	0.0001	1.00
	Others: Unchanged father	−0.0492	0.95
Occupation × Ancestors' occupation	Professionals: low	−0.1288	0.88
	Professionals: medium	−0.0254	0.97
	Professionals: high	0.1542	1.17
	Managers: low	−0.0601	0.94
	Managers: medium	0.1498	1.16
	Managers: high	−0.0897	0.91
	Others: low	0.1889	1.21
	Others: medium	−0.1244	0.88
	Others: high	−0.0645	0.94
Occupation × Age at arrival	Professionals: 0–6	0.1945	1.21
	Professionals: 7–11	0.1255	1.13
	Professionals: 12–18	0.0805	1.08
	Professionals: 19+	−0.4005	0.67
	Managers: 0–6	−0.0283	0.97
	Managers: 7–11	−0.0698	0.93
	Managers: 12–18	0.0512	1.05
	Managers: 19+	0.0469	1.05
	Others: 0–6	−0.1662	0.85
	Others: 7–11	−0.0557	0.95
	Others: 12–18	−0.1317	0.88
	Others: 19+	0.3536	1.42

Notes: Panel (b) lists the parameter estimates of the log-linear model (of the general type $\log_e F_{ij} = \mu + G_i + H_j + GH_{ij}$) and the anti-logs of these estimates (of the general type $F_{ij} = e^{\mu} e^{Gi} e^{Hj} e^{GHij}$). These anti-logs allow us to calculate odds ratios between predicted cell frequencies. For example, for those among the former refugees who had a father who had been a professional in Europe, the estimated odds of being professionals themselves (rather than being in the "other" occupational category) were 1.43/.72 or 1.99 : 1. For those among the former refugees whose father had worked in an "other" occupation in Europe, those estimated odds were 0.78/1.31 or 0.60 : 1. Hence, the odds of being professionals themselves (rather than in the "other" category) were more than three (1.99/.60 = 3.3) times as high for those with a father who had been a professional in Europe as for those whose father had been in the "other" occupational category.

14. We also wondered whether, in addition to the effect of father's occupation, there was an effect of metropolitan birth place (Vienna or Berlin), hypothesizing that growing up in a metropolitan environment (as part of or close to the Jewish elite and perhaps exposed to particularly rich intellectual opportunities) may have conveyed additional advantages. Controlling for their father's occupation, the young refugees who had come from Vienna or Berlin were indeed more likely than those from other areas in Central Europe to be professionals. However, in the extensive model with several independent variables estimated above, the variable of metropolitan birthplace dropped below the statistical significance level.

15. Another approach to explain this pattern that has been occasionally discussed is to assume that some genetic trait conducive to socioeconomic success is being passed from one generation to the next. We lack the means and expertise to consider this hypothesis.

16. The following is an example of a less active approach: "[European origins and migration] hindered me in that I didn't have any contacts." Making contacts was one of the strategies that helped newly arrived refugees succeed. The perception of closing opportunities, both in terms of cultural and social capital, is encapsulated in the following quote: "Many opportunities were denied to me in moving from Germany. These include cultural opportunities, friendships and relationships and financial—we had very poor income in the US and no savings."

17. These statistics exclude the listees of *Men and Women of Science*. If they were included, the percentages would rise slightly.

18. Once 3-way interactions were included, we found that the relationship between grandfathers' occupation and child's occupation was stronger for the children of the elite refugees than for the children of the elite non-refugees. For instance, for the children of refugees, the odds ratio between the estimated odds for someone with a grandfather in the "other" category to be in the "other" category (rather than in the professional category) and the odds for someone with a grandfather who had worked in the professions to be in the "other" category was 4.2 times as high as for the children of the comparison group. This result suggests a lower intergenerational social mobility among the refugee families than among the non-refugee families in the elite sample.

19. The following is to illustrate why the two variables, family situation at arrival and age at arrival, should be viewed together. Here is a prima facie perhaps surprising result: Those who arrived without their parents reported, on average, that they *more* frequently thought about their life in Europe than did those who came with at least one parent. Those arriving without parents also tended to think that their early upbringing in Europe had influenced their later life somewhat more strongly than did the other group, on average. Although one might think that the children who came without their parents were less exposed to stories about the old times back in Europe than were those who came with parents, those who had come without their parents now think more often about their life in Europe and feel more influenced by it. A partial explanation of this result is certainly the correlation between arriving without parents and age at arrival: The older the children were at arrival, the more likely

they were to arrive alone; and, as we shall see below, older arrival cohorts thought more frequently about their life in Europe, and believed that their later life was more strongly influenced by their early upbringing in Europe. This is what one might expect.

20. The results were generated by ANOVA statistical procedures including as predictors the dichotomous parent variable (arriving with no parent vs. arriving with at least one parent), the age at arrival variable (containing four levels: 0–6 years, 7–12 years, 13–18 years, 19+ years), and their interaction.

21. The statistically significant differences reported in the following are sometimes rather small. Because of the large Ns involved, our analyses had a great deal of statistical power and thus were able to detect even small differences.

22. Again, the absence of a correlation does not mean that individuals' life trajectories were independent of their family circumstances during and after immigration. For instance, living alone and living in an immigrant community might, through *different* mechanisms, have led to the *same* types of outcomes, on average.

23. Furthermore, they reported lower levels of sadness and guilt in the early phases after arrival, as well as lower levels of current feelings of anger, sadness, and guilt. These differences were also reflected in the two composite measures of emotions.

24. On this effect, there were no significant interactions with the father's profession or with gender.

25. When looking at the genders separately, there were four traits that correlated significantly with age at arrival for both men and women: interested in learning, hardworking, achievement-oriented, and interested in food.

26. There was, however, an interaction: Among the oldest and the youngest arrival cohorts, the ones arriving without parents felt more European than those arriving with parents. The opposite was the case among the two middle cohorts.

27. We distinguished three groups: arrival years 1933–37, arrival years 1938–41, and arrival years 1942–49. The majority of our participants (65 percent) was in the second group. The time period of arrival was obviously correlated with the age at arrival, but the point to be made here was that the time period of arrival added no statistically significant explanatory power once age at arrival was considered.

28. This policy was in line with the high priority placed on "assimilating" immigrants into the American mainstream, and also perhaps with the intention of minimizing an Anti-Semitic backlash against the refugees.

29. The levels were: No other refugees; relatively few other refugees; relatively numerous other refugees.

30. See Garmezy and Rutter (1988), Janoff-Bulman (1992), and Werner and Smith (1989, 1992), as well as the contributions in Tedeschi, Park, and Calhoun (1998).

31. How satisfied are you with your life in general?
    very dissatisfied □   *dissatisfied* □   *somewhat dissatisfied* □
    somewhat satisfied □   *satisfied* □   *very satisfied* □

32. *Shortly after you arrived in the United States,* how did you feel about your migration and the events that led to it? By circling the appropriate number, please rate the extent to which you had each of the following feelings. You may add and rate an additional feeling on the last line.

	None	Slight	Considerable	Intense
Anger	0	1	2	3
Sadness	0	1	2	3
Guilt	0	1	2	3
Gratitude	0	1	2	3
_____	0	1	2	3

We realize, of course, that the reports of the former refugees' emotions from half a century ago might not be entirely accurate, but somehow tainted by their current situation or by memory problems. Hence they need to be taken with a grain of salt.

33. *Currently,* how do you feel about your migration and the events that led to it? By circling the appropriate number, please rate to which extent you have each of the following feelings. You may add and rate an additional feeling on the last line.

	None	Slight	Considerable	Intense
Anger	0	1	2	3
Sadness	0	1	2	3
Guilt	0	1	2	3
Gratitude	0	1	2	3
_____	0	1	2	3

34. Because age at arrival was associated with family situation at arrival (younger refugee children having been more likely to arrive with parents), the results reported here are from ANOVAs that included these two variables and their interaction.

35. There was also a significant interaction. Among the youngest arrival cohort, the level of current anger was higher among those who arrived without parents than among those who arrived with parents. Among the other groups, such a difference did not exist.

242   Notes

36. Additional examples: "Wanted to succeed to prove that emigration and dislocation could be overcome as handicaps." And, "It probably helped. As an immigrant and outsider, I tried harder." "I have always been very ambitious for myself and my family." "Wanted to belong and be like everyone else." "Understanding of sacrifices. Need to become successful in life and financially."

37. Such a theme was also evident in our study of women in science (Sonnert and Holton 1995a, 1995b).

38. "Yes, that [transition to the U.S.] of course created difficult relational problems in our family, and I think in a way I was the parent and they were the children."

39. Other examples for a revenge impulse: "That you have to fight for justice to be done to make sure the Germans pay for their deeds. (They did reimburse us for passage, etc., after many years)." "I joined the [military] . . . in Sept. 1939. At the time I felt the US would be involved in the war and felt an obligation to be involved; first to get rid of Hitler and second to get even."

40. For example, "I was fortunate to escape and that gives me responsibilities to assist others."

41. "Grin and bear it. Every day is my birthday. Can wait—the Elohim know me. I still can be of use, make jokes, be grateful for luxuries. Free as a bird, pass on my many tricks to improve to others if they like my advice—this 'makes my day!' "

42. "I feel strongly that we must learn from the events of the Holocaust to prevent from happening again. That the whole world needs to ask, 'How did we allow it to happen?' And find those answers—because all of us have an obligation to make this a better world."

43. "I have strong family values and take great pride in my Jewish heritage. I am not a religious person, but take great pride in my people and their accomplishments. Before we boarded ship in Rotterdam, the Jewish Temple there had services to pray for our safe voyage and while at the temple I met a young girl who had been my classmate at the Jewish School I attended in [German city]. She was only 10 years old and had been sent through 'The *Kindertransport*' to live with strangers. She started crying when she saw me, because she was so lonely for her family. I felt so sad for her that in my mind in later years, she became 'Anne Frank.' I have been crying for her ever since."

44. "I appreciate my close ties to my husband, children and grandchildren. I am an activist, speak up against injustice, make sure our heritage is preserved."

45. Another former refugee who had had a distinguished professional career said, "I thank our *Führer*, basically, because who knows what could have happened in Austria if I'd stayed there." Another participant made the following comment: "I grew up in a racially mixed community (1/3 Italian, 1/3 Black, 1/3 else) which probably only existed in the US in those days. As most of my family is elitist, I would have grown up with elitist tendencies and probably would have been a banker had we remained in Vienna. Instead I plugged into democracy and population diversity and am also doing what I really love to do. I have a much more interesting life than I would have had in Europe, and I am much less elitist."

7 Anguish—Privatized Costs, Socialized Benefits

1. For instance, "We were very poor when we arrived. I went to work at an early age—12 years old. I always felt as an outsider—always felt deprived. Life was difficult." Or, "I thought often of a sense of loss—of few things that I had, of our apartment, of the ability to play on the sidewalk, and being cut-off suddenly from playing with my friends. I have never felt completely settled and have developed no attachment to belongings or to living spaces." In the words of a third participant, "Could not make good friends like I had, even though I am a friendly person, I think, but there is something missing." Similarly, another said, "There was little sense of 'belonging' beyond our family life and traditional American experiences such as Boy Scouts and summer camps. I have remained somewhat of an individualist. I am not a joiner." Finally, "Always feeling different; learning to be careful; learning to be a people-pleaser."

2. The passage continues, "Yet as I have gotten older and understand the stress and difficulties my parents were put through, and how difficult the transition was for them, I admire their courage and foresight. I only hope and pray that future generations need not bear witness to what happened in those years."

3. One participant described himself as "The unwanted and hunted Jew. Trust no one and nothing. Very depressing."

4. This difference became statistically nonsignificant when the variables of family situation at arrival and age at arrival were considered jointly in an ANOVA model. As discussed earlier, there was a strong relationship between these two variables (children who were older at arrival were also more likely to arrive unaccompanied). All other reported differences were statistically significant in joint models.

5. The anger level was now slightly lower.

6. In the following quote, the experience of early upheaval led to the appreciation of stability and family. "Although, quite young, the constant flight and camp internment during ages 3 to 5, the subsequent relative stability in Switzerland during ages 5 to 8, yet still in Europe suffering in the throes of war, the absence of my father from ages 3 to 8 when we were reunited in the US. All had a sobering and lasting effect. Because of all that I value social stability and a strong family relationship most highly."

7. Children in families undergoing socioeconomic decline have been found to suffer from various socioemotional problems (McLoyd and Wilson 1991).

8. "I have blocked from memory a portion of time, 1938–39. I think there are some tensions I hold in my body from this."

9. In an interesting case, one former refugee said he lived in a kind of imaginary past. "My friends were all over the world. I didn't know anybody. I slowly made friends, but I have the sad tendency of living in the past, and eradicating the bad parts, fantasizing about the good ones. I think this is pretty much how it was. And I always kept wondering if I would ever again have a place as nice as the one we had in Vienna."

8   Epilogue: Lessons for Current Refugees

1. On young immigrants, see, for instance, Booth, Crouter and Landale (1997), Suárez-Orozco and Suárez-Orozco (2001), Waters (1997), and, more generally, Foner (2000). Other contributions of interest include Pedraza and Rumbaut (1996), Perlmann and Waldinger (1998), Portes (1996), Portes and Rumbaut (1996), and Waldinger (1997).

Appendix

1. Also included were the small groups of refugees born in Saarland and Danzig, two originally German regions that, after World War I, were detached from Germany, but where German cultural factors continued (education, language, etc.). In the following "born in Germany or Austria" is shorthand for the cumbersome "born in Germany, Austria, Saarland, or Danzig."
2. In addition, non-refugees started coming to America, mostly "GI brides" (Central European women married by American military personnel serving in the postwar occupation), but also a numerically small, but interesting (and to some degree controversial) group of experts recruited by the United States government for the beginning the cold war in what was called *Operation Paperclip*.
3. We thank our Faculty Aide, Tina Wang, for her meticulous and dependable gathering and preparing of the *Who's Who* data.
4. The *International Biographical Dictionary* does not include American-born individuals, so that no comparison group could be formed from this source.

Bibliography

Alba, R. D., and Nee, V. (2003). *Remaking the American Mainstream: Assimilation and Contemporary Immigration*. Cambridge, MA: Harvard University Press.

American Men & Women of Science. 20th ed. (1998–1999). New Providence, NJ: R.R. Bowker.

Angress, W. T. (1988). *Between Fear & Hope: Jewish Youth in the Third Reich*. New York: Columbia University Press.

Ash, M. G., and Söllner, A. (Eds.) (1996). *Forced Migration and Scientific Change: Emigré German-Speaking Scientists and Scholars After 1933*. Cambridge, UK: Cambridge University Press.

Ashworth, M. (1982). The cultural adjustment of immigrant children in English Canada. In Nann, R. C. (Ed.), *Uprooting and Surviving: Adaption and Resettlement of Migrant Families and Children*. Boston, Dordrecht, Holland: Reidel, 77–83.

Bader, A. (1995). *Adventures of a Chemist Collector*. London: Weidenfeld and Nicolson.

Baumel, J. T. (1990). *Unfulfilled Promise-Rescue and Resettlement of Jewish Refugeee Children in the United States, 1934–1945*. Juneau, AK: Denali Press.

Bentwich, N. (1953). *The Rescue and Achievement of Refugee Scholars: The Story of Displaced Scholars and Scientists, 1932–1952*. The Hague: M. Nijhoff.

Benz, U. and Benz, W. (Eds.) (1992). *Sozialisation und Traumatisierung: Kinder in der Zeit des Nationalsozialismus*. Frankfurt a. M.: Fischer Taschenbuch Verlag.

Benz, W. (1998). Die jüdische Emigration. In C.-D. Krohn et al. (Eds.), *Handbuch der deutschsprachigen Emigration, 1933–1945*. Darmstadt: Primus, 5–16.

Berghahn, M. (1984). *German-Jewish Refugees in England: The Ambiguities of Assimilation*. New York: St. Martin's Press.

Berry, J. W. (1990). Psychology of Acculturation. In Padilla, A. M. (Ed.), *Acculturation: Theory, Model, and Some New Findings*. Boulder, CO: Westview, 9–25.

Bloom, W. (1990). *Personal Identity, National Identity and International Relations*. Cambridge, UK: Cambridge University Press.

Booth, A., Crouter, A. C., and Landale, N. S. (Eds.) (1997). *Immigration and the Family: Research and Policy on U.S. Immigrants*. Mahwah, NJ: Lawrence Erlbaum Associates.

Bourdieu, P. (1983). Ökonomisches Kapital, kulturelles Kapital, soziales Kapital. In Kreckel, R. (Ed.), *Soziale Ungleichheiten*, Göttingen: Schwartz, 183–98.

Bourdieu, P. (1990). *The Logic of Practice.* Translated by R. Nice. Stanford, CA: Stanford University Press.

Boyers, R. (Ed.) (1972). *The Legacy of the German Refugee Intellectuals.* New York: Schocken Books.

Bradley, E. (2005). *The Way Home: A German Childhood, an American Life.* New York: Pantheon.

Brody, D. (1956). American Jewry, the Refugees and Immigration Restriction (1932–1942). *Publications of the American Jewish Historical Society* 45, no. 27, 220–7.

Buriel, R., and de Ment, T. (1997). Immigration and Sociocultural Change in Mexican, Chinese, and Vietnamese American Families. In Booth, A., Crouter, A. C., and Landale, N. (Eds.), *Immigration and the Family: Research and Policy on U.S. Immigrants.* Mahwah, NJ: Lawrence Erlbaum Associates, 165–200.

Cazden, R. E. (1970). *German Exile Literature in America 1933–1959: A History of the Free German Press and Book Trade.* Chicago: American Library Association.

Cesarani, D. (2000). Introduction. In Harris, M. J., and Oppenheimer, D., *Into the Arms of Strangers: Stories of the Kindertransport.* London, UK: Bloomsbury, 1–19.

Cohen, N. W. (1984). *Encounter with Emancipation: The German Jews in the United States, 1830–1914.* Philadelphia, PA: Jewish Publication Society of America.

Coll, C. G., and Magnuson, K. (1997). The Psychological Experience of Immigration: A Developmental Perspective. In Booth, A., Crouter, A. C., and Landale, N. (Eds.), *Immigration and the Family: Research and Policy on U.S. Immigrants.* Mahwah, NJ: Lawrence Erlbaum Associates, 91–131.

The Complete Marquis Who's Who on CD-ROM (Winter 2002–2003). New Providence, NJ: Marquis Who's Who.

Coser, L. (1984). *Refugee Scholars in America: Their Impact and Their Experiences.* New Haven, CT: Yale University Press.

David, R. L. (1996). *Ein Kind unserer Zeit: Autobiographische Skizzen eines jüdischen Mädchens: Kindheit in Fränkisch-Crumbach, Kindertransport nach England, Leben im Exil.* Frankfurt a. M.: dipa-Verlag.

Davie, M. R. (1947). *Refugees in America: Report of the Committee for the Study of Recent Immigration from Europe.* New York: Harper & Brothers.

Davie, M. R., and Koenig, S. (1945). *The Refugees Are Now Americans.* Public Affairs Pamphlet No. 111. New York: Public Affairs Committee.

Davis, M. F. (1977). *Transforming Suffering Into Love: The First Ten Years of the Newcomers Christian Fellowship.* M. Div. thesis. Union Theological Seminary.

de Leon Siantz, M. L. (1997). Factors that Impact Developmental Outcomes of Immigrant Children. In Booth, A., Crouter, A. C., and Landale, N. (Eds.), *Immigration and the Family: Research and Policy on U.S. Immigrants.* Mahwah, NJ: Lawrence Erlbaum Associates, 149–61.

Delpard, R. (1994). *Überleben im Versteck: Jüdische Kinder 1940–1944.* Bonn: Verlag J. H. W. Dietz Nachfolger.

Drucker, O. L. (1995). *Kindertransport.* New York: Henry Holt & Co.

Duggon, S. P. H., and Drury, B. (1948). *The Story of the Emergency Committee in Aid of Displaced Scholars.* New York: Macmillan.

Duncan, O. D. (1961). A Socioeconomic Index for All Occupations. In Reiss, A., Jr. (Ed.), *Occupations and Social Status*. New York: Free Press, 109–38.

Dwork, D. (1991). *Children With a Star: Jewish Youth in Nazi Europe*. New Haven, CT: Yale University Press.

Eckfeld, R. (2002). *Letzte Monate in Wien: Aufzeichnungen aus dem australischen Internierungslager 1940/41*, Krist, M. (Ed.). Vienna: Turia und Kant.

Eliel, E. L. (1990). *From Cologne to Chapel Hill*. Washington, DC: American Chemical Society.

Elon, A. (2002). *The Pity of It All: A History of Jews in Germany, 1743–1933*. New York: Metropolitan Books.

Enzie, L. L. (Ed.) (2001). *Exile and Displacement: Survivors of the Nazi Persecution Remember the Emigration Experience*. New York: Peter Lang.

Epstein, H. (1979). *Children of the Holocaust: Conversations with Sons and Daughters of Survivors*. New York: G. P. Putnam's Sons.

Epstein, H. (1997). *Where She Came From: A Daughter's Search for her Mother's History*. Boston: Little, Brown.

Erichsen, R. (1998). Fluchthilfe. In C.-D. Krohn et al. (Eds.), *Handbuch der deutschsprachigen Emigration, 1933–1945*. Darmstadt: Primus, 62–81.

Erikson, E. H. (1970). Autobiographic Notes on the Identity Crisis. *Daedalus* 99, 730–59.

Espenshade, T. J., and Fu, H. (1997). An Analysis of English-Language Proficiency Among U.S. Immigrants. *American Sociological Review* 62, 288–305.

Fleming, D., and Bailyn, B. (Eds.) (1969). *The Intellectual Migration: Europe and America, 1930–1960*. Cambridge, MA: Belknap Press.

Fermi, L. (1971). *Illustrious Immigrants: The Intellectual Migration from Europe, 1930–41*. Revised ed. Chicago: University of Chicago Press.

Fittko, L. (1985). *Mein Weg über die Pyrenäen: Erinnerungen 1940/41*. Munich: Carl Hanser.

Fogelman, E. (1993). The Psychology Behind Being a Hidden Child. In Marks, J. (Ed.), *The Hidden Children: The Secret Survivors of the Holocaust*. New York: Fawcett Columbine, 292–307.

Foner, N. (2000). *From Ellis Island to JFK: New York's Two Great Waves of Immigration*. New York: Russell Sage Foundation.

Foster, E. (1990). *Reunion in Vienna*. Riverside, CA: Ariadne Press.

Freud, A., and Burlingham, D. T. (1943). *War and Children*. New York: Medical War Books.

Freud, S. (2001). New identities for the New Century. *Families in Society* 82, 335–44.

Friedländer, S. (1979). *When Memory Comes*. New York: Farrar, Straus, Giroux.

Friedländer, V. (2004). *Die Kinder von La Hille: Flucht und Rettung vor der Deportation*. Berlin: Aufbau Taschenbuch Verlag.

Fry, V. (1992). *Assignment-Rescue: An Autobiography*. New York: Scholastic.

Fuchs, G. (1992). Kriegskinderheime in London 1940–1945: Anna Freuds Hampstead Nurseries. In Benz, U., and Benz, W. (Eds.), *Sozialisation und Traumatisierung: Kinder in der Zeit des Nationalsozialismus*. Frankfurt a. M.: Fischer Taschenbuch Verlag, 58–69.

Gans, H. J. (1979). Symbolic Ethnicity: The Future of Ethnic Groups and Cultures in America. *Ethnic and Racial Studies* 2, 1–20.

Gans, H. J. (1982). *The Urban Villagers: Group and Class in the Life of Italian-Immigrants.* New York: Free Press.

Garmezy, N., and Rutter, M. (Eds.) (1988). *Stress, Coping, and Development in Children.* Baltimore: Johns Hopkins University Press.

Gartner, L. P. (1964). The Jews of New York's East Side, 1890–1893. *American Jewish Historical Quarterly* 53, 264–84.

Gates, G. G. (1955). *A Study of Achievement and Adjustment of German-Jewish Refugee Students in American Public High Schools of the San Francisco Bay Area.* Ed.D. dissertation. University of California, Berkeley.

Gay, P. (1998). *My German Question: Growing up in Nazi Berlin.* New Haven: Yale University Press.

Gellman, I. F. (1971). The St. Louis Tragedy. *American Jewish Historical Quarterly* 61, 144–56.

Gershon, K. (1989). *We Came as Children: A Collective Autobiography.* London: Papermac.

Gilbert, M. (1996). *The Boys: Triumph Over Adversity.* London, UK: Weidenfeld & Nicolson.

Gill, A. (2005). *Interrupted Journeys: Young Refugees From Hitler's Reich.* London: Simon & Schuster.

Gillman, P., and Gillman, L. (1980). *"Collar the Lot!" How Britain Interned and Expelled Its Wartime Refugees.* London: Quartet Books.

Glazer, N., and Moynihan, P. D. (1963). *Beyond the Melting Pot.* Cambridge: M.I.T. Press.

Göpfert, R. (1997). *Der jüdische Kindertransport von Deutschland nach England.* Frankfurt a. M.: Campus Verlag.

Gordon, M. M. (1964). *Assimilation in American Life: The Role of Race, Religion, and National Origins.* New York: Oxford University Press.

Gottlieb, A. Z. (1998). *Men of Vision: Anglo-Jewry's Aid to Victims of the Nazi Regime, 1933–1945.* London: Weidenfeld & Nicolson.

Grunwald, H. (1997). *One Man's America: A Journalist's Search for the Heart of His Country.* New York: Doubleday.

Hahn, H. (1982). *On the Way to Feed the Swans.* New York: Tenth House Enterprises.

Hall, P. (2001). *Cities in Civilization.* New York: Fromm International.

Handbuch der deutschsprachigen Emigration, 1933–1945. C.-D. Krohn et al. (Eds.). Darmstadt: Primus.

Hansen-Schaberg, I. (1998). Kindheit und Jugend. In C.-D. Krohn et al. (Eds.), *Handbuch der deutschsprachigen Emigration, 1933–1945.* Darmstadt: Primus, 81–94.

Häntzschel, H. (1998). Geschlechtsspezifische Aspekte. In C.-D. Krohn et al. (Eds.), *Handbuch der deutschsprachigen Emigration, 1933–1945.* Darmstadt: Primus, 101–17.

Harris, M. J., and Oppenheimer, D. (2000). *Into the Arms of Strangers: Stories of the Kindertransport.* London: Bloomsbury.

Heilbut, A. (1983). *Exiled in Paradise: German Refugee Artists and Intellectuals in America, From the 1930s to the Present*. New York: Viking Press.

Heims, S. J. (Ed.) (1987). *Passages from Berlin: Recollections of Former Students and Staff of the Goldschmidt Schule*. South Berwick, ME: Atlantic Printing.

Helmreich, W. B. (1996). *Against All Odds: Holocaust Survivors and the Successful Lives They Made in America*. New Brunswick, NJ: Transaction Publishers.

Hertling, V. (1998). *Mit den Augen eines Kindes: Children in the Holocaust, Children in Exile, Children under Fascism*. Amsterdam, Netherlands: Editions Rodopi.

Hirsch, J. (2003). *Survivor Guilt and Transgenerational Transmission of Trauma in Jewish Holocaust Survivors and Their Children*. Doctoral dissertation. California School of Professional Psychology, San Francisco: Bay Campus.

Hirsch, J., and Hirsch, E. (1961). Berufliche Eingliederung und wirtschaftliche Leistung der deutsch-jüdischen Einwanderung in die Vereinigten Staaten (1935–1960). In *Twenty Years American Federation of Jews From Central Europe, Inc. 1940–1960*, New York: American Federation of Jews From Central Europe, Inc., 41–70.

Hoffman, E. (2004). *After Such Knowledge: Memory, History, and the Legacy of the Holocaust*. New York: Public Affairs.

Holton, G., and Sonnert, G. (2004). What Happened to the Austrian Refugee Children in America? A Report from Research Project 'Second Wave.' In Stadler, F. (Ed.), *Österreichs Umgang mit dem Nationalsozialismus: Die Folgen für die wissenschaftliche und humanistische Lehre*, Vienna, New York: Springer, 171–92.

Hughes, H. S. (1975). *The Sea Change: The Migration of Social Thought, 1930–1965*. New York: Harper & Row.

Ingrisch, D. (2004). *Der dis/kontinuierliche Status des Seins: Über vom Nationalsozialismus aus Österreich vertriebene (und verbliebene) intellektuelle Kulturen in lebensgeschichtlichen Kontexten*. Frankfurt a. M.: Peter Lang Europäischer Verlag der Wissenschaften.

Jackman, J. C., and Borden, C. M. (1983). *The Muses Flee Hitler: Cultural Transfer and Adaption, 1930–1945*. Washington, DC: Smithsonian Institution Press.

Janoff-Bulman, R. (1992). *Shattered Assumptions: Towards a New Psychology of Trauma*. New York: Free Press.

Jason, P. K., and Posner, I. (Eds.) (2004). *Don't Wave Goodbye: The Children's Flight from Nazi Persecution to American Freedom*. Westport, CT: Praeger.

Kagan, J. (2002). *Surprise, Uncertainty, and Mental Structures*. Cambridge, MA: Harvard University Press.

Kagan, J., and Reznick, J. S. (1986). Shyness and Temperament. In Jones, W. H., Cheek, J. M., and Briggs, S. R. (Eds.), *Shyness: Perspectives on Research and Treatment*. New York: Plenum, 81–90.

Kaganoff, N. M. (1966). Organized Jewish Welfare Activity in New York City (1848–1860). *American Jewish Historical Quarterly* 56, 27–61.

Kahana, B., Harel, Z., and Kahana, E. (1988). Predictors of Psychological Well-being Among Survivors of the Holocaust. In Wilson, J. P., Harel, Z., and Kahana, B. (Eds.), *Human Adaption to Extreme Stress: From the Holocaust to Vietnam*. New York: Plenum, 171–92.

Kanner, M. A., and Kugler, E. R. (1997). *Shattered Crystals*. New York: C.I.S. Publishers.

Kaplan, M. A. (1998). *Between Dignity and Despair: Jewish Life in Nazi Germany*. New York: Oxford University Press.

Katznelson, I. (1981). *City Trenches: Urban Politics and the Patterning of Class in the United States*. New York: Pantheon.

Keilson, H. (1992). Trennung und Traumatisierung: Jüdische Kinder im Untergrund während deutscher Besatzung 1940–1945. In Benz, U., and Benz, W. (Eds.), *Sozialisation und Traumatisierung: Kinder in der Zeit des Nationalsozialismus*. Frankfurt a. M.: Fischer Taschenbuch Verlag, 40–57.

Keller, M., and Keller, P. (2001). *Making Harvard Modern: The Rise of America's University*. New York: Oxford University Press.

Kent, D. (1953). *The Refugee Intellectual*. New York: Harper & Brothers.

Kestenberg, J. S., and Brenner, I. (1996). *The Last Witness: The Child Survivor of the Holocaust*. Washington, DC: American Psychiatric Press.

Kestenberg, J. S., and Kahn, C. (Eds.) (1998). *Children Surviving Persecution: An International Study of Trauma and Healing*. Westport, CT: Praeger.

Kettler, D., and Lauer, G. (2005). *Exile, Science, and Bildung: The Contested Legacies of German Emigre Intellectuals*. New York: Palgrave Macmillan.

Kirchheimer, G. D., and Kirchheimer, M. (1997). *We Were So Beloved: Autobiography of a German Jewish Community*. Pittsburgh, PA: University of Pittsburgh Press.

Kranzler, D., and Landesman, D. (1998). *Rav Breuer: His Life and His Legacy: A Biography of Rav Dr. Joseph Breuer*. New York: Feldheim.

Kreider, R. M., and Fields, J. M. (2002). Number, Timing, and Duration of Marriages and Divorces: 1996. Washington, DC: U.S. Department of Commerce, Census Bureau.

Krist, M. (2001). *Vertreibungsschicksale: Jüdische Schüler eines Wiener Gymnasiums 1938 und ihre Lebenswege*. Vienna: Turia & Kant.

Krohn, C. D. (1993). *Intellectuals in Exile: Refugee Scholars and the New School for Social Research*. Amherst, MA: University of Massachusetts Press.

Laqueur, W. (1992). *Thursday's Child Has Far To Go: A Memoir of the Journeying Years*. New York: Charles Scribner's Sons.

Laqueur, W. (2001). *Generation Exodus: The Fate of Young Jewish Refugees from Nazi Germany*. Hanover, NH: University Press of New England.

Lerner, G. (1971). *The Woman in American History*. Menlo Park, CA: Addison-Wesley.

Lerner, G. (1986–93). *Women and History*. 2 vols. New York: Oxford University Press.

Lerner, G. (2002). *Fireweed: A Political Autobiography*. Philadelphia: Temple University Press.

Les Prix Nobel 2000. Stockholm: Imprimerie Royale.

Leverton, B., and Lowensohn, S. (1990). *I Came Alone, Stories of the Kindertransport*. Sussex, UK: The Book Guild Ltd.

Levine, R. F. (2001). *Class, Networks, and Identity: Replanting Jewish Lives from Nazi Germany to Rural New York*. Lanham, MD: Rowman & Littlefield Publishers.

Lowenstein, S. M. (1989). *Frankfurt on the Hudson: The German-Jewish Community of Washington Heights, 1933–1983, Its Structure and Culture*. Detroit, MI: Wayne State University Press.

Luckmann, B. (1981). Exil oder Emigration: Aspekte der Amerikanisierung an der "New School for Social Research" in New York. In Frühwald, W., and Schieder, W. (Eds.), *Leben im Exil: Probleme der Integration deutscher Flüchtlinge im Ausland, 1933–1945*. Hamburg: Hoffmann und Campe, 227–34.

Marks, J. (1993). *The Hidden Children: The Secret Survivors of the Holocaust*. New York: Fawcett Columbine.

McLoyd, V., and Wilson, L. (1991). The Strain of Living Poor: Parenting, Social Support, and Child Mental Health. In Huston, A. C. (Ed.), *Children in Poverty*. Cambridge, UK: Cambridge University Press, 105–35.

Mecklenburg, F. (1995). The Occupation of Women Émigres: Women Lawyers in the United States. In Quack, S. (Ed.), *Between Sorrow and Strength: Women Refugees of the Nazi Period*. Washington, DC: German Historical Institute, 289–99.

Medawar, J. S., and Pyke, D. (2001). *Hitler's Gift: The True Story of the Scientists Expelled by the Nazi Regime*. New York: Arcade Publishing.

Mendes-Flohr, P. (1999). *German Jews: A Dual Identity*. New Haven, CT: Yale University Press.

Merton, R. K. (1996). *On Social Structure and Science*. Chicago: The University of Chicago Press.

Meyerhof, W. (2002). *In the Shadow of Love: Stories from My Life*. Santa Barbara, CA: Fithian Press.

Möller, H. (1984). *Exodus der Kultur: Schriftsteller, Wissenschaftler und Künstler in der Emigration nach 1933*. Munich: C. H. Beck.

Morse, A. D. (1968). *While Six Million Died: A Chronicle of American Apathy*. New York: Random House.

Moser, J. (1991). Österreich. In Benz, W. (Ed.), *Dimension des Voelkermords: Die Zahl der jüdischen Opfer des Nationalsozialismus*. Munich: Oldenbourg, 67–93.

Nairn, T. (1975). The modern Janus. *New Left Review* 94 (Nov.–Dec.), 3–29.

Neubauer, R. (1966). *Differential Adjustment of Adult Immigrants and Their Children to American Groups (The Americanization of a Selected Group of Jewish Immigrants of 1933–1942)*. Doctoral dissertation. Teachers College, Columbia University.

Neuringer, S. M. (1980). *American Jewry and United States Immigration Policy, 1881–1953*. New York: Arno Press.

Newman, J. (n.d.). *Kinder Transporte: A Study of Stresses and Traumas of Refugee Children* (n.p.).

Nicholas, L. N. (2005). *Cruel World: The Children of Europe in the Nazi Web*. New York: A. A. Knopf.

Office of Immigration Statistics (2004). *2003 Yearbook of Immigration Statistics*. Washington, DC: Department of Homeland Security. (http://uscis.gov/graphics/shared/aboutus/statistics/ybpage.htm).

Oropesa, R. S., and Landale, N. S. (1997). In Search of the New Second Generation: Alternative Strategies for Identifying Second Generation Children and Understanding their Acquisition of English. *Sociological Perspectives* 40, 429–55.

Österreicher im Exil, Grossbritannien 1938–1945: Eine Dokumentation (1992). Ed. by Dokumentationsarchiv des österreichischen Widerstandes. Vienna: Österreichischer Bundesverlag.

Ottenheimer, F. (2000). *Escape and Return: Memories of Nazi Germany.* Kearney, NE: Morris Publishing.

Papanek, E. (1980). *Die Kinder von Montmorency.* Vienna: Europaverlag.

Papanek, E., with Linn, E. (1975). *Out of the Fire.* New York: William Morrow & Co.

Papanek, H. (1973). Men, Women and Work: Reflections on the Two-Person Career. *American Journal of Sociology* 78, no. 4, 852–72.

Papanek, H. (1998). Exile or Emigration: What Shall We Tell the Children? Exil oder Auswanderung: Was sagen wir den Kindern? In Hertling, V. (Ed.), *Mit den Augen eines Kindes: Children in the Holocaust, Children in Exile, Children under Fascism.* Amsterdam: Editions Rodopi, B. V., 220–36.

Pedraza, S., and Rumbaut, R. G. (1996). *Origins and Destinies: Immigration, Race, and Ethnicity in America.* Belmont, CA: Wadsworth Publishing Company.

Perlmann, J., and Waldinger, R. (1998). Are the Children of Today's Immigrants Making It? *Public Interest* 132 (Summer), 73–96.

Perloff, M. (2004). *The Vienna Paradox: A Memoir.* New York: New Directions Publishing Corp.

Pfanner, H. F. (1983). *Exile in New York: German and Austrian Writers After 1933.* Detroit: Wayne State University Press.

Portes, A. (Ed.) (1996). *The New Second Generation.* New York: Russell Sage Foundation.

Portes, A., and Rumbaut, R. G. (1996). *Immigrant America: A Portrait.* 2nd ed. Berkeley, CA: University of California Press.

Portes, A., and Rumbaut, R. G. (2001). *Legacies: The Story of the Immigrant Second Generation.* New York: Russell Sage Foundation.

Portes, A., and Zhou, M. (1993). The New Second Generation: Segmented Assimilation and its Variants. *Annals of the American Academy of Political and Social Sciences* 530, 74–96.

Pozetta, G. E. (Ed.) (1991). *Ethnicity, Ethnic Identity, and Language Maintenance.* New York: Garland Publishing.

Proudfoot, M. J. (1957). *European Refugees: 1939–52. A Study in Forced Population Movement.* London, UK: Faber and Faber.

Putnam, R. (1995). Bowling Alone: America's Declining Social Capital. *Journal of Democracy* 6, no. 1, 65–78.

Quack, S. (1995a). *Zuflucht Amerika: Zur Sozialgeschichte der Emigration deutsch-juedischer Frauen in die USA, 1933–1945.* Bonn: J. H. W. Dietz.

Quack, S. (Ed.) (1995b). *Between Sorrow and Strength: Women Refugees of the Nazi Period.* Washington, DC: German Historical Institute.

Raven, D., and Krohn, W. (2000). Edgar Zilsel: His Life and Work (1891–1944). In Raven, D., and Krohn, W. (Eds.), *Edgar Zilsel: The Social Origins of Modern Science,* (Boston Studies in the Philosophy of Science, vol. 2000), Dordrecht: Kluwer Academic Publishers, xxi–lxii.

Ressler, E. M., Boothby, N., and Steinbock, D. J. (1988). *Unaccompanied Children: Care and Protection in Wars, Natural Disasters, and Refugee Movements.* New York: Oxford University Press.

Röder, W. (1998). Die politische Emigration. In C.-D. Krohn et al. (Eds.), *Handbuch der deutschsprachigen Emigration, 1933–1945.* Darmstadt: Primus, 16–30.

Röder, W., and Strauss, H. A. (Eds.) (1980–1983). *Biographisches Handbuch der deutschsprachigen Emigration nach 1933* (International Biographical Dictionary of Central European Emigres, 1933–1945). Munich: K.G. Saur.

Rosenkranz, H. (1978). *Verfolgung und Selbstbehauptung: Die Juden in Österreich, 1938–1945*. Vienna: Herold.

Rosenthal, D. A. (1987). Ethnic Identity Development in Adolescents. In Phinney, J. S., and Rotheram, M. J. (Eds.), *Children's Ethnic Socialization: Pluralism and Development*. Newbury Park, CA: Sage Publications, 156–79.

Rosenthal, R., and Rosnow, R. L. (1984). *Essentials of Behavioral Research: Methods and Data Analysis*. New York: McGraw-Hill.

Rosovsky, N. (1986). *The Jewish Experience at Harvard and Radcliffe*. Cambridge, MA: Harvard University Press.

Ruggles, S., Sobek, M., et al. (1997). *Integrated Public Use Microdata Series: Version 2.0*. Minneapolis: Historical Census Projects, University of Minnesota (http://www.ipums.umn.edu).

Rumbaut, R. G. (1991). The Agony of Exile: A Study of the Migration and Adaption of Indo-Chinese Refugee Adults and Children. In Athey, J. L., and Ahearn, F. L. (Eds.), *Refugee Children: Theory, Research, and Services*. Baltimore, MD: Johns Hopkins University Press, 53–91.

Rumbaut, R. G. (1994). The Crucible Within: Ethnic Identity, Self esteem, and the Segmented Assimilation Among Children Immigrants. *International Migration Review* 28, 748–94.

Rumbaut, R. G. (1997a). Introduction: Immigration and Incorporation. *Sociological Perspectives* 40, 333–8.

Rumbaut, R. G. (1997b). Ties that Bind: Immigration and Immigrant Families in the United States. In Booth, A., Crouter, A. C., and Landale, N. S. (Eds.), *Immigration and the Family: Research and Policy on U.S. Immigrants*. Mahwah, NJ: Lawrence Erlbaum Associates, 3–46.

Rumbaut, R. G., and Portes, A. (Eds.) (2001). *Ethnicities: Children of Immigrants in America*. Berkeley: University of California Press.

Saenger, G. (1941). *Today's Refugees, Tomorrow's Citizens: A Story of Americanization*. New York: Harper & Brothers.

Schütz, A. (1944). The Stranger: An Essay in Social Psychology. *American Journal of Sociology* 49, no. 6, 449–507.

Segal, L. (1964). *Other People's Houses*. New York: Harcourt, Brace & World.

Segal, L. (1985). *Her First American*. New York: Alfred A. Knopf.

Simpson, J. H. (1939). *The Refugee Problem*. London: Oxford University Press.

Slezkine, Y. (2004). *The Jewish Century*. Princeton: Princeton University Press.

Sokal, M. M. (1984). The Gestalt Psychologists in Behaviorist America. *American Historical Review* 89, 1240–63.

Sonnert, G. (1986). *Nationalismus und Krise der Moderne: Theoretische Argumentation und empirische Analyse am Beispiel des neueren schottischen Nationalismus*. Frankfurt a. M.: Athenäum.

Sonnert, G. (1988). Nationalism Between Modernization and Demodernization. *Canadian Review of Studies in Nationalism* 15, no. 1–2, 43–51.

Sonnert, G., with the assistance of Holton, G. (1995a). *Gender Differences in Science Careers: The Project Access Study*. ASA Rose Book Series. New Brunswick, NJ: Rutgers University Press.

Sonnert, G., with the assistance of Holton, G. (1995b). *Who Succeeds in Science? The Gender Dimension*. New Brunswick, NJ: Rutgers University Press.

Sonnert, G., and Holton, G. (2004). Younger, But Still Successful: Project Second Wave Examines What Became of the Young Central European Refugees in America. *Aufbau*, February 26.

Sonnert, G., and Holton, G. (2006). "The Grand Wake for Harvard Indifference": How Harvard and Radcliffe Students Aided Young Refugees from the Nazis. *Harvard Magazine*, (Sept.–Oct.), 50–55.

Soyer, D. (1997). *Jewish Immigrant Associations and American Identity in New York, 1880–1939*. Cambridge, MA: Harvard University Press.

Spaulding, E. W. (1968). *The Quiet Invaders: The Story of the Austrian Impact Upon America*. Vienna: Österreichischer Bundesverlag für Unterricht, Wissenschaft und Kunst.

Stadler, F. (Ed.) (1987). *Vertriebene Vernunft I: Emigration und Exil österreichischer Wissenschaft, 1930–1940*. Vienna: Jugend und Volk.

Stadler, F. (Ed.) (1988). *Vertriebene Vernunft II: Emigration und Exil österreichischer Wissenschaft, 1930–1940*. Vienna: Jugend und Volk.

Stanley, I. (1957). *The Unforgotten*. Boston: Beacon Press.

Steinberger, J. (2005). *Learning About Particles: 50 Privileged Years*. Berlin, New York: Springer.

Stephan, A. (1998). Die intellektuelle, literarische und künstlerische Emigration. In C.-D. Krohn et al. (Eds.), *Handbuch der deutschsprachigen Emigration, 1933–1945*. Darmstadt: Primus, 30–46.

Strauss, H. A. (1980–1981). Jewish Emigration from Germany: Nazi Policies and Jewish Responses. In *Leo Baeck Institute Yearbook*, 25, 313–361 and 26, 343–409.

Strauss, H. A. (1981). Zur sozialen und organisatorischen Akkulturation deutsch-jüdischer Einwanderer der NS-Zeit in den USA. In Frühwald, W., and Schieder, W. (Eds.), *Leben im Exil: Probleme der Integration deutscher Flüchtlinge im Ausland, 1933–1945*. Hamburg: Hoffmann und Campe, 235–59.

Strauss, H. A. (1983). Jews in German History: Persecution, Emigration, Acculturation. In Strauss, H. A., and Röder, W. (Eds.), *International Biographical Dictionary of Central European Emigrés 1933–1945*. Munich: K. G. Saur, xi–xl.

Strauss, H. A. (1987). *Essays on the History, Persecution, and Emigration of German Jews*. New York: K. G. Saur.

Strauss, H. A., Fischer, K., Hoffmann, C., and Söllner, A. (Eds.) (1991). *Die Emigration der Wissenschaften nach 1933: Disziplingeschichtliche Studien*. Munich: K. G. Saur.

Suárez-Orozco, C., and Suárez-Orozco, M. M. (2001). *Children of Immigration*. Cambridge, MA: Harvard University Press.

Suedfeld, P. (Ed.) (2001). *Light from the Ashes: Social Science Careers of Young Holocaust Refugees and Survivors*. Ann Arbor, MI: University of Michigan Press.

Suleiman, S. R. (2002). The 1.5 generation: Thinking about Child Survivors and the Holocaust. *American Imago: Studies in Psychoanalysis and Culture* 59, 277–95.

Synnott, M. G. (1979). *The Half-Opened Door: Discrimination and Admissions at Harvard, Yale, and Princeton, 1900–1970.* Westport, CT: Greenwood Press.

Szajkowski, Z. (1971). The Attitude of American Jews to Refugees from Germany in the 1930's. *American Jewish Historical Quarterly* 61, 101–43.

Tartakower, A., and Grossmann, K. R. (1944). *The Jewish Refugee.* New York: Institute of Jewish Affairs of the American Jewish Congress and World Jewish Congress.

Taylor, S. E. (2005). On Healthy Illusions. *Daedalus* 134 (Winter), 133–5.

Tec, N. (1993). A Historical Perspective: Tracing the History of the Hidden-Child Experience. In Marks, J., *The Hidden Children: The Secret Survivors of the Holocaust,* New York: Fawcett Columbine, 273–91.

Tedeschi, R. G., Park, C. L., and Calhoun, L. G. (Eds.) (1998). *Posttraumatic Growth: Positive Change in the Aftermath of Crisis.* Mahwah, NJ: Lawrence Erlbaum Associates.

Thompson, E. P. (1963). *The Making of the English Working Class.* New York: Vintage Books.

Timms, E., and Hughes, J. (Eds.) (2003). *Intellectual Migration and Cultural Transformation: Refugees from National Socialism in the English-Speaking World.* Vienna: Springer.

Trahan, W. W. (1998). *Walking With Ghosts: A Jewish Childhood in Wartime Vienna.* New York: Peter Lang.

Turner, B. (1991). *. . . And the Policeman Smiled: 10,000 Children Escape from Nazi Europe.* London: Bloomsbury.

Tutas, H. E. (1975). *Nationalsozialismus und Exil: Die Politik des Dritten Reiches gegenüber der deutschen politischen Emigration, 1933–1939.* Munich: Hanser.

van der Kolk, B. A., McFarlane, A. C., and Weisaeth, L. (Eds.) (1996). *Traumatic Stress: The Effects of Overwhelming Experience on Mind, Body, and Society.* New York: Guilford Press.

Waldinger, R. (1997). Second Generation Decline? Children of Immigrants, Past and Present-A Reconsideration. *International Migration Review* 31, 893–922.

Waldinger, R. (Ed.) (2001). *Strangers at the Gates: New Immigrants in Urban America.* Berkeley, CA: University of California Press.

Waldinger, R., and Der-Martirosian, C. (2001). The Immigrant Niche: Pervasive, Persistent, Diverse. In Waldinger, R. (Ed.), *Strangers at the Gates: New Immigrants in Urban America,* Berkeley, CA: University of California Press, 228–71.

Waldinger, R., and Lee, J. (2001). New Immigrants in Urban America. In Waldinger, R. (Ed.), *Strangers at the Gates: New Immigrants in Urban America,* Berkeley, CA: University of California Press, 30–79.

Walter, H.-A. (1984). *Deutsche Exilliteratur 1933–1950,* vol. 2 *Europäisches Appeasement und überseeische Asylpraxis.* Stuttgart: J. B. Metzler.

Waters, M. C. (1990). *Ethnic Options: Choosing Identities in America.* Berkeley, CA: University of California Press.

Waters, M. C. (1997). Immigrant Families at Risk: Factors that Undermine Chances for Success. In Booth, A., Crouter, A. C., and Landale, N. (Eds.), *Immigration and the Family: Research and Policy on U.S. Immigrants.* Mahwah, NJ: Lawrence Erlbaum Associates, 79–87.

Waters, M. C. (1999). *Black Identities: West Indian Immigrant Dreams and American Realities.* New York: Russell Sage Foundation.

Watts, I. N. (2000). *Remember Me: A Search for Refuge in Wartime Britain.* Toronto: Tundrabooks.

Weil, R. A. (1991). *Through These Portals: From Immigrant to University President.* Chicago: Roosevelt University.

Werner, E. E., and Smith, R. S. (1989). *Vulnerable but Invincible: A Longitudinal Study of Resilient Children and Youth.* New York: Adams, Bannister, Cox.

Werner, E. E., and Smith, R. S. (1992). *Overcoming the Odds: High Risk Children from Birth to Adulthood.* Ithaca, NY: Cornell University Press.

Wetzel, J. (1992). Ausgrenzung und Verlust des sozialen Umfelds: Jüdische Schüler im NS-Staat. In Benz, U., and Benz, W. (Eds.), *Sozialisation und Traumatisierung: Kinder in der Zeit des Nationalsozialismus,* Frankfurt a. M.: Fischer Taschenbuch Verlag, 92–102.

Whiteman, D. B. (1993). *The Uprooted: A Hitler Legacy: Voices of Those Who Escaped before the "Final Solution."* New York: Plenum Press.

Who's Who in American Jewry. (1980). Los Angeles, CA: Standard Who's Who.

Wyman, D. S. (1968). *Paper Walls: America and the Refugee Crisis, 1938–1941.* Amherst, MA: University of Massachusetts Press.

Wyman, D. S. (1984). *The Abandonment of the Jews: America and the Holocaust, 1941–45.* New York: Pantheon Books.

Zander, W. (1992). Kinder und Jugendliche als Opfer: Die traumatisierenden Einflüsse der NS-Zeit und des Zweiten Weltkrieges. In Benz, U., and Benz, W. (Eds.), *Sozialisation und Traumatisierung: Kinder in der Zeit des Nationalsozialismus.* Frankfurt a. M.: Fischer Taschenbuch Verlag, 128–40.

Zhou, M., and Bankston, C. L. (1998). *Growing up American: How Vietnamese Children Adapt to Life in the United States.* New York: Russell Sage Foundation.

Zuroff, E. (2000). *The Response of Orthodox Jewry in the United States to the Holocaust: The Activities of the Vaad ha-Hatzala Rescue Committee, 1939–1945.* New York: Yeshiva University Press.

Index

Printed in the United States
69458LVS00001B/109-150